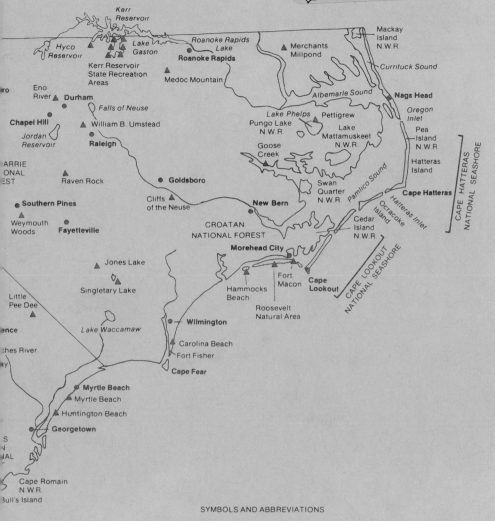

SYMBOLS AND ABBREVIATIONS

| | |
|---|---|
| ● | **Cities** |
| ▲ | **State Parks** |
| N.W.R. | **National Wildlife Refuge** |
| M.B.R. | **Migratory Bird Refuge** |

# Birds of the Carolinas

# Birds

## of the Carolinas

Eloise F. Potter, James F. Parnell,

and Robert P. Teulings

in association with the Carolina Bird Club, Inc.

The University of North Carolina Press   Chapel Hill

© 1980 The University of North Carolina Press

All rights reserved

Manufactured in the United States of America

ISBN 0-8078-1399-0

Library of Congress Catalog Card Number 79-14201

Library of Congress Cataloging in Publication Data

Potter, Eloise F      1931–
  Birds of the Carolinas.

  Bibliography: p.
  Includes index.
    1. Birds—North Carolina.   2. Birds—South Carolina.   3. Birds—Virginia.
  4. Birds—Tennessee.   5. Bird watching—North Carolina.   6. Bird watching—
  South Carolina.   7. Bird watching—Virginia.   8. Bird watching—
  Tennessee.   I.   Parnell, James F., joint author.   II.   Teulings, Robert P.,
  1934–     joint author.   III.   Title.
  QL684.N8P67   598.2'9756   79-14201
  ISBN 0-8078-1399-0

*The University of North Carolina Press is grateful to the family of the late
Helen Thornton Brooks of Greensboro, North Carolina, for its generous support
of the publication of this book.*

# Contents

# Preface

We are indebted to the many photographers who submitted color transparencies for our consideration. Their generous cooperation made possible the publication of this book. Most of the donors are members of Carolina Bird Club, but a few are friends from distant states. A credit line appears with each picture.

References used in preparing the species accounts are *South Carolina Bird Life* by Alexander Sprunt Jr. and E. Burnham Chamberlain (1949, revised by E. Milby Burton 1970); *Birds of North Carolina* by T. Gilbert Pearson, C. S. Brimley, and H. H. Brimley (1942, revised by David L. Wray and Harry T. Davis 1959); *Notes on the Birds of the Great Smoky Mountains National Park* by Arthur Stupka (1963); *Birds of the AEC Savannah River Plant Area* by Robert A. Norris (1963); *South Carolina Birds of the Foothills* by Jay Shuler (1966); A. C. Bent's *Life Histories of North American Birds* (20 volumes, 1919–1958); *Chat*, volumes 1–43 (1937–1979); *American Birds* (formerly *Audubon Field Notes*), volumes 17–31 (1963–1977); "The Fall Migration of Land Birds Along the Bodie Island–Pea Island Region of the Outer Banks of Northeastern North Carolina" by Paul W. Sykes Jr. (Master's thesis, Department of Zoology, North Carolina State University, 1967); "Spring Migration Routes and Patterns of the Parulidae in North Carolina and the Southeastern United States" by Harry E. LeGrand Jr. (Master's thesis, Department of Zoology, North Carolina State University, 1973); *Birds of Charlotte and Mecklenburg County, North Carolina* by Elizabeth B. Clarkson (privately printed, Charlotte, N.C., 1970); *Endangered and Threatened Plants and Animals of North Carolina* by John E. Cooper, Sarah S. Robinson, and John B. Funderburg (North Carolina State Museum, Raleigh, N.C., 1977); and *Atlas of Colonial Waterbirds in North Carolina Estuaries* by J. F. Parnell and Robert F. Soots Jr. (North Carolina Sea Grant Program, Raleigh, N.C., 1979). *Birds of the World* by Oliver L. Austin Jr. (1961) was a valuable source of information on the orders and families of birds.

J. H. Carter III, David S. Lee, and Harry E. LeGrand Jr. reviewed the manuscript and added significant unpublished data on current ranges, relative abundance, and habitat preferences. Gladys Baker, Dr. Paul Hosier, Dr. Donald A. McCrimmon, Dr. Thomas L. Quay, Dr. Marcus B. Simpson Jr., and Elizabeth P. Teulings also read the manuscript and made many constructive suggestions. John O. Fussell III, J. Merrill Lynch, Chris Marsh, Wendell P. Smith, and Michael Tove gave us the benefit of their field experience and unpublished distributional data. Roxie C. Laybourne provided guidance and comment concerning our arrangement of the species accounts. The bird topography illustration (page 396) was prepared by Nikki Bane.

Many friends, whether they could offer us bird pictures and field data or not, gave us something very special—encouragement. Foremost among these very important people is Frances Parnell, who was our gracious hostess during the weekends spent evaluating slides and revising the manuscript. Faced with a multitude of decisions, authors must not underestimate the value of a pleasant place to work, a delicious meal, and a cheerful conversation, all of which Frances unfailingly provided according to our needs.

# Birds of the Carolinas

# Introduction

Few regions in North America have a richer bird life than the Carolinas. North and South Carolina offer great diversity of land form, climate, and vegetation, resulting in habitat suitable for a remarkable diversity of birds. The two states stretch from the high mountain forests of western North Carolina to the semitropical islands of the South Carolina low country. Within their borders occur most of the major plant communities of eastern North America. On the high mountain peaks, birds characteristic of the spruce-fir forests of Canada are to be found. In the low country of southeastern South Carolina, birds usually associated with Florida occur regularly. In regions between these two extremes, one may see most of the species found in eastern North America. No less than 415 species have been recorded in these two states, and as many as 184 species have been found on a single day by a group of observers participating in an organized bird census. Roger Tory Peterson in his *Field Guide to the Birds* lists 514 species from the area generally east of the 100th meridian. Thus, about 80% of all the species occurring in eastern North America have been officially recorded in the Carolinas.

This richness of bird life has led to a very rich history of ornitho- logical exploration in the Carolinas. Arthur T. Wayne, an early Carolina ornithologist, commented that more birds were made known to science from South Carolina than from any other state. Many well-known early ornithologists spent time in the Carolinas. J. J. Audubon, Mark Catesby, and Alexander Wilson all wrote of the Carolinas; and Dr. John Bachman, William Brewster, J. S. Cairns, M. S. Curtis, and Wayne added much to our early knowledge of Carolina bird life.

The first book devoted exclusively to the birds of the region was Wayne's *Birds of South Carolina*, which was published as a contribution of the Charleston Museum in 1910. This was followed in 1919 by the appearance of *Birds of North Carolina* by T. Gilbert Pearson, C. S. Brimley, and H. H. Brimley, as a part of the Geological and Economic Survey.

In 1942 a second edition of *Birds of North Carolina* was prepared by the same authors and published by the North Carolina State Museum through the N.C. Department of Agriculture. In 1959 David L. Wray and Harry T. Davis revised the 1942 edition.

In 1949 *South Carolina Bird Life* was written by Alexander Sprunt Jr. and E. Burnham Chamberlain. It was revised in 1970 by E. Milby Burton.

In addition to these major works, several other regional books have been published. The bird life of the Carolinas has been featured in many works of a wider geographic scope. See the suggested reading list for information on these volumes.

More recently many professional and amateur ornithologists have contributed significantly to the knowledge of Carolina bird life. Their papers may be found regularly in *Chat, Auk, Wilson Bulletin,* and other ornithological journals. Even with the wealth of information available on the birds of this region, there is still much for the present-day student of birds to contribute. Knowledge of life histories of most Carolina birds remains inadequate, and the habitat requirements, behavior, and population fluctuations of all species need further work.

*Birds of the Carolinas* is designed to introduce you to the remarkably diversified avifauna of the region and to stimulate your interest in birds. As you travel about the Carolinas and become familiar with the various habitats that offer exciting opportunities for bird-watching, you will come to understand why the contemporary bird student must both practice and preach conservation. We are watching as salt marshes are filled and developed, swamps channeled and drained, forests cleared, and air polluted. Birds require a place to live, clean air, and unpoisoned food, as we do. The rich biological heritage of the Carolinas will be lost without strong support for habitat preservation and restoration of a clean environment.

Only informed and enthusiastic citizens can work together effectively to influence local, state, and federal governments to preserve our natural heritage and thus maintain a wholesome environment for both man and his avian neighbors.

# Bird Identification

It is natural to want to learn to identify birds. Most people feel a real closeness to wildlife, and birds are the most accessible and colorful of the animals with which we associate. As any experienced birder knows, however, it is not always easy to identify birds in the field. Achieving competence in the skill of species identification requires patience and lots of practice.

A major problem involves plumage differences within a species. Often males and females are quite different in appearance. Females are usually cryptically colored, an advantage during incubation of eggs. If males assist with incubation, they may also be protectively colored. If the male does not assist with incubation, he is often brightly colored. Bright plumage has an advantage during courtship, serving to attract females and to repel other males. For example, Cardinals and most warblers have brightly colored males and relatively inconspicuous females.

To further complicate identification, males may lose their bright colors in the fall, and until the following spring may look much like the females. In other cases immature birds may appear quite different from adults. For example, the Herring Gull's plumage is different during each of its first 3 years.

Thus, you may have to learn several color patterns to be able to identify members of a single species. With a little effort, however, you can learn to identify both sexes of those species that come to your feeders or nest in your yard. Each time you become thoroughly familiar with one species, a new one is a little easier to identify.

Although plumages may differ considerably within some species, other external characters are less variable. Bills and feet are particularly useful in identification. Bill size and shape relate very closely to food habits and are usually relatively constant for both sexes and all ages. However, bill color often changes with attainment of sexual maturity. The short, powerful bills of Cardinals and sparrows are designed for crushing seeds whole, while the slender bills of warblers are adapted for catching insects. Similarly, the long legs of wading birds are good field characters, and differences in their leg colors are helpful in identifying many species.

The behavior of birds is also a great help in making identifications. Each species goes about its daily activities in characteristic ways. You can probably recognize most of your friends by their ways of walking, talking, or gesturing. Birds are just as easy. Look for differences in behavior among species. Do they feed by searching for insects at the tips of branches, or do they dart out from exposed perches to catch insects in midair? Do they walk or hop? Are they calm or fidgety? With a little patience you will find that you can recognize many species by their actions without ever seeing plumage patterns or colors. The advanced birder who identifies a bird by a mere flicker of movement in a thicket is using such information.

There are many such clues to the identity of birds. The secret is to become familiar with as many aspects of their lives as possible and to notice birds wherever you go. Daily contact will add to your knowledge, and soon you will find that you know a great deal more than you suspected. You may even be startled to realize that you have passed, without thought, from bird identification to bird study and have begun an avocation that will give you much pleasure throughout life.

Several aids can make identifying birds easier. First, obtain a good pair of binoculars. Buy the best pair you can afford. With proper care, good binoculars will last a lifetime, and they will add a whole new dimension to your activities. Seven- or eight-power glasses are generally considered best for bird identification, and

the lighter the weight, the easier they are to use. Next, purchase a good field guide to the birds of your region. If there is a bird club in your area, by all means join. Most bird clubs have programs and field trips that help inexperienced bird-watchers develop confidence in their ability to identify birds. Carolina Bird Club provides such help for residents of North and South Carolina.

One of the joys of bird-watching is to discover an unexpected bird, one outside the region generally accepted as its normal range. Birds usually spend their lives within definite boundaries. They may, for example, nest in Canada and spend the winter in the Carolinas, thus making long migratory trips twice each year. Most have definite breeding ranges, migratory pathways, and winter homes. Use this knowledge to your advantage. When you first identify a new bird, look immediately to see if it belongs where you have found it. *Birds of the Carolinas* gives the residence status and range in the Carolinas for all species that have been recorded here within the last 100 years. If the range or season of occurrence does not fit, check to see if a similar species should be present. The chances are that the bird in question was a species that was supposed to be present in your area rather than a wanderer from another region. If after a careful check it still appears to be a stranger, have a friend verify your identification. Even experts try to have their unusual sightings corroborated by another experienced observer. If it develops that you really do have something special, notify the people at the nearest museum of natural history, college or university biology department, or local bird club. They can often provide expert assistance with identification, and they will be interested in learning about your find.

# Migration Through the Carolinas

Each fall millions of birds travel from their breeding grounds in the northern United States and Canada to wintering areas in the southern United States or in Central or South America. The Carolinas are located along the migratory routes of many such birds and twice yearly are flooded with transients. Their passage adds much excitement to bird study.

The manner by which birds navigate during migration is of great interest to ornithologists and has been extensively studied. Although much is yet to be learned, it appears that many migrants use celestial clues in their navigation. Most small, weak-flying birds such as sparrows and warblers migrate by night. Experiments indicate that they are able to navigate by reference to stars. Most strong fliers such as swallows and hawks are diurnal migrants. They apparently find their way by orienting to the sun. In both cases there must be internal clocks that allow the birds to adjust their flight paths to changes in relative positions of celestial objects.

The timing of the passage through an area is often closely associated with the weather. In the eastern United States autumn is a time of cold fronts and prevailing northerly or northwesterly winds. Most fall migrants follow these tail winds southward. Northwesterly winds tend to push birds eastward, and there is often a massive buildup of land birds along the coast. The Outer Banks of North Carolina act as a natural funnel. Birding there in the fall is often spectacular. At dawn nocturnal migrants often can be seen flying in off the ocean and seeking shelter in the first available cover.

In spring, warm fronts followed by southerly winds and cold fronts followed by northerly winds alternate. Most small land birds move northward on the tail winds associated with warm fronts. As cold fronts pass and northerly winds prevail, the migratory movement is temporarily halted, perhaps even reversed. The birds pause to feed and rest until conditions are again favorable for migration. Thus, the best time to find large numbers of migrant land birds in spring is shortly after the passage of a cold front, when thickets and forests will often be filled with colorful transients.

In contrast to the events in the fall, spring wind patterns do not push migrating birds to the coast. As a result, the passage of land birds northward is much more spectacular in the piedmont and mountains. Food supply is another factor in this westward displacement. The coastal plain is primarily an evergreen area, whereas the piedmont and mountains have more deciduous vegetation. As new leaves burst forth in spring, there is a corresponding sudden emergence of defoliating insects that provide a bounty of food in deciduous forests. The northward movement of insectivorous birds coincides with this abundant food supply. This appears to be the reason that many song birds normally select a route northward through the deciduous forests of the piedmont and mountains.

Although the migrations of small land birds are much influenced by weather and food supply, the movements of larger birds such as shorebirds and waterfowl appear less closely related to seasonal variables. For example, the arrival of wintering Canada Geese at Lake Mattamuskeet usually coincides with the full moon in October regardless of weather conditions. Most shorebirds and many waterbirds such as scoters generally migrate along the coast. However, in years of low water levels when extensive mudflats appear around inland lakes, migrating shorebirds are usually found far inland in considerable

numbers. Heavy late summer and early fall rains may result in the formation of temporary marshes. Waterfowl may use such sites in passage. Thus, while major passageways are recognized, birds migrate over all portions of the Carolinas. The occurrence of suitable weather and habitat conditions will result in stopovers in unusual places. Bird-watchers can use knowledge of these weather conditions to good advantage.

There are predictable differences between South and North Carolina in the times of appearance of migrants. Spring migrants may reach southeastern South Carolina as much as a month before the same species can be found in the higher mountains of the Carolinas. Fall migrants generally arrive in North Carolina a little earlier than in South Carolina. Arrival and departure dates given in this book, unless otherwise stated, are approximations based on average dates from several widely separated points. The reader should expect to notice many local and seasonal variations during several years of bird-watching.

# Annual Cycle

As days begin to lengthen in late winter, inner physiological changes are initiated that prepare a bird for migration and reproduction. Migrant species become restless, and by April and May migration is at a peak. Permanent residents may nest in the same vicinity where they winter, and some will begin nesting while the weather is still quite cold. The Great Horned Owl may begin laying eggs in December, and by January the American Woodcock may have begun its spectacular courtship flights. By early April many permanent resident species will have begun nesting. Migrants arriving from farther south may not begin nesting activities until much later, perhaps as late as June in mountain habitats.

As the urge to begin the reproductive process takes hold, the males of many species establish territories, areas from which other males of their species are excluded. Small land birds usually advertise territory ownership by singing. This song has a dual function: It warns other males away from the territory and attracts prospective mates. Birds such as herons and egrets may have very small territories restricted to the distance members of a pair can reach while standing on the nest. They must forage outside their territories, often at a considerable distance from the nesting colony. Most small land birds have territories large enough to provide all the necessities for raising a brood.

Females attracted to a territory are vigorously courted by the resident male. He may sing, perform plumage displays, dance, or make acrobatic flights, all in an effort to attract the female. The final choice of mate appears to be up to the female.

Pair formation is usually for a season, but may be for only a single brood, or in some species for life. One mate at a time, monogamy, is the rule among birds; but polygamy, the situation in which an individual may have more than one mate at the same time, is not uncommon. In gallinaceous birds, such as the Turkey, one male may mate with several females, each of which then raises a brood of young. In some shorebirds, such as the Spotted Sandpiper, the role of the sexes may be reversed. In this case one female may mate with several males. She provides each male with a clutch of eggs that he incubates to hatching, and he tends the young.

Pair formation is followed by nest construction, egg laying, incubation, hatching, and care of young. Incubation may begin with the laying of the first egg or may be delayed until the clutch is nearly complete. Consequently, eggs may hatch almost at once, on several consecutive days, or at even longer intervals in some large birds. The condition of the young at hatching is often closely correlated with the nature of the nest. Birds whose offspring are precocial (covered with down and able to follow parents almost immediately after hatching) often lay their eggs in simple depressions in the ground. Birds whose offspring are altricial (hatched naked, blind, and helpless) use nesting cavities or carefully camouflaged nests, which help to keep the young safe until they are well feathered and able to move about quickly enough to hide from predators. For birds that raise more than one brood, the nesting season may extend throughout the summer, but some single-brooded early nesters may have finished rearing their families by early June. Details of life histories of many birds are poorly documented. Local and regional studies on nesting habits and development of young are worthwhile endeavors. To encourage the gathering of data from all parts of the country, national programs have been organized. One of the most successful is the Nest Record Card Program of the Cornell Laboratory of Ornithology, Cornell University, Ithaca, N.Y. Staff members collect and analyze information reported by amateur as well as professional ornithologists.

Feathers are a unique characteristic of birds. Feathers provide a lightweight covering that sheds water, helps the bird regulate its body temperature, and makes flight possible. During late summer and early autumn most birds, both adults and young of the year, renew all or part of their plumage. Some birds also undergo a partial molt in late winter or early spring. Normally only a few feathers drop out at a time, and new ones, each encased in a protective sheath, quickly emerge from the underlying feather follicles. Only the keenest observer can detect these subtle day-to-day changes in the plumage. Sometimes, particularly after heavy or prolonged rainfall, molting birds drop many feathers all at once. For a week or so birds with bald heads or only two crooked tail feathers are all over the place.

Birds have to keep their plumage neatly arranged and well cared for at all seasons, but during the molting period they devote a great deal of time to grooming. When the rate of feather growth is most rapid, the bird-watcher is most likely to see birds water-bathing, preening, scratching themselves, sunbathing, and anting. Sunbathing and anting are two behavior patterns that are of particular interest. Sunbathing birds often position themselves with wings spread and body flattened against the ground in full sunlight and fluff the body feathers. They may remain motionless for long periods of time, or they may scratch and preen while sunning. Sometimes a bird assumes a sunbathing position at an anthill, allowing the ants to crawl into the plumage. Thrusting its beak into the plumage and grasping an ant, the bird crushes the insect or causes it to spray its supply of acid. At other times birds snatch ants from the ground and apply them to their plumage.

Several hypotheses have been advanced to explain sunbathing and anting. However, the fact that these habits have been observed most frequently during the months of the year when birds normally molt strongly indicates that the warmth of the sun and the acids excreted by ants are used to soothe the skin during periods of rapid feather growth.

Late summer to early autumn is a leisurely time for birds. Young are on the wing, molt is largely completed, temperatures are mild, and food is abundant. For many species there is a renewal of song and even an occasional pursuit flight or courtship feeding.

At this time of year immature birds may wander in all directions away from their nesting localities. Herons and egrets, for example, often appear at inland sites far from the breeding colonies and away from the normal migratory lanes.

Fall migration actually begins in summer for many species and extends into late November or even early winter for others. Winter is a time of intense feeding activity as birds require great amounts of energy to counteract severely cold weather. In fall and winter small land birds often feed in loose flocks containing several species. As the days begin to lengthen in late winter, the reproductive urge again takes precedence and the annual cycle begins anew.

# Bird Habitats

Birds have tremendous potential for travel. Their ability to fly means that birds can easily traverse barriers that are impassable to most animals. Yet we do not find Ruffed Grouse along the coast, but in the mountains; we do not typically find gulls and terns in mountain forests, but rather along coastal waterways. Although birds have the potential for far-ranging movement, they are generally found only in those regions and habitats where they can best make a living. Thus, we know that the Ruffed Grouse is a forest bird, the Killdeer a bird of open fields, and the Canvasback a duck of open waters. The key to the abundance and diversity of birds in the Carolinas is in the diversity of the landscape.

Mount Mitchell in western North Carolina rises to 6,684 feet (2,025.7 m) and is the highest point in eastern North America. On Mount Mitchell and other peaks of the southern Appalachian Mountains are spruce-fir forests very similar to those found in Canada. In the coastal counties of the Carolinas there are vast swamplands and estuaries reminiscent of more tropical regions. At Mount Mitchell, winter temperatures may remain below freezing for weeks at a time, while at Charleston the winter temperatures seldom reach the freezing point. Between these extremes lie an almost endless variety of oak-hickory forests, pine forests, floodplain forests, lakes, ponds, bogs, backyards, old fields, and other plant communities. Each community has its characteristic birds—birds that function best in the particular complex set of circumstances that make up a particular habitat; birds that, in spite of their mobility, will usually be found in the habitat for which they are best fitted.

## MOUNTAIN HABITATS

The western counties of both Carolinas rise into the Blue Ridge Mountains. In extreme western North Carolina lie the Great Smoky Mountains. Mountain forests add much to the diversity of bird habitats in the Carolinas, and here many birds characteristic of northern forests reach their southern limits.

At the highest elevations, southern extensions of the great northern coniferous forests are found (Fig. 1). These forests are generally isolated units at elevations above 4,500 feet (1,380 m). Dominant trees are Fraser fir and red spruce. In such forests several nesting birds more characteristic of the forests of the northeastern United States and Canada occur.

Fig. 1. *Northern coniferous forest in western North Carolina*
Paul Hosier

For example, the Golden-crowned Kinglet, Red-breasted Nuthatch, and Black-capped Chickadee reach the southern limits of their breeding in these high forests.

Dense shrub thickets called rhododendron or heath balds develop on many mountain peaks. These distinct mountain communities are known primarily for dazzling summer displays of rhododendron flowers. They are also excellent places to observe such characteristic mountain nesting birds as the Canada, Black-throated Blue, and Chestnut-sided Warblers and the Carolina race of the Dark-eyed Junco.

Deciduous forests dominate all except the driest and most southerly mountain slopes. This general forest type is highly variable depending on altitude, slope direction, moisture, and substrate, but oaks dominate. Magnificent oak-chestnut forests once occurred on the higher slopes, but the chestnut is now essentially gone, having been destroyed by blight. The present-day oak forests, however, remain important and extensive (Fig. 2). Characteristic breeding bird species of the more elevated, moist, deciduous-forest-covered slopes are the Solitary Vireo, Black-throated Blue Warbler, and Rose-breasted Grosbeak. The lower and drier oak-dominated forests are the summer homes for a host of small land birds that we associate with piedmont deciduous forests. Carolina Chickadees, Tufted Titmice, Red-eyed Vireos, Black-and-white Warblers,

Fig. 2. *Mixed oak forest in Blue Ridge Mountains of western North Carolina*
Paul Hosier

Hooded Warblers, and Scarlet
Tanagers are usually common.

In moist fertile coves throughout the mountains beautiful cove
forests develop. Here a great diversity of deciduous tree species
occur. It is in this habitat that
mountain herbaceous wildflowers
reach their peak of development.
Coves are the summer homes for
many birds including Scarlet Tanagers and Black-and-white
Warblers.

Whenever forests are timbered
or burned, characteristic patterns
of plant succession occur that
eventually lead to a redevelop-
ment of the mature forest. Each
stage of this succession will have
characteristic birds. Of particular
interest in the mountains are the
dense thickets of shrubs and

saplings typical of cutover forests.
Here such interesting mountain
species as Canada and Golden-
winged Warblers find conditions
suitable for nesting. As the forests
mature these species will seek out
other cutover or otherwise disturbed areas. Because the locations of such habitats are
determined by human activity,
the observer must seek them out
and be prepared to find new locations every few years.

Small cool streams characterized by pools and rapids drain the
high mountains, flowing through
mountain valleys and into the
piedmont. Such streams are often
lined with characteristic streamside forests (Fig. 3). Hemlocks are
usually the dominant overstory
tree associated with a dense

Fig. 3. *Hemlock forest adjacent to mountain stream*
Walter Biggs

understory of rhododendron and mountain laurel. Here nest the Blackburnian and Canada Warblers. A recently discovered southern Appalachian population of the Swainson's Warbler also nests in this habitat, apparently isolated from the better-known coastal plain population.

On dry slopes with thin soils, shortleaf and Virginia pine may be dominant. Here bird life is quite similar to that of piedmont pine forests. Typical birds are Blue Jays, Carolina Chickadees, and Solitary Vireos.

Of particular interest are the high rocky cliff faces such as those at Whiteside Mountain, Mount Mitchell, Chimney Rock, and Table Rock. Here and at other such high rocky outcrops, one

may find scattered groups of Common Ravens. While they apparently breed regularly in the mountains, nests are difficult to find and actual reports of nesting are few.

Many of our highest mountain peaks are to be found in the Great Smoky Mountains National Park, lying along the border between North Carolina and Tennessee. All major mountain habitats occur within this park and all of the characteristic mountain birds may be found there.

A popular approach to mountain bird-watching is to travel the Blue Ridge Parkway, which extends across North Carolina from Virginia to the Great Smoky Mountains. This scenic highway passes through most mountain habitats. Overlooks, picnic areas, and campgrounds provide easy access to excellent birding sites.

A number of parks and national forests in the mountains of North and South Carolina offer undisturbed mountain habitats, trails to remote areas, and generally exciting birding.

It is through the deciduous forests (Fig. 4) of the piedmont and mountains that most small land birds pour northward during the spring migration. Birding is often spectacular in spring, and it is at this time of year that bird-watchers are most strongly attracted to the mountains. As summer arrives, the spectacular passage wanes, but the forests still contain many interesting birds. For example, 23 species of warblers have been recorded nesting in the Great Smoky Mountains National Park in western North Carolina and eastern Tennessee. In the Carolinas many of these warblers nest only in the mountain forests.

Autumn brings a southward movement that is not spectacular in the mountains because much of the concentration of fall migrants is along the coast. In fall, however, hawk migration may be exciting, and birders often gather at favored locations to watch the passage.

Even in winter there is interest. People hardy enough to brave the wind and cold may find Snow Buntings on a mountain bald or a flock of White-winged Crossbills feeding in conifers. Mountain bird feeders often attract large numbers of the finches that sometimes pour out of the northern forests into all parts of our region, even to the coast.

PIEDMONT HABITATS

Although parts of the mountains are farmed, and pastures and open fields are common, the mountain slopes are generally forested, and the bird life is generally that of the forest. As one moves down the slopes into the foothills and rolling country of the piedmont, the forests become more broken, and the hand of man is more evident. From the air this portion of the Carolinas looks like a great patchwork quilt, with cultivated fields, brushy overgrown fields, pastures, and woodlots mixed without apparent order. This pattern persists eastward until the extensive swamp forests of the coastal plain are encountered.

The piedmont offers a range and abundance of bird life that parallels the diversity of the habitat. Farm ponds provide shelter for small numbers of waterfowl and shorebirds; fields are populated by sparrows, quail, and other ground birds; and each stage in the successional pattern from abandoned field to mature deciduous forest has its characteristic complement of birds.

Most of the central portion of the Carolinas is much modified by man. Only the flood plains of riv-

Fig. 4. *Piedmont oak-hickory forest*
Robert F. Soots Jr.

ers flowing out of the mountains and down to the ocean have retained a semblance of their original wildness (Fig. 5), and often these are the only blocks of mature forests remaining. Such areas usually provide excellent opportunities to observe many kinds of birds.

The original forest of the piedmont was dominated by a variety of oaks and hickories. Scattered stands of this forest type remain. The best examples are generally to be found in state parks, such as Umstead State Park near Raleigh, N.C. Much of the original deciduous forest has been cleared and converted to farmland. A more recent trend has been the replanting of abandoned farmland to forests, primarily of loblolly pines.

This change from deciduous to coniferous forests has undoubtedly resulted in shifts in the abundance of many piedmont birds.

The Carolina Sandhills lie along the border between the coastal plain and the piedmont and overlap the two Carolinas. Here the soil is poor, and until recently vast stands of longleaf pine and scrub oak dominated. This is an important habitat of the endangered Red-cockaded Woodpecker. Large acreages of this habitat type are preserved in the Fort Bragg Military Reservation (Fig. 6) and in wildlife refuges in both North and South Carolina. Weymouth Woods Sandhills Nature Preserve near Southern Pines, N.C., also protects a small tract of mature longleaf pine with its attendant

Fig. 5. *Flood plain of Cape Fear River in Raven Rock State Park, N.C.*
James F. Parnell

Fig. 6. *Longleaf pine forest in Carolina Sandhills*
J. H. Carter III

Fig. 7. *Man-made impoundment in piedmont*
Courtesy U.S. Army Corps of Engineers

Red-cockaded Woodpeckers.

A number of large dams have been built in the piedmont and upper coastal plain. While the resulting impoundments often have destroyed large acreages of lowland forests, they now provide much habitat for waterbirds where little existed before (Fig. 7). In recent years, observations of ducks, geese, and other typically coastal waterbirds have greatly increased in the interior. Of particular interest has been the establishment of colonies of Cliff Swallows nesting on the dams and bridges at several large man-made lakes in the Carolina piedmont, notably at Lake Hartwell in western South Carolina and at Kerr Lake in northeastern North Carolina. Cliff Swallows are not known to have nested in the Carolinas prior to the establishment of these large reservoirs.

COASTAL PLAIN HABITATS

The lower coastal plain of the Carolinas is a land of swamps, rivers, floodplain forests, extensive bays or pocosins, and pine forests. Some lands have been cleared, and farming is important to the economy; but vast swamplands remain heavily wooded, and the harvesting of pines for use in the manufacture of plywood and paper products is a major industry. When the coastal plain is viewed from the air, forests obviously predominate.

Coastal plain habitats are diverse and birds abundant. In the lowland swamps and forests one may still find conditions approaching wilderness (Fig. 8). Here travel on foot is often difficult, and myriad insects add to the discomfort. Nevertheless, the rewards of a visit may be great. The bird life is often spectacular but still poorly known.

The swamp forests of eastern Carolina consist primarily of stands of cypress and tupelo. Usually flooded for most of the year, these forests are important wintering grounds for waterfowl, especially Wood Ducks and Mallards. Wood Ducks also nest extensively in swamp forests (Fig. 9).

Flood plains are closely associated with swamps, and at certain times of the year the two are difficult to separate. Swamps are under water almost continuously, whereas alluvial forests are usually flooded only at times of high water and are dry for much of the year. Flood plains and swamps generally support a great diversity of bird life. They are summer homes for many insectivorous birds such as the coastal plain population of the Swainson's Warbler.

Inland freshwater marshes are not abundant in North Carolina but are relatively extensive in coastal South Carolina as remnants of the earlier rice-growing industry. Such marshes (Fig. 10) are highly productive, and they

Fig. 8. *Coastal swamp in Brunswick County, N.C.*
James F. Parnell

Fig. 9. *Cypress swamp near*
*Charleston, S.C.*
James F. Parnell

Fig. 10. *Old rice fields at Magnolia*
*Gardens near Charleston, S.C.*
James F. Parnell

usually sustain large and diverse bird populations at all seasons. During the fall and winter these marshes are of major importance to waterbirds such as puddle ducks, American Coots, and Pied-billed Grebes. In summer they are occupied by Red-winged Blackbirds, various herons and egrets, gallinules, and small insectivorous birds.

There are few natural lakes in the coastal plain, but several large man-made systems such as the Santee-Cooper reservoir in South Carolina augment natural ones such as Lake Waccamaw in North Carolina. Large lakes have significant value as wintering areas for waterfowl, especially if, as at Lake Mattamuskeet, there are associated freshwater marshes. In summer these lakes may be important feeding or nesting areas for birds such as the Osprey and Great Blue Heron.

In addition to these large bodies of water, there are many smaller lakes and ponds scattered throughout the coastal plain. Old mill ponds and municipal water reservoirs provide valuable habitat and excellent birding. Farm ponds are generally numerous and, especially when surrounded by pasturelands, regularly attract small numbers of waterfowl, long-legged waders, and shorebirds.

There are two basic types of pine-dominated upland forest in the coastal plain. On dry sandy soils along the coast, extensively in South Carolina and into the southern edge of North Carolina, occur stands of longleaf pine, turkey oak, and wiregrass. These open forests, maintained by periodic fires, have an avifauna characterized by the Red-cockaded Woodpecker, Bachman's Sparrow, and Brown-headed Nuthatch. Most rich coastal plain soils are vegetated by forests dominated by loblolly pine. These forests are often quite dense with well-developed understories. They have been extensively logged and cleared to provide agricultural lands and now often remain only as woodlots. They are the homes for many familiar birds such as Pine Warblers, Tufted Titmice, Cardinals, and Rufous-sided Towhees.

Many places in the coastal plain offer excellent birding. Two are especially impressive. Lake Mattamuskeet National Wildlife Refuge lies in Hyde County in northeastern North Carolina. This refuge centers around a shallow lake 7 miles (11.3 km) wide and 15 miles (24 km) long. The lake is surrounded by hundreds of acres of managed freshwater marshes. The Lake Mattamuskeet Refuge is the winter home for thousands of Whistling Swans, Canada Geese, and ducks. The marshes also provide prime habitat for rails and long-legged waders, while adjacent loblolly pine forests and cultivated lands attract a variety of upland birds.

In South Carolina the Francis Marion National Forest located in

24

Charleston and Berkeley Counties provides all of the coastal plain habitats. The forest is especially extensive and wild, and one may expect to see breeding Swallow-tailed Kites. This is also the site of the last known Carolina observations of the extremely rare and endangered Bachman's Warbler.

Fig. 11. *Cape Point on the Outer Banks of North Carolina*
James F. Parnell

COASTAL HABITATS

Coastal Carolina may be thought of as a vast intermingling of ocean and land. The mixing of the warm saline waters of the Atlantic and silt-laden fresh waters from upland areas has helped to create a rich and diverse estuarine environment. Intermittent barrier islands separate these shallow estuaries from the ocean. In North Carolina these barrier beaches are broken only by a series of narrow inlets, but in South Carolina the barrier is often broken by large isolated embayments and river mouths. The upper portion of this barrier beach system, known as the Outer Banks (Fig. 11), often reaches to within 20 to 40 miles (32–65 km) of the Gulf Stream; and sounds and bays separate it from the mainland by as much as 25 miles (40 km). Farther south the barrier islands may be only a few hundred yards from the mainland.

Most of the Outer Banks of North Carolina lie within the boundaries of the Cape Hatteras and Cape Lookout National Sea-

Fig. 12. *Freshwater ponds on Bull's Island, S.C.*
James F. Parnell

shores. One of the largest of South Carolina's barrier islands, Bull's Island, is a part of the Cape Romain National Wildlife Refuge (Fig. 12). Behind the barrier beaches lie shallow open sounds and bays and extensive salt marshes. North Carolina has a series of interconnected sounds, such as Pamlico and Core; but South Carolina has a series of isolated embayments, such as historic Bull's Bay and Port Royal Sound. Along the borders of these bays occur the extensive salt marshes and flats so much a part of the estuary.

Salt marshes and flats are the key to the productivity of the estuaries. By photosynthesis they convert solar energy into huge quantities of plant tissue—food that eventually provides energy to the animals of the estuary and coastal waters. Without these marshes, the estuaries would be unable to support their vast populations of invertebrates, fish, and birds.

The coast of the Carolinas has undergone tremendous change in recent years. Man has increased his use of the estuaries greatly as he has harvested seafood and waterfowl from coastal waters, constructed marinas for his boats, and built commercial and residential structures on the barrier beaches or on land created by the destruction of the salt marshes. He has modified the very face of the barrier beaches as he has destroyed the maritime forests, built roads and bridges, and attempted to stabilize the dunes. He has even opened and closed inlets between the ocean and sounds. Such changes have been generally detrimental to the coastal wildlife, and what we see now is only a remnant of vast populations of earlier times. Conservation efforts are under way, but existing programs must be greatly strengthened and broadened if we are to retain the coastal beaches and estuaries as places of exceptional natural riches.

The coast is a very special place to bird-watchers, for the combination of diversity of habitat and rich food supply has resulted in a wealth of bird life at all seasons.

The shallow water of the Atlantic Ocean overlying the continental shelf represents the most easterly bird habitat of the Carolinas. Loons, grebes, Gannets, and several species of gulls winter regularly, and such rare visitors as jaegers occur often enough to excite expectations.

Major migratory routes for many waterbirds lie off the coast. Each spring and fall thousands of shearwaters and petrels pass the Carolinas, mostly well offshore. Closer inshore such birds as loons, scoters, and other waterfowl pass in sometimes spectacular numbers. Cape Point near Buxton, N.C., is perhaps the best place in the Carolinas to witness this migration (Fig. 11). Here pelagic birds sometimes come very close inshore as they round the point.

In autumn the barrier islands provide a corridor for the southward passage of large numbers of land birds. Many species of passerines can be found in the shrub thickets and maritime forests. Spectacular flights of hawks also occur. The barrier beaches in autumn are perhaps the best places in the Carolinas to see the rare Peregrine Falcon.

The wild and remote sandy shores of the Carolinas once teemed with bird life and provided nesting sites for thousands of terns and many shorebirds. As people and vehicles have come in increasing numbers, only a few of our beaches remain truly wild. One of these is the magnificent

Fig. 13. *Palms and sea oats on beach at Bull's Island, S.C.*
James F. Parnell

strand of Bull's Island (Fig. 13). On nearby Cape Island several species of terns still nest on natural beaches. No such large colonies of nesting birds remain on North Carolina's beaches, although occasional colonies of Least Terns and Black Skimmers can be found.

The bird life of the beaches remains spectacular, however, as many species of shorebirds migrate southward along the beaches in the fall and back northward a few months later in the spring. A few such as the Black-bellied Plover and Dunlin will make the beaches their winter home. Willets, American Oyster-catchers, and Wilson's Plovers will nest in the sand and grasses just behind the foredunes.

Beaches are also favorite resting and foraging places for gulls and terns. In fall and winter, when surf fishermen provide bountiful food in the form of trash fish, the beaches are crowded with Herring and Ring-billed Gulls. In summer they are largely replaced by the familiar black-headed Laughing Gull and several species of terns.

The Carolinas have no extensive naturally occurring rocky coasts, but in a few small ways man has created a facsimile of this more northern habitat. As man has attempted to protect beaches and inlets, he has often built rock jetties. These large piles of rock extending out from beaches or lying adjacent to inlets or ship channels are similar enough to rocky shorelines to attract vagrant birds associated with this habitat farther north. Thus one may find Purple Sandpipers fairly regularly wintering on the jetties at Fort Macon near Atlantic Beach, at Wrightsville Beach, and even at Charleston. Various sea ducks, including an occasional eider, may be found diving in the rough waters adjacent to such jetties.

Mudflats and sandflats are especially important coastal bird habitats (Fig. 14). Sandflats are usually associated with inlets or with overwash zones where wind and tide have moved beach sands to the rear of the barrier islands. Mudflats are usually associated with quieter portions of the estuary where fine sediments are being deposited. Such flats are often intertidal and are exposed to use by birds for only a part of each day. When these flats are exposed by the falling tide, a bounteous food supply is made available, and many species of shorebirds and long-legged waders find sustenance here. As the returning tide covers the food supply, the birds retreat to the sandflats, which are

Fig. 14. *Mudflats in the Cape Romain National Wildlife Refuge near McClellanville, S.C.*
James F. Parnell

often above high tide, to loaf until the next feeding period.

During the spring and fall migrations, when shorebirds are most numerous in the Carolinas, it is possible to find thousands of individuals of several species feeding actively on favored flats, such as those just to the south of the North Pond at the Pea Island National Wildlife Refuge or between the mainland and Bull's Island at the Cape Romain National Wildlife Refuge.

Along the inside of the barrier islands, adjacent to the mainland, and in fact wherever water is shallow and well protected, marshes develop. We generally think of the vast acreages of smooth cordgrass when we think of salt marshes in the Carolinas (Fig. 15). This is the species that dominates most of the areas twice flooded and twice exposed by the daily tidal rhythm. These salt marshes are of primary importance to the maintenance of the abundance and diversity of estuarine life.

There are also other kinds of coastal marshes. Those flooded only by spring tides will generally be occupied by grasses such as saltmeadow cordgrass. Still less saline areas flooded only by irregular storm tides, such as the vast marshes adjacent to the mainland on the western edge of Pamlico Sound, will be generally dominated by black needle rush.

Birds use all of these grasslands. The extensive regularly flooded

28

Fig. 15. *Low salt marsh at Smith Island, N.C.*
James F. Parnell

marshes are a very special environment, and only a few species of birds live there. Clapper Rails are abundant all year, and Seaside Sparrows nest at scattered locations and winter throughout the marsh. Other rails are present during the migratory periods, and some winter here along with Sharp-tailed Sparrows and American Bitterns.

In northeastern North Carolina, Snow Geese winter in the upper portions of the marshes and on grassy upland meadows. Canada Geese and some ducks also feed regularly in these marshes and meadows. Some shorebirds, such as the Whimbrel, show an affinity for the short-grass meadows; and many species of shorebirds forage

in the more open portions of these coastal grasslands.

The bays and sounds are places of constant change. In Pamlico Sound in northeastern North Carolina, the lunar tidal change is only a few inches, but winds may result in nonrhythmic tides of over 2 feet (0.6 m). In Bull's Bay lunar tidal differences of over 5 feet (1.5 m) are experienced. Thus what is open water occupied by diving ducks one morning may the same afternoon be a mudflat or oyster bar occupied by several species of shorebirds.

Sounds and bays are traditional wintering grounds for vast numbers of waterfowl. The lore of both Carolinas is filled with stories of the abundance of ducks and geese

Fig. 16. *Ducks, geese, and swans over marsh at Lake Mattamuskeet National Wildlife Refuge in northeastern North Carolina*
James F. Parnell

as recently as the early part of this century. Although we are unlikely to witness such massive flights of ducks and geese ever again, we may still see impressive remnants of those huge flocks at refuges such as the Lake Mattamuskeet National Wildlife Refuge (Fig. 16). The shoals of Pamlico Sound still provide eelgrass for wintering Canada Geese, Brant, and many species of ducks. Charleston Harbor still winters thousands of scaup. Puddle ducks of several species still feed along the edges of the sounds and over the shallow shoals.

In summer waterfowl are replaced by gulls and terns, which nest on the sandy islands and feed their young on the bounty of the shallow, rich estuary. Black Skimmers, Laughing Gulls, and at least five species of terns nest in colonies ranging from a few pairs to 10 to 20 thousand mixed pairs (Fig. 17). Brown Pelicans are presently known to nest at four locations in the Carolinas: on a sandy shoal behind Ocracoke Inlet and on a dredged-material island in the Cape Fear River in North Carolina as well as at Cape Romain and Deveaux Bank in South Carolina. On these isolated, windswept islands one may still see a remnant of the grandeur of the coastal wilderness of the Carolinas.

Birds are abundant at all seasons along the coast of the Carolinas, but several places are especially significant. In South Carolina the

Fig. 17. *Royal Tern colony on the lower Cape Fear River near Southport, N.C.* James F. Parnell

Cape Romain National Wildlife Refuge, located opposite McClellanville, offers spectacular birding at any season. Although portions of the refuge containing the large tern colonies are closed to the public, Bull's Island, accessible only by boat, is open to visitors. Throughout the refuge, extensive salt marshes, tidal creeks, fresh marshes and ponds, maritime forests, and a spectacular natural beach provide great diversity of habitat.

In northeastern North Carolina, the Cape Hatteras National Seashore and Pea Island National Wildlife Refuge occupy over 70 miles (110 km) of barrier beach, marshes, sounds, inlets, and manmade freshwater ponds. The entire area is easily accessible by car. While bird-watching is good at any season, fall, winter, and spring are better than summer. Offshore trips to the nearby Gulf Stream provide the best regional access to pelagic birds.

Altogether, the Carolina coast offers outstanding opportunities for bird-watching, indeed some of the best places in the eastern United States. In addition to the Outer Banks and Cape Romain, there are Fort Macon near Morehead City, Fort Fisher near Wilmington, Huntington Beach State Park, and the entire Charleston Harbor area. Bird students visiting the Carolina coast will find that each habitat has its own characteristic bird life. By spending a little time in each habitat, one can usually compile a remarkable list of species during a single weekend afield.

# Conservation in the Carolinas

Conservation is a tradition in the Carolinas, where people have participated in the nation's conservation efforts since the 1800s. Recently we have shared the rush of environmental concern and have profited greatly from this newly kindled interest. Historically, conservation interests have been expressed in several ways. The protection of certain species such as long-legged waders was an especially significant first step, followed by success in the management and protection of both species and habitat. Today, we find ourselves concerned not only with these issues but also with the management of the increasing numbers of people wishing to use our natural resources.

Species protection originally meant the restriction of the taking of certain birds or their nests and eggs. All migratory birds are now protected by federal law, although there are regulated hunting seasons on some species. More recently, all nonmigratory hawks and owls have been given protected status and may not be killed legally.

Recent federal legislation has established lists of rare and endangered plants and animals, and both North and South Carolina have established state lists. Official recognition of rare and endangered plants and animals will encourage further scientific study of these species and their habitat requirements. The scientific data provide guidelines for state and federal agencies that are involved in land management, industrial development, pollution abatement, highway location, stream channelization, and other activities that significantly influence the environment.

The protection of habitat is a relatively new idea. It was first implemented in this country with the establishment of national and state wildlife refuge systems. State and national parks and forests also provide protection, albeit often coincidental to other purposes. It is only in very recent years that habitat units have been managed specifically for nongame species. An excellent example involves the management of state and federal lands for the rare and endangered Red-cockaded Woodpecker.

The problem of habitat destruction remains as the most serious conservation issue concerning birds. Each species must have an adequate amount of appropriate habitat. The strict enforcement of antishooting laws will not help in the least if habitat is not maintained. As man continues to modify the landscape on an ever increasing scale, we face the very real problem of the complete elimination of some species from the Carolinas and the severe reduction of numbers of others. The species in serious trouble have the most rigid habitat requirements (e.g., beach nesters and occupants of mature forests) or restricted habitat (e.g., the spruce-fir forests of western North Carolina). Unless commitments are made to maintain suitable areas of living space, we will see our avifauna continue to diminish.

Although pesticides continue to be a serious problem, some areas of the Carolinas appear to have escaped massive damage. For example, Ospreys and wading birds have suffered losses in lower South Carolina, apparently due to pesticide-induced thinning of eggshells. On the other hand, in North Carolina, Osprey reproduction appears normal. Perhaps we have begun to reverse the dangerous trend of excessive pesticide use in time for Carolina bird life.

Human population density is a major problem. As our numbers increase, we continue to place severe pressures on our wild neighbors. We must slow population growth as well as increase awareness of the natural environment if the Carolinas are to remain a very special place for both people and wildlife.

There are several important conservation organizations in the Carolinas. For many years, the South Carolina Fish and Game Commission and the North Caro-

lina Wildlife Resources Commission have effectively managed and protected game species. Citizens' groups have also been important for many years. The Carolina Bird Club, formed in 1948 by combining clubs in North and South Carolina, actively promotes both conservation and bird study. The North Carolina and South Carolina Wildlife Federations have served as conservation arms of hunters and fishermen. The National Audubon Society has local chapters scattered throughout the Carolinas. They are strongly conservation oriented and work for local, regional, and national conservation issues. Many other state and national organizations have included birds in their broad conservation interests.

Of major importance is the work of civic clubs, garden clubs, and other local organizations. They respond strongly to local conservation needs and are often instrumental in the preservation of actual habitat units such as parks and refuges. They are led by local people and work on local projects—and that is where the action is.

# Species Accounts

Included in the species accounts are all birds reported from North Carolina or South Carolina under circumstances that leave little or no doubt as to the authenticity of the occurrence. The great majority of the species are supported by a specimen collected in the Carolinas and deposited in the Charleston Museum, the North Carolina State Museum of Natural History, or the U.S. National Museum. A few species have been included on the basis of a recognizable photograph supported by a convincing published account of the occurrence. Provided a species is readily identifiable under field conditions, some birds have been listed on the basis of three or more independent sight records supported by convincing details published in a state bird book or ornithological journal.

Some species accounts conclude with the parenthetical phrase, hypothetical status. These birds are included on the basis of apparently valid reports that fail to meet the criteria listed above. Such records await the accumulation of additional supporting data. All first occurrences of species frequently kept in captivity (waterfowl, falcons, popular cage birds) are considered hypothetical even if supported by a specimen or an excellent photograph.

We have omitted accidental or exotic species recorded in our region more than 100 years ago and not supported by subsequent records from the Carolinas.

Nomenclature generally follows the American Ornithologists' Union *Check-list of North American Birds* (fifth edition, Baltimore, 1957) and its current supplements (*Auk* 90:411–419 and 93:875–879). For shorebirds the scientific names and species order follow the recommendations of Joseph R. Jehl Jr. in "Relationships in the Charadrii (Shorebirds): A Taxonomic Study Based on Color Patterns of the Downy Young" (San Diego Society of Natural History, memoir 3, 1968). Obsolete common names still in general use (sometimes for a race formerly regarded as a species) are noted in parentheses following the presently adopted ones. Colloquial names are placed within quotation marks.

The value in inches (centimeters) following the common and scientific names of each species is the approximate length of the bird as measured from the tip of the bill to the tip of the tail. For some pelagic species that have unusually long wings in proportion to body size, the wingspan (W) is given in addition to the length (L).

Species accounts have four principal subheadings: range, nesting habits, feedings habits, and description.

RANGE

Range includes statements of seasonal abundance, residence status, and distribution in the Carolinas. Data on habitat preference and seasonal abundance refer specifically to the situation in the Carolinas. Such information is based on the authors' personal knowledge, the comments of experienced field observers who reviewed the manuscript, or the current literature on Carolina bird life.

Terms of residence status are defined as follows:

*Permanent resident:* The species is present throughout the year and breeds in the given region. Some species, particularly shorebirds, can be found in the Carolinas all 12 months of the year, but they do not breed here and therefore are not considered to be permanent residents.

*Summer resident:* The species arrives in the spring, breeds, and departs before winter.

*Winter resident:* The species arrives in late summer or autumn, remains all winter, and departs in spring.

*Summer or winter visitor:* The species is present only part of a given season and generally is somewhat erratic in its occurrence, although it is expected to be present with some degree of regularity. Summer visitors do not breed, not even when they are present regularly throughout the season as is the case with some pelagic birds.

*Spring or fall transient:* The species passes through the region during migration.

*Accidental:* This term refers to birds found outside their normal range.

*Straggler:* This term refers to birds found during a season when the species usually is absent.

Residence status is uncertain for some species. In such cases the period of observation has been noted, and a determination of status must await additional data and further analysis. Residence status may change as species shift range boundaries or migration routes.

Listed below are the terms of relative abundance used in this book. They are based on the probability of seeing a given species during several hours of active bird-watching at the proper season and in suitable habitat as well as on the number of reports in the literature.

*Abundant:* Always expect to see a large number of individuals. Example: Royal Tern on the coast in summer.

*Very common:* Always expect to see a moderate number of individuals. Example: Cardinal.

*Common:* Almost always expect to see a moderate number of individuals. Example: Tufted Titmouse.

*Fairly common:* Usually expect to see a few individuals. Numerous reports in the literature. Example: Ruby-throated Hummingbird in summer.

*Uncommon:* Expect to see a small number of individuals occasionally. Regular reports in the literature. Example: Gray-cheeked Thrush as a spring or fall migrant.

*Rare:* Expect to see no more than one individual per year. Few reports in the literature. Example: Nashville Warbler.

*Very rare:* Expect to see less than one individual every five seasons. Very few reports in the literature. Example: Black-headed Gull.

NESTING HABITS

For birds breeding in the Carolinas, the species accounts include an outline of the reproductive process: nest construction, clutch size (number of eggs most commonly found), egg description (smooth and ovate unless otherwise stated), incubation period, and care and development of young. To emphasize the importance of similarities, the pattern of nesting behavior is given under the appropriate order or family heading.

For many species, details of the reproductive cycle were not available directly from the Carolinas, and data were taken from the general literature, principally Bent's *Life Histories.* We hope that *Birds of the Carolinas* will encourage readers to watch closely those species whose habits are poorly known and to investigate any occurrence or behavior that appears to be unusual. The chief purpose of *Chat,* the quarterly journal of Carolina Bird Club, is to help local bird-watchers and professional biologists communicate with each other. Ornithology remains a field of science in which the contributions of informed amateurs are both needed and welcomed.

FEEDING HABITS

Major foods are listed for each species. This does not imply that these are the only foods eaten. Food resources in the Carolinas may differ from those available in other parts of the species' range. Feeding methods also are given. In some cases the feeding habits are essentially the same for all birds in a family or order, and the reader is referred to the appropriate heading.

DESCRIPTION

A brief description is provided for all species except those of hypothetical status. The descriptions are designed to supplement the photographs, which cannot possibly illustrate all plumages of the more than 400 species found in the Carolinas; and they generally emphasize the characteristics that separate similar species. Short descriptions are inadequate for positive identification of some species. Field guides, more detailed works such as some of the books mentioned in the suggested reading list, or even museum collections should be consulted in difficult cases.

# Birds of the Carolinas

# Order Gaviiformes: Loons

Loons have webbed toes and obtain their food, primarily fish not considered suitable for table use, by diving and pursuing their prey underwater. Their legs are set so far back on their heavy bodies that they move on land with great difficulty, usually sliding from shore to water much like a seal. Because they can take flight only by pattering along the surface of open water for a considerable distance, loons become stranded if they mistake wet pavement for water during night migrations.

# Family Gaviidae: Loons

### Common Loon
*Gavia immer*
28–36 in. (70–90 cm)

*Range:* Common Loons begin moving southward in early October and are common winter residents in Carolina coastal waters until mid-May. Nonbreeding birds occasionally remain throughout the summer. Small numbers of Common Loons are found regularly on large inland lakes, mostly during migrations.

*Feeding habits:* See comments on order.

*Description:* This diver's bill is dark, stout, and evenly tapered. Summer plumage is black with white spots arranged in bands across the back. Winter plumage is unspotted gray above and white below.

Common Loon, winter
James F. Parnell

## Red-throated Loon
*Gavia stellata*
24–27 in. (60–68 cm)

*Range:* The Red-throated Loon is
a fairly common to common
winter resident in coastal waters
from mid-October to mid-May,
but it rarely occurs inland. This
species is seen primarily on the
ocean, where it generally
outnumbers the Common Loon.

*Feeding habits:* See comments on
order.

*Description:* The Red-throated
Loon is similar to the Common
Loon but smaller with a shorter
and slightly uptilted bill. In
spring, the adult has a reddish
throat patch.

*Red-throated Loon, winter*
James F. Parnell

# Order Podicipediformes: Grebes

Grebes resemble ducks when seen at a distance, but they are readily distinguished by their slender necks and pointed bills (except Pied-billed). Unlike the webbed toes of most other birds that are adept at swimming and diving, the toes of grebes are individually lobed with horny flaps. Grebes feed largely on insects, crustaceans, and small fish.

# Family Podicipedidae: Grebes

## Red-necked Grebe
(Holboell's Grebe)
*Podiceps grisegena*
17–22 in. (43–56 cm)

*Range:* Usually occurring from November through March, the Red-necked Grebe is a rare winter resident along the Carolina coast, where it is found mainly in salt water. It is a very rare visitor inland.

*Feeding habits:* See comments on order.

*Description:* The Red-necked Grebe is a stocky, long-necked diver similar to the Horned Grebe. Winter plumage is gray. Summer plumage is dark above with cinnamon on the neck and upper breast. The contrast between the dark neck and the light cheek and throat patch is distinctive in all plumages.

## Horned Grebe
*Podiceps auritus*
12–15 in. (30–38 cm)

*Range:* Horned Grebes are common winter residents of our coastal waters from late October to early May, and they may be locally common visitors on large inland lakes. A few Horned Grebes, often wearing nuptial plumage, linger into late spring; but there is no evidence of nesting in the Carolinas.

*Feeding habits:* See comments on order.

*Description:* Winter plumage is dark gray with white face and neck. Summer plumage is black above with cinnamon neck and underparts and conspicuous buffy ear tufts.

*Horned Grebe, winter*
James F. Parnell

# Eared Grebe
*Podiceps nigricollis*
12½–13½ in. (31–34 cm)

*Range:* The Eared Grebe is a rare but apparently regular migrant and winter visitor on the Carolina coast from mid-December to late April. This Western species has been found at several large piedmont lakes. First recorded in South Carolina in January 1959 and in North Carolina in December 1964, the species seems to be increasing in numbers along our coast.

*Feeding habits:* See comments on order.

*Description:* The Eared Grebe is similar to the Horned Grebe and thus easily overlooked. Winter plumage is gray with a white throat and white ear patches. Summer plumage is black with cinnamon sides and buffy ear tufts. The bill appears thinner than that of the Horned Grebe.

# Western Grebe
*Aechmophorus occidentalis*
22–29 in. (56–73 cm)

*Range:* The Western Grebe is a very rare accidental on the Carolina coast, appearing sporadically from late November to late June. Inland, the species has been reported in Wake County, N.C., twice during December.

*Feeding habits:* See order.

*Description:* Dark above and white below, this large grebe is distinguished by its long straight neck and long needle-like bill. The cheek, throat, and foreneck are white.

# Pied-billed Grebe
*Podilymbus podiceps*
12–15 in. (30–38 cm)

*Range:* Found in the Carolinas at all seasons, the Pied-billed Grebe is most abundant in fresh waters along the coast from September until May. It winters commonly on lakes and ponds throughout the inland counties. Breeding records come chiefly from the swamps, rice fields, small ponds, or bogs of the coastal region, but nesting does occur inland.

*Nesting habits:* Mating may take place in late February on the South Carolina coast, but a slightly later date probably is the case northward and inland. Built by both adults, the nest is a little floating island of rushes, aquatic grasses, and water-logged debris, usually anchored to emergent vegetation. Incubation of the five to seven brown-stained eggs lasts 23 to 24 days, and only one brood is raised each season. The downy young are heavily streaked on the head, back, and sides. They are able to swim shortly after hatching and often are carried on the backs of the adults even during dives.

*Pied-billed Grebe*
William G. Cobey

*Feeding habits:* See comments on order.

*Description:* This species is the "Water-witch," "Didapper," or "Hell-diver" familiar to everyone who lives near a farm pond. When disturbed, the Pied-billed Grebe almost never flies. Instead it dives, or sinks like a submarine, and swims underwater to a sheltered nook where it remains hidden with only its head above water until danger has passed. This habit gives the impression that the bird dives and never returns to the surface. The Pied-billed Grebe is a brown bird with a thick bill. It frequently displays its white under-tail coverts. Summer adults have a black throat patch and a bold black band around the bill.

# Order Procellariiformes: Tube-nosed Swimmers

Tubenoses are wide-ranging sea birds that normally come ashore only to breed on remote islands. They include fulmars, shearwaters, petrels, storm-petrels, and albatrosses. Although some of these birds are quite numerous in our offshore waters in summer, they do not breed in the Carolinas and therefore are called summer visitors rather than summer residents. Most of our tubenoses nest in the South Atlantic during our winter season and migrate to the North Atlantic during our summer; but individuals that have not reached sexual maturity remain at sea during the breeding season. Thus, some of these birds may occur in Carolina waters throughout the year.

Named for the tubular external nostrils on their upper mandibles, tubenoses eat small fish, squid, and crustaceans. Like many other pelagic species, tubenoses swallow much salt water in the course of feeding and preening, thus taking in more sodium chloride than their renal systems can excrete. In a highly concentrated form, the surplus salt is discharged externally through nasal glands. Tubenoses also discharge through the mouth and nostrils a foul-smelling stomach oil that is rich in vitamins A and D. Fulmars are noted for using the oil in nest defense.

## Family Diomedeidae: Albatrosses

Although albatrosses are seen in Carolina waters from time to time, no published account to date contains convincing details of specific identification.

## Family Procellariidae: Shearwaters and Petrels

### Northern Fulmar
*Fulmarus glacialis*
L 19 in., w 42 in. (L 48 cm, w 106 cm)

*Range:* The Northern Fulmar nests in the Arctic and around the British Isles. The species was first reported from the Carolinas during the 1970s, but its status along our coast has not yet been determined. Fulmars, mostly in the light phase, have been recorded in spring and fall off

*Northern Fulmar, light phase*
Michael Tove

Cape Hatteras, and one was reported from Charleston County, S.C., in March 1978.

*Feeding habits:* Fulmars have a taste for waste fish thrown overboard from boats, and they regularly follow fishing boats and cannery ships.

*Description:* The light-phase Northern Fulmar resembles an adult Herring Gull with a stubby yellow bill, heavy head and neck, and gray rump and tail. At close range the fulmar's nasal tubes clearly distinguish it from a gull. The white of the fulmar's head, neck, and underparts is often stained yellowish by discharged stomach oil. Flight is stiff with alternate periods of flapping and gliding. The long wings have light patches on the upper surface near the base of the primaries. Dark-phase birds are dusky above and below, lack the light wing patches, and generally resemble shearwaters; but the stubby yellow bill remains a good field mark when the birds come close to boats.

## Cory's Shearwater
*Puffinus diomedea*
L 19 in., w 44 in. (L 48 cm, w 112 cm)

*Range:* Cory's Shearwaters are generally fairly common summer visitors offshore from mid-May to early November. They are locally abundant at the peak of spring and fall migration when thousands may be seen in a single day and large numbers may pass close inshore.

*Feeding habits:* See comments on order.

*General comments on shearwaters:* Members of boating parties sometimes see large numbers of shearwaters off the Carolina coast from May to October, but mostly in late summer. Long-winged birds with slender hooked bills, shearwaters skim the troughs between waves, seldom follow ships, and rarely visit our beaches except after storms. Ashore, look for shearwaters at capes and inlets, particularly along the Outer Banks.

*Description:* Cory's Shearwater is dark brown with white underparts and a yellow bill.

## Greater Shearwater
*Puffinus gravis*
L 18 in., w 45 in. (L 45 cm, w 115 cm)

*Range:* The Greater Shearwater is a fairly common summer visitor

*Greater Shearwater*
Richard A. Rowlett

off the Carolina coast during June and July, the period of peak abundance. Winter stragglers are very rarely recorded.

*Feeding habits:* See comments on order.

*Description:* Dark above and white below with a distinct black cap and a black bill, the Greater Shearwater has a white band at the base of its tail.

## Sooty Shearwater
*Puffinus griseus*
L 16 in., W 43 in. (L 40 cm, W 110 cm)

*Range:* The Sooty Shearwater is generally fairly common off the Carolina coast from late May to mid-June, the period of peak abundance. It is a very rare winter straggler along the Outer Banks.

*Feeding habits:* See comments on order.

*Description:* The Sooty Shearwater is a uniform dark gray-brown above and below except for its whitish wing linings.

## Manx Shearwater
*Puffinus puffinus*
L 13 in., W 32 in. (L 33 cm, W 81 cm)

*Range:* Manx Shearwaters are rare on the Atlantic Coast. There are several spring, fall, and early winter records from the Outer Banks and adjacent offshore waters.

*Feeding habits:* See comments on order.

*Description:* Dark upperparts and white underparts contrast sharply with the black crown, which extends well below the eye. The tail is relatively short and rounded. Manx Shearwater has a black bill and pink feet. Its wing beat and flight are relatively fast.

## Little Shearwater
(Allied Shearwater)
*Puffinus assimilis*
L 10 in., W 24 in. (L 25 cm, W 61 cm)

*Range:* The Little Shearwater normally ranges over the eastern Atlantic Ocean, but an exhausted storm-blown bird was found near Charleston, S.C., in August 1883. Two birds thought to be this species were seen off Oregon Inlet in November 1978.

*Feeding habits:* See comments on order.

*Description:* Black above and mostly white below, this species is similar to the Manx and Audubon's Shearwaters but smaller. The Little Shearwater flies with more flapping and less gliding. The black of its crown does not extend below the eye, and its feet are bright blue.

## Audubon's Shearwater
*Puffinus lherminieri*
L 11 in., w 26 in. (L 28 cm, w 66 cm)

*Range:* Audubon's Shearwater is generally fairly common off the Carolina coast in July and August, the period of peak abundance.

*Feeding habits:* See comments on order.

*Description:* Audubon's is a small shearwater that is dark above and white below and has no white on the rather long tail. Relatively short wings and long tail help distinguish Audubon's from other small black-and-white shearwaters.

## Black-capped Petrel
*Pterodroma hasitata*
L 14–18 in., w 35 in. (L 36–45 cm, w 89 cm)

*Range:* Black-capped Petrels were first reported from South Carolina offshore waters in 1966 and North Carolina offshore waters in 1972. Although this Caribbean species is generally considered rare and accidental off the Atlantic Coast of the United States, it appears to be a regular, though uncommon, summer visitor from mid-May to early November along the western edge of the Gulf Stream off North Carolina. A few sight records

suggest that the species may be present throughout the year.

*Feeding habits:* See comments on order.

*Description:* A large petrel, dark above and light below, the Black-capped has a distinctive white band across the hind neck and a broad white V at the base of the tail. A band of white also separates the black bill from the black crown. This species is easily confused with the Greater Shearwater, which has black lores and forehead.

## South Trinidad Petrel
(Trindade Petrel)
*Pterodroma arminjoniana*
L 15 in., w 38–40 in. (L 38 cm, w 96–100 cm)

*Range:* A dark-phase female South Trinidad Petrel was collected off Oregon Inlet on August 20, 1978. This specimen constitutes the second published record for North America. The species breeds in the Southern Hemisphere and is not believed to wander widely.

*Feeding habits:* See comments on order.

*Description:* Although similar in size and flight to the Black-capped Petrel, the South Trinidad Petrel is less heavily built and has a longer tail. Plumage is highly variable and lacks easily recognized field marks. Reference to books on pelagic birds is recommended.

# Family Hydrobatidae: Storm-Petrels

## White-faced Storm-Petrel
(Frigate Petrel)
*Pelagodroma marina*
8 in. (20 cm)

*Range:* This fall transient may not be as rare or irregular in North Carolina offshore waters as the several records indicate. Sightings have occurred from late August to early October. Two White-faced Storm-Petrels were seen near Oregon Inlet on October 2, 1971, after the passage of a hurricane. All other occurrences were well off Oregon Inlet.

*Feeding habits:* See comments on order. This is a nocturnal feeder.

*Description:* Dark above with a gray rump, this species is the only North Atlantic petrel with white underparts and a white face. Its dark legs are so long that the orange-webbed feet extend beyond the tip of the tail during its erratic, wavering flight.

## Leach's Storm-Petrel
*Oceanodroma leucorhoa*
L 8 in., W 19 in. (L 20 cm, W 48 cm)

*Range:* This spring and fall transient is found in Carolina offshore waters from mid-May to late June and from mid-September to late October or early November. Leach's Storm-Petrel probably is not as rare as our few published records indicate.

*Feeding habits:* See comments on order. Leach's Storm-Petrels are not attracted to chum in our waters and thus appear to be largely nocturnal feeders during migration.

*Description:* Commonly called "Mother Cary's Chickens," this and the next two species resemble Purple Martins with white rumps. Most storm-petrels flutter over the waves singly or in flocks with their webbed feet dangling and pattering on the surface of the water. Leach's, however, does not patter, and its flight is much like that of a Common Nighthawk, only low on the water rather than overhead. Leach's has a forked tail, prominent white rump, gray wing patch, and dark feet. Harcourt's is almost identical to Leach's except that the tail is less deeply forked and the rump patch is less clearly defined. Wilson's is similar to Leach's, but the tail is rounded and the dark feet have bright yellow webs.

## Harcourt's Storm-Petrel
*Oceanodroma castro*
L 9 in., W 18 in. (L 22 cm, W 45 cm)

*Range:* Harcourt's Storm-Petrel occurs accidentally in the Carolinas. All records to date are storm-blown birds found along the coast in June 1972.

*Feeding habits:* See comments on order.

*Description:* See Leach's Storm-Petrel.

## Wilson's Storm-Petrel
*Oceanites oceanicus*
L 7 in., W 16 in. (L 17 cm, W 40 cm)

*Range:* Wilson's Storm-Petrels are common summer visitors off the Carolina coast from mid-May to mid-October.

*Feeding habits:* See comments on order. Flocks quickly gather around boats when waste fish and other foods are thrown overboard.

*Description:* See Leach's Storm-Petrel.

*Wilson's Storm-Petrel*
Richard A. Rowlett

# Order Pelecaniformes: Pelicans and Allies

All birds of this order are large aquatic fish-eaters with a gular pouch. These are the only birds that have all four toes connected by webs, the hind toe being turned partly forward toward the innermost front toe.

# Family Phaethontidae: Tropicbirds

## Red-billed Tropicbird
*Phaethon aethereus*
36–42 in. (91–103 cm)

*Range:* Although it breeds in the Caribbean, the Red-billed Tropicbird is very rarely reported in the eastern United States and adjacent offshore waters. An adult and an immature collected off Oregon Inlet on May 16, 1979, constitute the only record for the Carolinas.

*Feeding habits:* The Red-billed Tropicbird dives for fish and squid, plunging vertically from a height.

*Description:* Larger than the White-tailed Tropicbird, the adult Red-billed is a predominantly white bird with black outer primaries, a mantle barred with black, greatly elongated central tail feathers, and a black line extending from one eye to the other across the nape. Immature birds are more heavily barred than adults, lack the long tail streamers, and have a yellowish bill. They are easily confused with immature White-taileds. Bill color is not a reliable field character even for adults.

## White-tailed Tropicbird
(Yellow-billed Tropic-bird)
*Phaethon lepturus*
28–32 in. (71–81 cm)

*Range:* An inhabitant of the tropical seas, the White-tailed Tropicbird breeds as far north as Bermuda where the "Longtail" is a popular tourist attraction. The species is a rare summer visitor offshore along the Carolina coast, and on very rare occasions storm-blown birds appear surprisingly far inland, once in Oconee County, S.C.

*Feeding habits:* The tropicbird dives for fish, plunging vertically from a height.

*Description:* This large white bird has an orange bill, a black eye line, and a black band running the length of the wing. Immatures are barred on the hind neck and upper back and lack the elongated central tail feathers that may add as much as 20 inches (50 cm) to the adults' total length.

# Family Pelecanidae: Pelicans

## White Pelican
*Pelecanus erythrorhynchos*
50–65 in. (127–165 cm)

*Range:* On rare occasions White Pelicans visit the Carolinas, chiefly the coastal region of South Carolina. The birds may be migrants flying to and from the wintering grounds in Florida, or possibly wanderers from the wintering population. Occurrences are erratic, as early as August and as late as mid-June, and in most cases appear to be the result of storms.

*Feeding habits:* The White Pelican scoops up fish while wading in shallows, often feeds in flocks, and does not dive.

*Description:* This large white bird has black wing tips and a wingspan of 8 to 9 feet (about 2.5 m). The White Pelican is well known for the capacious pouch suspended from its lower mandible.

## Brown Pelican
*Pelecanus occidentalis*
42–54 in. (107–137 cm)

*Range:* Although recently endangered by pesticide residues in some of its primary food sources, the Brown Pelican has managed to survive as a breeding species on the Carolina coast. Some colonies again are enjoying normal nesting success. Found

*White Pelicans*
James F. Parnell

*Brown Pelican, breeding plumage*
William G. Cobey

*Brown Pelicans in nesting colony*
James F. Parnell

chiefly about coastal inlets, these permanent residents may be seen resting on sandbars, gliding above the breakers, or diving for fish from heights of 10 to 30 feet (3–9 m). Generally less abundant in North Carolina than in South Carolina, Brown Pelicans are locally fairly common to very common in the vicinity of breeding colonies. There are only a few nesting sites in the Carolinas.

*Nesting habits:* All the Brown Pelican nesting sites in the Carolinas are located on small, uninhabited coastal islands. The carefully protected colony at Cape Romain is one of the most spectacular sights that bird-watchers might hope to see in our region. Here ground-level nests of seaweed, marsh grass, and debris are built a foot (30 cm) or more high. The male gathers nest materials, and the female does the building. Both parents incubate the three chalky white blood-stained eggs, which may be laid as early as mid-March and require 28 days for hatching. At first the nestlings are naked, blind, and helpless. Their reddish skin turns black, and at 10 to 12 days of age they are covered with white down and have well-developed pouches. Both parents feed the young, which cannot fly until about 9 weeks old and are still dependent at this stage. Only one brood is raised each year; however, if clutches are destroyed, females will renest.

*Feeding habits:* The Brown Pelican dives for small fish, plunging from the air or from the surface of the water.

*Description:* This large gray-brown bird has a predominantly white head that contrasts with the dark bill and gular pouch. Pelicans fly with the neck and head doubled back on the shoulders. Wingspan of the Brown Pelican is 6 to 7 feet (about 2 m).

# Family Sulidae: Boobies and Gannets

### Blue-faced Booby
(Masked Booby)
*Sula dactylatra*
26–34 in. (66–86 cm)

### Brown Booby
(White-bellied Booby)
*Sula leucogaster*
26–29 in. (66–73 cm)

*Range:* Birds of the tropical seas, boobies very rarely reach the Carolina coast. The Blue-faced Booby has been seen in both North and South Carolina (hypothetical status). The Brown Booby has been recorded several times from South Carolina where a specimen was taken of an immature bird. Boobies found in Carolina waters probably are storm-blown birds.

*Feeding habits:* Boobies capture fish by diving both from the air and from the surface of the water.

*Description:* Boobies are similar to Gannets. The Blue-faced Booby is a dark bird with light underparts and light patches on its rump and upper back. The bill is blue in the adult. Both adults and immatures have blue feet. The Brown Booby is a dark bird with a white belly, yellow bill, and yellow feet. Immatures are uniformly dark above with light brown underparts.

## Gannet
*Morus bassanus*
35–40 in. (89–102 cm)

*Range:* Gannets are common winter residents along the Carolina coast, especially the Outer Banks, from November to April. Occasionally they appear in early October and linger into June. Sometimes Gannets move close to the beaches or visit inlets, but most often they are found offshore.

*Feeding habits:* Folding their wings, Gannets plunge headlong into the water from heights of 40 feet (12 m) or more, making a great splash as they dive upon shoaling herring and menhaden. Like pelicans and boobies, they have a system of air sacs under the skin to help cushion their impact with water and to give them buoyancy. These sacs can be inflated and collapsed at will.

*Description:* The adult Gannet is white with a long, pointed bill; pointed tail; and slender, pointed, black-tipped wings. Its wingspan is 6 feet (1.8 m). Immatures are

*Gannet*
Paul W. Sykes Jr.

*Gannet, immature acquiring adult plumage*
Paul W. Sykes Jr.

brown mottled with white. They gradually become predominantly white and are easily mistaken for boobies.

# Family Phalacrocoracidae: Cormorants

## Great Cormorant
*Phalacrocorax carbo*
32–36 in. (81–91 cm)

*Range:* Among the vast numbers of Double-crested Cormorants that winter in the coastal waters of the Carolinas, keen observers occasionally find one or two Great Cormorants, usually immature birds. Great Cormorants have been seen irregularly in our region from mid-October to late April. They are considered rare.

*Feeding habits:* Cormorants capture small fish by diving from the surface and swimming underwater.

*Description:* The adult Great Cormorant is black with a white patch at the base of its bill. White nuptial plumes appear on the flanks in spring. Immatures are brownish with the belly lighter than the neck and breast. The yellow bill is heavier than that of the Double-crested Cormorant.

## Double-crested Cormorant
*Phalacrocorax auritus*
22–36 in. (56–91.5 cm)

*Range:* The Double-crested Cormorant is present in the coastal region throughout the summer in small numbers, and it is known to nest at Lake Ellis in eastern North Carolina. Arrival of birds from northern breeding grounds in autumn increases the

*Double-crested Cormorants, immature on left*
Heathcote Kimball

coastal winter resident population to many thousands and brings a few cormorants to inland rivers and lakes. Spring migration also brings an increase in inland sightings in April and May. Standing at Hatteras Inlet in winter, one may watch thousands of Double-crested Cormorants, in one black skein after another, flying from Pamlico Sound to the ocean in the morning and returning at evening.

*Nesting habits:* Using sticks, rubbish, and a wide variety of other coarse materials, both adults participate in the building of the nest. The first year it is a flimsy affair; but after being refurbished for use in subsequent years, it becomes a substantial structure. A favored site for nesting is in stunted cypresses along the heavily forested shore of a lake. Thirty or more nests may be placed in a single living tree, which is soon killed by the birds' excrement. The peak of laying in North Carolina probably is in early May, and the three or four pale bluish eggs have a soft, chalky outer layer. Both adults incubate the eggs, and the incubation period is about 4 weeks. The altricial young are fed by both parents during their 3 to 4 weeks of nestling life. Young fly at 5 to 6 weeks and become independent at 10 weeks. The species is single-brooded.

*Feeding habits:* Cormorants usually feed on small fish, diving from the surface of the water and outswimming their prey.

*Description:* Cormorants are dark goose-like birds with short legs, webbed toes, a long neck, a small gular pouch, and a beak sharply hooked at the tip. Immature birds are dull brownish in color, but adults are mostly black with a greenish or coppery sheen to some of the plumage. Double-crested Cormorants are so named because they grow a few curly filaments above and behind the eyes during the mating season. These nuptial plumes drop out soon after nesting has begun. Cormorants often perch with wings outspread and sometimes swim with their bodies submerged and only their snake-like necks and heads above water.

# Family Anhingidae: Darters

### Anhinga
(Water Turkey)
*Anhinga anhinga*
32–36 in. (81–91 cm)

*Range:* The "Snake Bird" is a fairly common permanent resident of the freshwater lakes, swamps, and rice fields of the low coastal region of South Carolina. It breeds sparingly northward to Lake Ellis in Craven County, N.C.

Anhingas very rarely appear as far north as Currituck Sound and inland in North Carolina to Rocky Mount and the Catawba River near Charlotte and in South Carolina to Richland County.

*Nesting habits:* Breeding usually begins in April in the Carolinas. Although solitary pairs are found, Anhingas tend to nest in groups, often in association with colonial

*Anhinga, female*
Elizabeth Conrad

birds such as herons and ibises. The nest is a substantial structure of sticks and twigs, often lined with green cedar or cypress foliage. It may be placed from 5 to 50 feet (1.5–15 m) or more above water. The male brings nesting materials to the female, who does the building. The three to five pale blue eggs have an uneven chalky coating and take about 25 to 28 days to hatch. Both parents incubate eggs and feed the altricial young. Nestlings quickly sprout a thick coat of short buffy-tan down and mature rapidly. If a 2-week-old chick should fall from the nest or depart hastily to escape a predator, it can swim and dive remarkably well upon first contact with the water.

*Feeding habits:* Anhingas capture fish while swimming underwater.

They hunt with the neck folded against the shoulders and strike to impale fish upon the sharply pointed bill. Surfacing, the successful darter tosses the fish into the air, catches it headfirst, and swallows it whole.

*Description:* The Anhinga's long wide tail readily separates it from the cormorant, which also has water-permeable flight feathers and "hangs itself out to dry." Females are black with a brown head, neck, and upper breast. Adult males are black with conspicuous white plumes in the wings and back. Anhingas often swim with only the snake-like head and neck above water. When soaring on rising air currents, Anhingas look like black crosses in the sky.

## Family Fregatidae: Frigatebirds

### Magnificent Frigatebird
(Man-o'-War Bird)
*Fregata magnificens*
37–45 in. (94–115 cm)

*Range:* The subtropical frigatebird is a rare summer visitor along the coast of the Carolinas, having been seen from early May to early September. The species is very rare in winter.

*Feeding habits:* The Magnificent Frigatebird spends most of its time at sea, feeding by snatching fish from the waves or by forcing weaker birds to disgorge their latest meal, which it then promptly devours.

*Description:* Easily recognized by its dark plumage and deeply forked tail, the frigatebird has crooked wings spanning 7 to 8 feet (2–2.5 m).

*Magnificent Frigatebird, female*
Robert F. Soots Jr.

# Order Ciconiiformes: Long-legged Waders

Birds of this order have long necks and long legs adapted for wading in shallow water where they feed upon aquatic animals. Long-legged waders generally nest in colonies, with both adults sharing in construction of the nest, incubation of eggs, and feeding of altricial young. Exceptions are noted in the species accounts. Usually the male selects a territory, often a site containing the remains of a nest used the previous year, and he may initiate construction as part of the mating ritual. After pair formation, the female usually shapes the nest while the male gathers material for her to use. Building may continue even after incubation is well under way. Many pairs perform elaborate ceremonies when one member relieves the other at the nest. Little or no effort is made to keep the nest clean.

The downy young have their eyes open at hatching but are unable to leave the nest. For most species accurate data are not available on the length of time chicks remain in the nest or their age at first flight. Young begin clambering about the nest trees almost as soon as the pinfeathers sprout, generally when only 10 to 20 days old. Most young waders probably can follow their parents on flights to the feeding grounds at 6 to 8 weeks of age. Although long-legged waders normally are single-brooded, females will lay replacement clutches if first sets of eggs are destroyed.

# Family Ardeidae: Herons and Bitterns

Often mistakenly called "cranes," herons have 15 to 17 vertebrae in their long necks. The bones are arranged so the neck readily assumes an S-shaped curve. Although a heron extends its neck when taking flight and landing, the airborne bird (unlike storks, ibises, cranes, and flamingos) holds its head near the body, thus appearing to have a short neck.

Although found in many other families of birds, powder-down reaches its highest development in the herons and is used by some authorities as the basis for determining relationships of the various species within the family. Powder-downs are specialized feathers that grow from certain spots on the breast, rump, and flanks of herons and bitterns. These feathers fray continually at the tip and provide powder used for dressing the other plumage. Once the powder-down has soaked up oil, grease, and slime, it is combed from the feathers by scratching with the serrated nail of the middle toe. After each

cleaning the plumage is water-
proofed with oil from the preen
gland.

The breeding plumes of many
herons were used to decorate
women's hats in the late 1800s.
This resulted in a massive systematic slaughter of nesting birds,
and several species were
approaching extinction before protective laws were passed in the
early 1900s. Action was taken in
time to save the birds, and populations of most species have
recovered to relatively good
numbers.

---

## Great Blue Heron
(Great White Heron)
*Ardea herodias*
45–54 in. (115–137 cm)

*Range:* Fairly common to
common in the Carolinas at all

seasons, but rare inland in summer, the Great Blue Heron is most
abundant toward the coast where
it nests in heavily wooded
swamps and river bottoms.

*Nesting habits:* Usually, but not
always, colonial in the breeding
season, Great Blue Herons may
begin nesting activities in March.
Nests are crude platforms of dead
sticks most likely placed near or
over water in the tops of tall trees,
often pines or cypresses, sometimes with several nests in a single tree. Four unmarked pale
greenish-blue eggs usually are
laid, and the incubation period is
about 28 days. Young herons of
this and other species will use
their sharp beaks to strike at curious naturalists and disgorge foul-
smelling partly digested food upon
intruders.

*Great Blue Heron*
Paul W. Sykes Jr.

*Feeding habits:* The Great Blue Heron feeds mostly on fish and other animals that live in or near water and hunts either by wading slowly through shallow water or by standing with neck folded and waiting to strike passing prey.

*Description:* The Great Blue Heron stands about 4 feet (1.2 m) tall and flies with slow and deliberate strokes on wings that spread to 7 feet (2 m). The bill measures about 6 inches (15 cm). From a distance the birds appear completely gray but very light on the head and neck. The Ward's Heron (*A. h. wardi*) is a race of the Great Blue that nests in southeastern South Carolina. Larger and paler than Great Blues breeding elsewhere in the Carolinas, individuals of this form occasionally wander north of the normal range.

Formerly considered a separate species, the Great White Heron (*A. h. occidentalis*) is now classified as a white morph of the Great Blue Heron. Breeding in extreme southern Florida, Great White Herons sometimes wander northward into the Carolinas. This form is our only completely white heron with yellow bill and legs.

---

## Green Heron
*Butorides striatus*
16–22 in. (40–56 cm)

*Range:* Breeding throughout the Carolinas, usually near marshes, ponds, or streams, Green Herons are common summer residents. A few birds remain through the winter along the coast.

*Green Heron*
William G. Cobey

*Nesting habits:* Although they may nest in loose colonies near heronries occupied by other species, Green Herons tend to be more solitary in both breeding and feeding behavior than other members of the family. Breeding usually begins in April. The nest is a loose platform of sticks and twigs placed anywhere from directly on the ground, or in a low bush, to 30 feet (9 m) high in a live oak or other large tree. Nests are sometimes found in dry woods, apple orchards, and other sites well removed from water. The pale greenish-blue eggs number four or five, incubation requires 17 days or slightly longer, and two broods may be raised in a season.

Little Blue Heron
William G. Cobey

*Feeding habits:* The Green Heron usually hunts by standing motionless at the edge of water, often leaning forward with the body in a horizontal posture, and striking at passing fish, frogs, crayfish, or other small aquatic animals.

*Description:* This small dark heron has a rather thick neck and a shaggy crest that is raised in alarm. Immatures are coarsely streaked and easily mistaken for bitterns or immature nightherons.

Little Blue Heron, immature
William G. Cobey

## Little Blue Heron
*Florida caerulea*
25–29 in. (63–73 cm)

*Range:* Little Blue Herons are common permanent residents of our coastal region, though less numerous in winter than during

the breeding season. Inland they occur most often during postbreeding dispersal from July through September, but spring visitors are not rare.

*Nesting habits:* Little Blues nest in colonies with other species of herons, usually occupying the lower branches of the nest trees. Depending on the vegetation, nest heights range from ground level to 10 or 15 feet (3–4.5 m). The nest may be a rickety platform of sticks 1 to 2 feet (30–60 cm) long or a substantial structure with a well-developed central depression. The four or five pale bluish-green eggs usually are laid in late April, and incubation requires about 23 days.

*Feeding habits:* Although Little Blue Herons usually feed in shallow water on fish and other small aquatic animals, they can survive in times of drought on insects obtained in grasslands.

*Description:* Adult Little Blue Herons are handsome slate-blue birds with maroon head and neck plumage. Immature birds are white with greenish legs and a dark-tipped bluish bill. "Calico Herons" are birds 1 to 2 years of age that are molting into the dark adult plumage. Adult Little Blue Herons are sometimes confused with dark-phase Reddish Egrets, which are larger birds with dark-tipped flesh-colored bills.

*Cattle Egret, breeding plumage*
James F. Parnell

---

## Cattle Egret
*Bubulcus ibis*
19–21 in. (48–53 cm)

*Range:* An Old World species that appeared in Venezuela in 1930, the Cattle Egret was breeding from Florida to Battery Island near Southport, N.C., by 1956. Today, the Cattle Egret is a common summer resident of coastal Carolina, occasionally lingering into winter. In South Carolina the species breeds inland to Barnwell, Calhoun, and Sumter Counties. In

April and May as well as after the breeding season, the Cattle Egret wanders far from the coast, even into the mountains.

*Nesting habits:* At first feared to be a serious threat to our native herons, the Cattle Egret apparently has had little adverse effect on them because it nests relatively late in the season. It lays clutches of four light blue eggs mostly in May and June when young of other species are well developed. Sometimes Cattle Egrets take over nests vacated by other herons instead of building their own. The incubation period is about 22 to 23 days, and young can fly short distances at about 40 days of age. Cattle Egret chicks are most easily recognized by the fact that when disturbed they disgorge ticks and insects instead of fish. Considerable evidence exists that some of our native herons prey on Cattle Egret nestlings as a convenient source of food for their own rapidly growing offspring.

*Feeding habits:* As their name implies, Cattle Egrets feed in pastures, picking ticks from the hides of cattle and capturing insects, amphibians, and mice stirred up by the grazing animals. Cattle Egrets also feed beside highways and airport runways, using moving vehicles as beaters.

*Description:* This small, short-necked white heron has yellow legs and bill. Adults in breeding plumage have buffy-orange patches on the crest, breast, and back; the bill may be orangish and the legs pinkish.

*Reddish Egret, dark phase*
Michael Tove

## Reddish Egret
*Dichromanassa rufescens*
27–32 in. (68–81 cm)

*Range:* A very rare accidental in the Carolinas, the Reddish Egret is most likely to be found along the coast from mid-April through September.

*Feeding habits:* The Reddish Egret often shows extremely active feeding behavior in shallow water, dashing about with wings partly open in pursuit of aquatic animals.

*Description:* Extreme care must be exercised in identifying this species, which is easily confused with the slightly smaller Little Blue Heron. Reddish Egrets occur in the typical dark phase and the less numerous white phase, with birds of both color phases having black-tipped flesh-colored bills. As is the case with the white morph of the Great Blue Heron, white-plumaged Reddish Egrets may be of any age or sex. Young white-phase birds look like adults of the same phase, but young dark-phase birds vary from light to dark gray with blackish bill, legs, and feet.

## Great Egret
(American Egret, Common Egret)
*Casmerodius albus*
37–41 in. (94–104 cm)

*Range:* The Great Egret is a common permanent resident of shallow waters along the coast, breeding in most coastal plain heronries and wandering throughout the piedmont and mountains in postbreeding dispersal, mostly from July through September.

Great Egret
James F. Parnell

*Nesting habits:* Nests and eggs are similar to those of the Great Blue Heron but smaller. Nesting usually begins in late March or April, and the incubation period is about 25 days. Once nearly extirpated by plume hunters for the millinery trade, the Great Egret has made an excellent recovery, as evidenced by the increase in the number of these birds wintering and nesting in the Carolinas.

*Feeding habits:* See comments on order.

*Description:* This is the largest white heron that occurs regularly in our area. Watch for the combination of yellow bill with black legs and feet.

## Snowy Egret
*Egretta thula*
22–26 in. (56–66 cm)

*Range:* The Snowy Egret is a common permanent resident along the coast, becoming less numerous in winter. Inland it is an uncommon visitor during post-breeding dispersal.

*Nesting habits:* The frail platform of sticks and twigs is placed in a bush or tree 1 to 30 feet (0.3–9 m) above ground in a mixed-species colony. The four or five blue-green eggs usually are laid in April or early May, and incubation takes about 22 days.

*Feeding habits:* Dashing about with wings spread, the Snowy Egret actively pursues fish and other aquatic animals in shallow water. It also pokes its toes cautiously among submerged plants and debris, apparently to lure small fish out of hiding without frightening them away. The Snowy sometimes hovers above water, descending suddenly upon its prey.

*Description:* This graceful white heron has a black bill, black legs, and bright yellow feet. Immediately before the mating season, the Snowy Egret grows decorative plumes called aigrettes, and at the same time its feet and unfeathered lores turn from bright yellow to golden orange or bright red. Only in recent years does the Snowy seem to have recovered adequately from the ravages of the plume hunters, its recurved aigrettes having been even more highly prized than the straight ones of the Great Egret as ornaments for women's hats in the late nineteenth century.

*Snowy Egret*
Elizabeth Conrad

## Louisiana Heron
(Tricolored Heron)
*Hydranassa tricolor*
24–28 in. (61–71 cm)

*Range:* A common permanent resident of the coastal region, the Louisiana Heron is less numerous in winter than during the breeding season. It is rare inland during postbreeding dispersal.

*Nesting habits:* Usually nesting about 1 to 15 feet (0.3–4.5 m) above ground in mixed-species colonies, the Louisiana Heron uses twigs to build a platform a little more than a foot (30 cm) in diameter. Nests may have a lining of twigs, grasses, or weed stems. In April or early May the female lays four or five bluish eggs that require about 21 days to hatch.

*Feeding habits:* While feeding, Louisiana Herons often stand or

*Louisiana Heron*
Haskell Hart

wade in water up to the belly. In shallow water the species tends to hunt by darting about in the manner of the Reddish and Snowy Egrets.

*Description:* This is a slate-blue heron with white underparts. Never the target of plume hunters, the Louisiana Heron is the most abundant native heron in the southeastern United States.

---

## Black-crowned Night-Heron
*Nycticorax nycticorax*
23–26 in. (58–66 cm)

*Range:* The Black-crowned Night-Heron is a common permanent resident along the coast, but it is generally rare to uncommon inland to the mountains during migrations and postbreeding· dispersal.

*Nesting habits:* Nests are highly variable, being placed mostly below 10 feet (3 m) high·and ranging from frail platforms of twigs to substantial structures used for several seasons. Black-crowneds frequently remove sticks from an old nest for use in contructing a new one. The three to five pale greenish-blue eggs usually are laid in April, and the incubation period is 24 to 26 days.

*Feeding habits:* Black-crowneds hunt at night, primarily by stalking fish, crayfish, snakes, and amphibians in shallow water.

*Description:* The adult Black-crowned Night-Heron has a black cap and back, gray wings, white

*Black-crowned Night-Heron*
Gilbert S. Grant

underparts, black bill, and yellow
legs. The immature is a streaky
brown bird that is easily confused
with the immature Yellow-
crowned Night-Heron and the
immature Green Heron. Gregarious at all seasons, Black-crowneds
can be seen at dusk flying in loose
flocks from roosts to feeding
places.

## Yellow-crowned
## Night-Heron
*Nyctanassa violacea*
22–28 in. (56–71 cm)

*Range:* Much less common than
the Black-crowned Night-Heron,
but more likely to be active by
daylight, the Yellow-crowned is a
permanent resident of the cypress
swamps, freshwater ponds, and
marshes of the coastal plain.
Migration, postbreeding dispersal,
and at least occasional breeding

*Black-crowned Night-Heron, immature*
Haskell Hart

bring the species into the piedmont, where it may be of considerably more frequent occurrence
than published records indicate.
The species tends to withdraw
from the inland counties in winter, but it occurs regularly along
the coast throughout the year.

*Nesting habits:* Rather solitary
birds, Yellow-crowned Night-

*Yellow-crowned Night-Heron*
William G. Cobey

*Yellow-crowned Night-Heron, immature*
Thomas Barnett

Herons nest in isolated pairs or in small groups, sometimes occupying the outer fringes of major heronries. The bulky nest usually is saddled on a limb high in a gum or cypress tree. Three or four blue-green eggs are laid in April or May, and incubation requires about 24 days.

*Feeding habits:* Yellow-crowneds are nocturnal feeders that eat mostly crabs, crayfish, and other crustaceans.

*Description:* The adult is a predominantly gray bird with a black bill and yellow legs. The bold black-and-white face pattern is accented by a touch of yellow just above the bill. Immatures are streaked with brown. Compared to the immature Black-crowned, the immature Yellow-crowned has a lighter-colored crown, a shorter and thicker bill, and longer legs.

## Least Bittern
*Ixobrychus exilis*
11–14 in. (28–35 cm)

*Range:* A fairly common to common summer resident of freshwater and brackish marshes of coastal Carolina, the Least Bittern also breeds in small numbers inland where extensive marshes are found. The species is a rare winter straggler near the coast.

*Nesting habits:* The nest is a platform of dried and living plants attached about a foot (30 cm) above shallow water, but near

*Least Bittern*
James F. Parnell

*Least Bittern with young at nest*
Morris D. Williams

open water, to an upright stem of a cattail or aquatic reed. Apparently both the male and the female shape the nest. The four or

five bluish-white eggs usually are laid in late April or early May, and incubation requires about 17 days. Young may leave the nest, at least temporarily, as early as the fifth day.

*Feeding habits:* Least Bitterns feed mostly on small fish, crustaceans, and insects.

*Description:* This diminutive heron is among our most secretive and well-camouflaged species. When alarmed, the Least Bittern will, like the larger American Bittern, freeze with its bill pointed skyward. Both sexes are dark above and light below with large buff and cinnamon wing patches. Immatures are similar, but the plumage pattern is less distinct.

*American Bittern*
Edward Burroughs

# American Bittern
*Botaurus lentiginosus*
24–34 in. (61–78 cm)

*Range:* Although known mostly as a fairly common winter resident, more numerous toward the coast than inland, the American Bittern may appear in marshes anywhere in the Carolinas during migration and postbreeding dispersal. The species nests at least locally near the coast, but the breeding range is not well known because very few nests have been found.

*Nesting habits:* The female alone builds the nest of rushes and marsh grasses on the ground in a marsh or meadow. The olive-buff eggs number three to five, and the incubation period is about 24 days. While the female is incubating eggs and caring for young, the male remains nearby; but the extent of his participation in the raising of the brood is unknown. Reports from other states suggest the possibility of polygamy.

*Feeding habits:* See comments on order.

*Description:* The American Bittern is predominantly brown with a yellow bill, greenish legs, and a bold black mark on the side of the neck. Blackish primaries and secondaries separate flying birds from similar species. Bitterns are noted for their habit of freezing with the bill pointed skyward and even swaying in the breeze to enhance their appearance as just another clump of brown marsh grass. Their weird pumping calls have given them the local names "Stake-driver" and "Thunder-pumper." In late April, listen for these calls at dawn and dusk in the marshes around Lakes Phelps and Mattamuskeet in North Carolina, around the freshwater ponds on Bull's Island in South Carolina, and around ponds on other barrier islands of both states. Although pumping suggests local breeding, such calls may be made at stops along the migratory route.

# Family Ciconiidae: Storks

Storks are strong-winged birds that fly with necks stretched straight ahead and long legs trailing behind. They differ from herons, bitterns, and ibises by having no powder-down or serrated middle toenail. Their hind toe is elevated above the other three, and all are partially webbed at the base. Adult storks, lacking muscles to their syrinx, are mute except for the rattling of their bills.

## Wood Stork
(Wood Ibis)
*Mycteria americana*
35–47 in. (89–120 cm)

*Range:* Our only native stork, the Wood Stork is a locally fairly common summer resident and uncommon winter resident of swamps, marshes, and mudflats in coastal South Carolina from near Georgetown southward. Although there is no positive evidence of successful breeding in the state, the birds have been found attempting to nest near Charleston. From June through early autumn Wood Storks wander northward and inland during post-breeding dispersal. A few birds reach southeastern North Carolina, and sightings sometimes occur inland to the mountains.

*Feeding habits:* Wood Storks feed together in an apparently cooperative manner. With one foot each bird stirs the mud and water ahead of it to frighten fish, reptiles, and amphibians from their hiding places; and each bird snatches in its bill whatever prey may come its way. A common feeding site is on the mudflats near the Ashley River Bridge

*Wood Stork*
William G. Cobey

within the city limits of Charleston.

*Description:* The adult is predominantly white with black flight feathers, dark legs and bill, and dark unfeathered head. The immature bird is similar, but it has a yellow bill.

# Family Threskiornithidae: Ibises and Spoonbills

Ibises and spoonbills have faces bare of feathers, lack powderdown, and have poorly developed voice boxes or none at all. Their toes are longer than the stork's, the hind toe being slightly elevated and the middle toenail being slightly scalloped. The bills of ibises are long, thin, and decurved, while those of the spoonbills are broad and flat. Ibises and spoonbills fly with their necks extended.

Glossy Ibis
Jack Potter

### Glossy Ibis
*Plegadis falcinellus*
19–26 in. (48–66 cm)

*Range:* First discovered breeding in the Carolinas in 1940 at Battery Island near Southport, N.C., the Glossy Ibis has increased rapidly until it now can be regarded as a permanent resident of shallow waters along our coast. The species is common in summer and rare to uncommon in winter from Bodie Island south. A few individuals and small flocks wander inland during postbreeding dispersal.

*Nesting habits:* Nesting at a low height in mixed colonies with White Ibises and various herons, the Glossy Ibis builds a substantial cup-shaped nest of sticks and twigs, sometimes with a lining of green vegetation. The three or four eggs are unmarked intense greenish-blue, and incubation requires 21 days.

*Feeding habits:* Favorite food items are crustaceans, grasshoppers, various insects, and small snakes.

*Description:* The Glossy Ibis is our only completely dark bird with a long decurved bill. Well-feathered preflight young are mostly black with some greenish highlights in the wing, pinkish or whitish patches on the throat and forehead, and decurved pinkish bills encircled by dark bands at the tip, middle, and base. Although young White Ibises are similar in appearance, they have white bellies, no light patches on throat and forehead, and no greenish highlights in the wing. Nestlings of the two species have almost identical bills, but the Glossy Ibis's bill turns black and the White Ibis's, pink.

White Ibis
Jack Potter

## White Ibis
*Eudocimus albus*
22–27 in. (56–68 cm)

*Range:* First discovered nesting in the Carolinas in 1922 at Fairlawn Plantation near Charleston, S.C., the White Ibis now is an abundant breeding bird in that area. In North Carolina the species nested at Lennon's Marsh near Lumberton in 1950, but a permanent colony was not established. White Ibises began nesting regularly on Battery Island near Southport in 1963 and at Phillips Island near Morehead City in 1971. Non-breeding birds have visited heronries northward to Pea Island, and continued range extension is expected. Common in summer and fairly common in winter, the White Ibis is most likely to be found in shallow water near her-

White Ibises, immatures
Richard A. Rowlett

onries. Not surprisingly, inland sightings of White Ibises have increased during the period of postbreeding dispersal as the coastal populations have proliferated and as the species has begun breeding some distance from the coast in southeastern South Carolina.

*Nesting habits:* White Ibis nests are low in trees or bushes or nearly on the ground in stands of spike-rush. Laid in late April or early May, the three or four greenish-white eggs are splotched with patches of light and dark brown. Incubation requires 21 days.

*Feeding habits:* Favorite food items are crayfish, cutworms, grasshoppers, and small snakes.

*Description:* The White Ibis is our only large white bird with pink legs, pink decurved bill, and black wing tips. For a description of the young, see Glossy Ibis.

## Roseate Spoonbill
*Ajaia ajaja*
30–34 in. (76–86 cm)

*Range:* Very rare visitors in the Carolinas, Roseate Spoonbills are most likely to be seen near the coast during the June to early autumn period of postbreeding dispersal.

*Feeding habits:* Spoonbills feed by wading with half-open bills immersed in shallow water. Swinging their heads from side to side, they grasp small aquatic animals with their bills and occasionally take some vegetable matter.

*Description:* The Roseate Spoonbill is our only mostly pink bird with a long dark bill that is flattened and becomes wider at the tip. Young birds are faintly pink with yellowish legs and bill. Color gradually intensifies with age.

# Family Phoenicopteridae: Flamingos

Flamingos have necks and legs longer in proportion to their body size than those of any other kind of bird, and they fly with necks straight before them and legs straight behind. Downy young are goose-like in appearance, and adults in flight honk much like geese.

## American Flamingo
*Phoenicopterus ruber*
about 50 in. (127 cm)

*Range:* Apparently a very rare autumn visitor on the Carolina coast from September to January, the American Flamingo tends to linger at one place a week or more. Because this exotic bird sometimes escapes from zoological gardens, all Carolina records are open to question. The natural occurrence of the species in our area is possible, however, particularly in the case of flamingos found in South Carolina prior to 1900.

*Feeding habits:* A flamingo feeds by immersing its sharply bent bill upside-down in shallow water. Muck is pumped through slits in the upper mandible to strain out minute edible plant and animal matter.

*Description:* The flamingo is our only all pinkish bird with a stout bill that is sharply bent downward and has a black tip.

# Order Anseriformes: Waterfowl

Anseriformes are web-footed aquatic birds that have flattened bills with serrated edges, or lamellae, which serve as strainers, permitting ejection of water and mud from the mouth during feeding. Swans and geese feed mostly on vegetable matter. Puddle ducks (e.g., Mallard, teals, wigeons) feed mostly on vegetable matter obtained by dabbling and tipping in shallow fresh water. Bay ducks (e.g., Canvasback, scaups) feed by diving from the surface and swimming underwater. In general they take more animal food than do surface-feeding species. Sea ducks (e.g., scoters, eiders) also are diving birds, feeding mostly on mollusks.

Waterfowl have bodies well insulated with down, which is used commercially to fill pillows, sleeping bags, comforters, and winter clothing. Ducks, geese, and swans generally breed in the northern and western portions of North America, often above the Arctic Circle. Large clutches of 8 to 14 unspotted pale greenish or creamy buff eggs are laid in nests lined with down the female has plucked from her own body. Eggs are covered with down when they are left unattended. Nests may be bulky mounds of plant materials and debris, in the case of swans; depressions in the ground, well lined with plant materials and concealed by natural vegetation, as with Mallards; or beds of moss, decaying wood chips, and other debris in natural cavities or man-made nest boxes, as with Wood Ducks. Incubation requires about a month for most waterfowl. The downy young are precocial, being able to walk and swim within a few hours after hatching.

On the secondary flight feathers of each wing, some ducks have a well-marked rectangle of color, the speculum. Often ducks can be recognized in flight at considerable distances because of their distinctive wing patterns. In summer, male ducks assume a drab eclipse plumage, which aids in concealing them during the period of about 2 to 4 weeks when they are flightless after having dropped their wing quills almost simultaneously. A second molt of the contour feathers prior to fall migration restores the colorful plumage after the flight feathers have been replaced. Females molt their flight feathers later in the summer than do the males, after the young are fully independent.

# Family Anatidae: Swans, Geese, and Ducks

## SUBFAMILY CYGNINAE: SWANS

### Mute Swan

*Cygnus olor*
50–61 in. (127–154 cm)

*Range:* Successfully introduced at many city parks and private waterfowl preserves, this European species is not known to breed in the wild in the Carolinas. It is possible that Mute Swans from the wild populations in New York, New Jersey, or the Chesapeake Bay area may wander into our region from time to time. (hypothetical status)

### Whistling Swan

*Olor columbianus*
47–58 in. (119–147 cm)

*Range:* Large flocks of Whistling Swans winter on Currituck Sound, at Lake Mattamuskeet,

and in the Pea Island National Wildlife Refuge. Inland and along the coast south of Pamlico Sound, the species is rare or uncommon. A few nonbreeding birds, possibly individuals too young to breed, bereft of mates, or wounded by hunters, may be found in summer at Pea Island. Whistling Swans mate for life and have been known to live for 70 years.

*Feeding habits:* Primary foods are roots and seeds of aquatic plants.

*Description:* The Whistling Swan is our only large completely white waterfowl with a long straight neck and a black bill. Immatures are dingy birds with the pinkish bill dark at the tip. Both adult and immature Mute Swans have a bill that is dark at the base.

*Whistling Swans, immature on right*
James F. Parnell

SUBFAMILY ANSERINAE: GEESE

## Canada Goose
*Branta canadensis*
30–43 in. (76–109 cm)

*Range:* An abundant winter resident in eastern North Carolina south to Cape Lookout, the Canada Goose normally does not breed in our area even though quite a few birds may spend the summer at Pea Island and a few other refuges. Some local nesting does occur, but it apparently involves introduced birds. Inland, geese tend to congregate in winter on large man-made lakes, but during migration they may visit surprisingly small farm ponds.

*Feeding habits:* Geese feed primarily on vegetable matter including roots, tubers, and seeds of aquatic plants. These birds are fond of rice, corn, and other grain crops, a characteristic that sometimes makes them unpopular with farmers. Because modern farming practices leave little grain in the fields in autumn, sportsmen at some places supply corn to attract migrating geese and to prevent their moving to areas with a greater abundance of natural food. Hunting over such baited fields is, of course, illegal.

*Description:* This dark goose has a black head and neck marked by a broad white chin strap. Watch for flocks flying in V formation.

*Canada Goose*
Charles Humphreys

## Brant

(Black Brant)
*Branta bernicla*
22–30 in. (56–76 cm)

*Range:* Once nearly extirpated by a blight that killed its chief source of food, the Brant appears to have made a good recovery. This small goose can be seen feeding and loafing on the tidal flats of Pamlico Sound around Hatteras Inlet from November until northward migration in March or April. South of Pamlico Sound the species is a rare winter visitor.

*Feeding habits:* The Brant feeds chiefly on eelgrass that grows in shallow salt water.

*Description:* This small dark goose wears a white clerical collar. A specimen of the very dark Western subspecies, the Black Brant (*B. b. nigricans*), was taken on Core Banks in 1964. Immatures lack the white neck marking.

## Barnacle Goose

*Branta leucopsis*
24–28 in. (61–71 cm)

*Range:* This Old World goose occurs very rarely along the Atlantic Coast southward to North Carolina. The Barnacle Goose is more likely to be seen in late autumn around Currituck Sound or at Pea Island than elsewhere in the state. There is no record for South Carolina.

*Feeding habits:* See Canada Goose.

*Description:* This small dark goose has a black neck with a black ridge extending onto the crown. The face is white.

## White-fronted Goose

*Anser albifrons*
26–30 in. (66–76 cm)

*Range:* A very rare winter visitor in the Carolinas, this species normally winters on the Gulf Coast

Brant
Richard A. Rowlett

or west of the Rocky Mountains. White-fronted Geese are seen most often in the Carolinas wherever large numbers of geese congregate either inland or along the coast.

*Feeding habits:* See Canada Goose.

*Description:* This is a gray goose with yellow legs. The adult has a white band of feathers completely encircling the base of the pink bill and irregular black bands across the underparts. The immature has a yellowish bill.

---

## Snow Goose
(Blue Goose)
*Chen caerulescens*
23–38 in. (58–96 cm)

*Range:* From early November to February or March, large numbers of Snow Geese winter at Lake Mattamuskeet, around Currituck Sound, and in the Bodie–Pea

Island area of North Carolina. Inland and south of Pea Island the species becomes rare.

*Feeding habits:* Snow Geese prefer the roots and tubers of coastal marsh plants.

*Description:* The Snow Goose and the Blue Goose are now classified as white-phase and dark-phase birds of a single species. White-phase birds far outnumber Blue Geese in the Carolinas, but dark-phase birds are not uncommon, especially at Lake Mattamuskeet. The adult Snow Goose is white with black wing tips and pink feet and bill. Immatures are dingy white with dark feet and bill. The adult Blue Goose is dark gray with a white head; its bill and feet are pink. Immatures are mostly dark gray with dark feet and bill.

Snow Geese
Michael Tove

Snow Goose, dark phase
Kenneth Knapp

## Ross' Goose
*Chen rossii*
about 20 in. (51 cm)

*Range:* The smallest and least abundant of our North American geese, this species breeds in the Arctic and winters almost exclusively in the interior valleys of California. The first Atlantic Coast record occurred in December 1967 when a single bird with a crippled leg appeared in North Carolina at Pea Island National Wildlife Refuge. The gimpy bird and at least one other Ross' Goose appeared in subsequent winters, once having lingered until early April.

*Feeding habits:* See Canada Goose.

*Description:* Ross' Goose is similar to a white-phase Snow Goose. Look for Ross' smaller size and stubby bill as well as the absence of the dark streak made by lamellae on the bill of the Snow Goose. When seen at very close range, the adult Ross' Goose has warty protuberances at the base of its bill.

## SUBFAMILY DENDROCYGNINAE: WHISTLING-DUCKS

## Fulvous Whistling-Duck
(Fulvous Tree Duck)
*Dendrocygna bicolor*
20 in. (51 cm)

*Range:* Since the 1950s the Fulvous Whistling-Duck has been an uncommon and erratic winter visitor in freshwater marshes and impoundments along the Carolina coast. Inland sightings are very rare and occur mostly in spring. Although individual birds may linger into June, there is no evidence of local breeding by this essentially Mexican species.

*Feeding habits:* The Fulvous Whistling-Duck feeds at night and does not dive. It eats corn, acorns, and various seeds.

*Description:* This tawny-brown goose-like duck has a dark bill, bluish feet, and white marks on the neck, sides, and rump. Its call is a shrill whistle.

*Fulvous Whistling-Duck*
John Erickson

SUBFAMILY ANATINAE: SURFACE-FEEDING DUCKS

## Ruddy Shelduck
*Tadorna ferruginea*
25 in. (64 cm)

*Range:* Three Ruddy Shelducks were taken from a flock of five in Currituck County, N.C., in 1886. In the absence of convincing evidence that this Eurasian species might occur naturally in North Carolina, the record at present must be regarded as representing birds escaped from captivity. The species is popular with waterfowl fanciers. (hypothetical status)

## Mallard
*Anas platyrhynchos*
21–27 in. (53–68 cm)

*Range:* A common winter resident of freshwater habitats throughout the region, the Mallard breeds locally in all sections of the Carolinas. Most of these nesting birds probably have reverted to the wild from introduced stock. The British name for the Mallard is "Stock Duck," a reference to the many domesticated strains derived from it.

*Nesting habits:* See comments on order.

*Feeding habits:* Mallards and other puddle ducks feed mostly on vegetable matter obtained by tipping-up in shallow water.

*Description:* The Mallard has a blue speculum bordered by white. The adult male has a yellow bill, green head, and white neck band. The female is mottled brown.

*Mallard, male*
William G. Cobey

*Mallard, female*
Bill Alexander

## Black Duck
*Anas rubripes*
20–26 in. (51–66 cm)

*Range:* The Black Duck is a fairly common winter resident throughout the Carolinas, but far more numerous toward the coast than inland. The species breeds regularly in northeastern North Carolina and to an unknown extent southward at least to the vicinity of Cape Romain National Wildlife Refuge in South Carolina and inland to the mountains.

*Nesting habits:* Nests are on the ground near water, and young leave the nest about mid-June.

*Feeding habits:* Black Ducks eat vegetable matter, snails, crustaceans, and insects.

*Description:* The Black Duck has a dark body, light head, and a violet speculum. White wing linings contrast with the dark body. The male has a yellow bill; the female, a mottled greenish one.

## Gadwall
*Anas strepera*
19–23 in. (48–58 cm)

*Range:* An uncommon to fairly common winter resident, the Gadwall is found throughout the Carolinas, though tending to be localized in distribution. The species has been nesting at Pea Island since 1939.

*Nesting habits:* Nests are often placed in the dense grasses along impoundment dikes, on small islands in the impoundments at Pea Island, or on islands of dredged material in Oregon Inlet.

*Black Duck*
William G. Cobey

*Gadwalls, male left, female right*
Bill Alexander

*Feeding habits:* Although the diet of the Gadwall is nearly 98% vegetable, the species dives much more frequently than do other surface-feeding ducks.

*Description:* This gray-brown duck has a dark bill and yellow feet. Its speculum is brown, black, and white with the white patch nearest the body.

# Pintail
*Anas acuta*
21–30 in. (53–76 cm)

*Range:* Pintails are abundant winter residents in northeastern North Carolina from September through April. The species becomes less common southward along the coast, and inland it is primarily an uncommon migrant. A pair of Pintails nested successfully in Guilford County in 1950.

*Feeding habits:* Pintails eat mostly the seeds of aquatic plants plus a few crustaceans and insects.

*Description:* The Pintail's name refers to the greatly elongated central tail feathers, which in some males may be nearly 10 inches (25 cm) long. These are long-necked, slender, agile ducks. The male has white underparts extending up the neck to a point behind the eye. The female is mottled brown. Both sexes have a metallic brown speculum with a white border on the trailing edge of the wing.

---

# Falcated Teal
*Anas falcata*
20 in. (51 cm)

*Range:* An adult male, obviously in poor health, was seen at an impoundment in Carteret County, N.C., in December 1974. Later its partially eaten carcass was preserved as a specimen. Falcated Teals taken in Alaska may be of natural occurrence, but birds found in the contiguous United States probably escaped from waterfowl fanciers. (hypothetical status)

Pintail, male
John L. Tveten

# Green-winged Teal
(Common Teal)
*Anas crecca*
12–16 in. (30–40 cm)

*Range:* Common winter residents in coastal Carolina, Green-winged Teals sometimes arrive in August and linger until early May, rarely throughout the summer. The species is generally uncommon inland. Stragglers from the European population, formerly called "Common Teal," are occasional visitors to coastal Carolina.

*Feeding habits:* Teals commonly associate with Pintails, sharing a preference for fresh water and for a diet consisting chiefly of seeds from aquatic plants.

*Description:* This is the smallest of our surface-feeding ducks. The male Green-winged Teal has a dark head with an oval patch of green about the eye, a white bar on the side of its body, and a green speculum. The female is mottled brown with a green speculum. The European Green-winged Teal is similar, but the male has no white bar on its body.

# Baikal Teal
*Anas formosa*
about 12 in. (30 cm)

*Range:* A hunter shot one of these Asian birds in North Carolina in 1912. The species is popular with waterfowl fanciers. (hypothetical status)

---

# Blue-winged Teal
*Anas discors*
14–16 in. (36–40 cm)

*Range:* Primarily a transient in most parts of the Carolinas, the Blue-winged Teal is fairly common inland and common along the coast, where small numbers remain throughout the winter. The species has been breeding occasionally at Pea Island since 1938, at Cape Romain since 1960, and in North Carolina's Onslow and Pamlico Counties since 1969.

*Nesting habits:* Nests are on the ground, and young leave them in June. The incubation period for this teal is only about 3 weeks, slightly shorter than average for larger waterfowl.

Green-winged Teal, male right, female left
Bill Alexander

Blue-winged Teal, male
William G. Cobey

*Feeding habits:* Food is about 70% seeds, with the animal matter being primarily snails, insects, and crustaceans.

*Description:* Both sexes have a green speculum and a large pale blue patch on the leading portion of each wing. The male has a white crescent on its face.

## Cinnamon Teal
*Anas cyanoptera*
15–17 in. (38–43 cm)

*Range:* Although common in the western United States, the Cinnamon Teal is a rare accidental in the Carolinas, usually found along the coast in winter or early spring.

*Feeding habits:* Cinnamon and Blue-winged Teals have similar feeding habits.

*Description:* The male Cinnamon Teal is solid cinnamon-red on the head and underparts. Otherwise plumages of this species are almost identical to those of the Blue-winged Teal.

## Garganey Teal
*Anas querquedula*
about 15 in. (38 cm)

*Range:* A drake Garganey Teal visited the Outer Banks of North Carolina in March 1957 and was positively identified by several competent observers. Because this European species has never before been recorded in the wild in North America, the bird is assumed to have escaped from a zoological garden or private waterfowl collection. (hypothetical status)

## European Wigeon
*Anas penelope*
17–21 in. (43–53 cm)

*Range:* A few of these Old World ducks appear along the Atlantic Coast of North America every fall. From October to mid-April, the species has been recorded in the Carolinas as far south as the Combahee River and as far west as Greenville, S.C.

*Feeding habits:* See American Wigeon.

*Description:* Similar to the American Wigeon, the male European has a rusty head with a creamy yellow crown. The female European has a brownish head with a dark cap.

## American Wigeon
(Baldpate)
*Anas americana*
18–23 in. (45–58 cm)

*Range:* A common winter resident that is more abundant along the coast than inland, the American Wigeon is generally present from October to April. Despite numerous June records from South Carolina, there is no evidence of breeding in that state.

*Feeding habits:* Wigeons are primarily plant-eaters, with small mollusks and insects composing less than 10% of their diet.

*American Wigeon, male*
John Trott

*Northern Shoveler, male*
Michael P. Schultz

Coastal birds sometimes feed heavily on certain kinds of green algae found in the intertidal zone. These birds take on a strong repugnant odor and are generally considered unpalatable.

*Description:* This brownish duck has a large white patch on the leading portion of each wing. Males have a light head with a green mask extending from one eye to the other around the back of the head. Females have a gray head. Both sexes have a blue bill that distinguishes this species from the dark-billed Gadwall.

## Northern Shoveler
*Anas clypeata*
17–22 in. (43–56 cm)

*Range:* A locally common winter resident along the coast, the Northern Shoveler occurs inland chiefly as an uncommon migrant. Mostly present from September through April, shovelers may linger into June, but there is no evidence of breeding in the Carolinas.

*Feeding habits:* All surface-feeding ducks have comblike lamellae along the edges of their bills, but in the shoveler these structures reach their highest development. Shovelers usually feed in very shallow water by digging into soft mud while swimming along with heads partly or completely submerged. The tongue, roof of the mouth, and soft edges of the bill have many nerves sensitive to touch and taste. These nerves, along with the lamellae, let shovelers filter out water, mud, and inedible items so they can feed on desirable mollusks, crustaceans, insects, and seeds. Although the shoveler's preference for animal matter sometimes makes it unpalatable, it is an economically valuable species because it consumes harmful insects.

*Description:* The greatly elongated bill is diagnostic. The male shoveler has a green head, and the female is mottled with brown. In flight both sexes show a large blue patch on the leading edge of each wing, but the large bill and the large amount of white on the male's body prevent confusion with the smaller Blue-winged Teal.

## Wood Duck
*Aix sponsa*
17–21 in. (43–53 cm)

Wood Duck, male
William G. Cobey

*Range:* A fairly common to common permanent resident throughout the Carolinas, the Wood Duck is more common in the swamps and wooded ponds and river bottoms of the coastal plain than in the western counties. The species is less numerous in winter than at other seasons.

*Nesting habits:* Mating takes place about midwinter, and the female usually builds her nest in a natural cavity in a dead or living tree standing in or near water. Nest boxes and abandoned chimneys may be used, and sometimes the nest is located a considerable distance from water. Eggs, creamy white and usually numbering 9 to 14, are laid from February to April, with the peak period of hatching in April and early May. A few second broods have been recorded. "Dump nests" may con-

tain up to 40 eggs deposited by more than one female. Only the hen incubates, but the strikingly colored drake remains more or less in attendance until time to molt into eclipse plumage. Usually on the morning of the day after hatching, the downy chicks respond to coaxing calls from the parent waiting below, claw their way to the entrance hole, and flutter down to the water or soft ground. Although the young can fly at 8 to 9 weeks, they hide and feed in emergent vegetation until August when the brood is strong upon the wing and ready to flock with other families.

*Feeding habits:* Vegetable matter constitutes about 90% of the Wood Duck's diet with favored items being cypress cones and galls, wild rice, pondweeds, water lily seeds, wild grapes, duckweed,

water elm seeds, acorns, beech-
nuts, and water hickory nuts. Animal food is nearly always insects.

*Description:* This is our only
native duck with a long,
smoothed-down crest. The male
Wood Duck has an irregular white
marking extending from his chin
and throat toward the eye and
nape. The female has a white eye
ring and a restricted white patch
on her chin.

## Mandarin Duck
*Aix galericulata*
about 17 in. (43 cm)

*Range:* A native of eastern Asia
and Japan, the Mandarin Duck is
popular with waterfowl fanciers
and is frequently used in scientific
studies. One shot near New Bern,
N.C., in 1972 at present must be
regarded as an escaped bird even
though its plumage revealed no
evidence of recent captivity.
(hypothetical status)

SUBFAMILY AYTHYINAE: DIVING DUCKS

## Redhead
*Aythya americana*
17–23 in. (43–58 cm)

*Range:* An uncommon winter
resident in the Carolinas, the Redhead is most likely to be found
from late October to mid-March
in the salty or brackish waters of
coastal sounds, bays, and estuaries. It is fairly common in Core
Sound and the lower part of Pamlico Sound in most years. Here
Redheads gather in closely packed
rafts of hundreds, or even thousands. A few birds visit inland
lakes and ponds, chiefly during
migration.

*Feeding habits:* The Redhead
dives from the surface and swims
underwater to obtain food, most
of which is vegetable matter.

*Description:* Redheads and Canvasbacks are so similar in appearance and behavior that many

Redhead, male
Robert Needham

Redhead, female
Bill Alexander

people are unable to tell them apart. Males of both species have cinnamon-red heads, black breasts, and generally gray bodies. The Canvasback is generally larger with a lighter body color. It has a flattened head-bill profile that makes the eyes appear to be almost on top of its head. The Redhead has a rounded head and a bluish bill with a dark tip. The female Redhead greatly resembles a female Ring-necked Duck, but the Redhead's bill has no white band across it.

*Ring-necked Duck, male*
Bill Alexander

## Ring-necked Duck
*Aythya collaris*
14–18 in. (35–45 cm)

*Range:* A common winter resident throughout the Carolinas from late October to April, the Ring-necked Duck prefers freshwater lakes and impoundments, and it is seldom seen in brackish and salt water.

*Ring-necked Duck, female*
Bill Alexander

*Feeding habits:* This is a diving duck with a predominantly vegetable diet.

*Description:* The species is named for the indistinct chestnut band encircling the neck of the adult male. The male has a solid black back and a prominent white bar on the side of the body. The brownish female has a white eye ring. Both sexes have a black-tipped blue bill with a distinct white band separating the black from the blue.

## Canvasback
*Aythya valisineria*
19–24 in. (48–61 cm)

*Range:* Once an extremely abundant winter resident in the sounds and bays of North Carolina and Virginia, the Canvasback was brought almost to the point of extinction by overshooting, botulism, and drainage and drought in the breeding grounds. Closed hunting seasons and habitat restoration projects appear to have

*Canvasback, male*
Bill Alexander

*Canvasback, female*
Bill Alexander

saved the species. In most years the Canvasback is a fairly common winter resident in coastal North and South Carolina from November to mid-April and an uncommon winter visitor inland.

*Feeding habits:* Canvasbacks gather in rafts to feed in fresh or brackish waters. Like the Red-head, this species dives from the surface and swims underwater to obtain food that is mostly vegetable matter.

*Description:* See Redhead.

# Greater Scaup
*Aythya marila*
16–21 in. (40–53 cm)

*Range:* Uncommon inland and even along the coast in South Carolina, the Greater Scaup is a fairly common winter resident only in Pamlico Sound and surrounding waters. The species is present from October to April.

*Feeding habits:* Although about half its food is vegetable, the Greater Scaup usually consumes enough shellfish to make its flesh unpalatable.

*Description:* Similar to male Ring-necked Ducks but larger, male scaup have a solid blue bill, gray back, and whitish sides. Greater and Lesser Scaup are difficult to distinguish from each other reliably either in the water or on the wing. Greaters have a longer white stripe in the wing and a more rounded head. Female Greaters and Lessers are brownish and have white surrounding the base of the solid blue bill.

*Greater Scaup, male*
Richard A. Rowlett

## Lesser Scaup
*Aythya affinis*
15–19 in. (38–48 cm)

*Range:* A fairly common to locally abundant winter resident and common transient throughout the Carolinas from October to May, the Lesser Scaup is found on fresh water far more often than the Greater. Nevertheless, large rafts of Lesser Scaup often occur along the coast. Although stragglers are found in summer, the Lesser Scaup is not known to breed in the Carolinas.

*Feeding habits:* Like the Greater Scaup, the Lesser sometimes feeds on shellfish and develops an undesirable flavor; at other times it feeds on plants and becomes highly palatable.

*Description:* See Greater Scaup.

---

## Common Goldeneye
(American Golden-eye)
*Bucephala clangula*
16–23 in. (40–58 cm)

*Range:* An uncommon winter resident from October to April, the Common Goldeneye is a coastal species that occurs inland as an uncommon migrant and rare winter visitor.

*Feeding habits:* Diving birds with a preference for deep water, goldeneyes often eat small mussels that give their flesh an unpalatable flavor.

*Description:* The male Common Goldeneye has black-and-white wings and body. Its dark greenish head is marked with a round

*Lesser Scaup, male*
James F. Parnell

*Lesser Scaup, female*
Edward Burroughs

*Common Goldeneye, male*
Heathcote Kimball

Common Goldeneye, female
James F. Parnell

Bufflehead, male
Bill Faver

white spot on the cheek. Except
for the head, it resembles the male
Bufflehead. In winter, the female
Common Goldeneye has a gray
body, cinnamon head, and white
collar.

## Barrow's Goldeneye
*Bucephala islandica*
16–23 in. (40–58 cm)

*Range:* There are no modern
records, and the few specimens
taken in North Carolina during
the nineteenth century are lost or
inadequately labeled. (hypothetical status)

## Bufflehead
*Bucephala albeola*
13–16 in. (33–40 cm)

*Range:* A fairly common to
common winter resident from
November through April or May,
the Bufflehead is more abundant
along the coast than inland. Birds
of this species tend to stay in
small flocks with a few individuals remaining on guard while the

others dive for food. At the beach,
look for Buffleheads in the breakers near piers and jetties as well as
in freshwater ponds and brackish
tidal waters.

*Feeding habits:* Buffleheads dive
for small aquatic animals.

*Description:* The male Bufflehead
is mostly white with a dark greenish head that is marked by a white
patch extending across the back of
the head from eye to eye. The
female is predominantly black
with an oval white cheek spot.

## Oldsquaw
*Clangula hyemalis*
Male 19–23 in. (48–56 cm)
Female 15–18 in. (38–45 cm)

*Range:* An uncommon winter
resident of North Carolina
sounds, bays, and offshore waters
from November to April, the
Oldsquaw is rare inland and in
coastal South Carolina. Stragglers,
probably injured birds, sometimes
are found in summer adorned in
full breeding plumage.

*Oldsquaw, winter male*
Michael Tove

*Oldsquaw, female*
Richard A. Rowlett

*Feeding habits:* A swift flier and expert diver, the Oldsquaw is a fish-eater that often has tough unpalatable flesh. Its small portion of vegetable food includes seaweed.

*Description:* The Oldsquaw is our only white-headed duck with completely dark wings. The male in winter has a dark patch surrounding the eye and extending toward the side of the neck. The female in winter has a black crown and a small dark cheek patch. Males have greatly elongated central tail feathers.

# Harlequin Duck
*Histrionicus histrionicus*
15–21 in. (38–53 cm)

*Range:* Very rare in winter along our coast as far south as Charleston County, S.C., the Harlequin Duck is usually found along rocky shores, but in the Carolinas it must settle for waters near piers and jetties. Although Harlequins rarely associate closely with other species of ducks, most of the few that have been seen in the Carolinas were feeding near flocks of Bufflehead.

*Feeding habits:* Harlequin Ducks feed mostly on mussels, crustaceans, and other small marine animals.

*Description:* The male Harlequin Duck is predominantly dark blue with white patches on the back, breast, and head. The female is mostly black with white spots before, behind, and below the eye.

# Common Eider
*Somateria mollissima*
23–27 in. (58–68 cm)

*Range:* A rare winter visitor in salt water along the Carolina coast southward to Charleston, the Common Eider has been found from early November to late June. Most sightings appear to involve first-winter birds, which tend to wander farther south than adults.

*Feeding habits:* The Common Eider dives for mollusks and crustaceans.

*Common Eider, female*
Chris Marsh

to submarine shoals to feed on shellfish.

*Description:* The brown female has a stubby bill with a frontal shield that slopes more steeply than that of the Common Eider. First-spring males have a yellow bill, black head, white foreparts, and black body and wings. Adult males have white wing patches and white foreparts that contrast with the predominantly black wings and body. The head is white with a blue-gray nape and an orange bill that flares broadly between the eyes.

*Description:* Females and first-winter males are brown with a dark bill that has a gently sloping frontal shield extending almost to the eyes. Females have a finely barred breast. Young males gradually acquire the black-and-white adult plumage. Adult males have a yellow bill, black crown, white cheek, and green nape.

## King Eider
*Somateria spectabilis*
19–25 in. (48–63 cm)

*Range:* Even rarer than the Common Eider along the Carolina coast southward to Charleston, the King Eider has been found from early October to late April. Usually a bird of the open sea, it sometimes occurs close to shore. Most King Eiders seen in the Carolinas are immature birds.

*Feeding habits:* King Eiders dive

## White-winged Scoter
*Melanitta deglandi*
19–24 in. (48–61 cm)

## Surf Scoter
*Melanitta perspicillata*
17–22 in. (43–56 cm)

## Black Scoter
(American Scoter, Common Scoter)
*Melanitta nigra*
17–21 in. (43–53 cm)

*Range:* Scoters are found along our coast from October to May, rarely into June. Although they may winter in sounds and bays or feed close to the beaches, they are usually seen offshore where they fly with rapid wing beats in long skeins just above the waves, swim in rafts, and dive for shellfish. The White-winged Scoter is uncommon. Relative abundance of Surf and Black Scoters varies considerably from one season to the next

*White-winged Scoter, male*
Michael Tove

and from place to place along our extensive coastline. Generally speaking, however, they are fairly common to common, becoming locally abundant in migration during October. Because "Sea Coots" are rarely hunted, little informa-

tion is available on their numbers and movements. Individuals of all three scoter species may visit inland waters during migration, but such occurrences are extremely rare.

*Feeding habits:* Scoters dive for shellfish.

*Description:* Scoters are large black sea ducks. The White-winged is easily recognized by the white speculum; the male has a white eye patch and a black knob above the orange bill. The male Surf Scoter has a white patch on the forehead and on the nape, and the male Black Scoter has an orange knob above the black bill. For identification of female scoters, consult a field guide.

## SUBFAMILY OXYURINAE: RUDDY AND MASKED DUCKS

### Ruddy Duck
*Oxyura jamaicensis*
14–17 in. (35–43 cm)

*Range:* A common winter resident from October to May, the Ruddy Duck is more numerous along the coast than inland. Nearly extirpated by market hunters, Ruddy Ducks have made a good recovery and can now be found in large rafts in our estuaries. Evidence of breeding has been obtained from Colleton and Charleston Counties in South Carolina and from Pamlico County in North Carolina.

*Nesting habits:* Although Ruddy

Ducks frequently appropriate an old coot or gallinule nest or lay eggs in the active nest of a grebe or another diving duck, the species is capable of building a very nice basketlike structure. Woven of reeds, rushes, flags, and other convenient marsh plants, the nest is built up 7 or 8 inches (17–20 cm) above water level. It is firmly attached to the surrounding living plants and usually is well concealed by them. Only sparsely lined, the nest often has a sloping platform of reeds leading to the water, which normally is about 2 or 3 feet (61–92 cm) deep at the

*Ruddy Duck, male*
Gilbert S. Grant

*Ruddy Duck, female*
James F. Parnell

nest site. Laying probably begins in April in the Carolinas. The species normally lays from 5 to 10 eggs, with the larger clutches often deposited in two layers because the eggs are surprisingly large for the size of the hen. Decidedly rough and granular, freshly laid eggs are dull white, but they become stained during the 25 to 26 days of incubation. Although the female does all the incubating, the male normally remains with her and helps tend the brood. Newly hatched Ruddy Ducks are very large and can dive for their food right away, unlike most other ducklings, which feed from the surface for several weeks.

*Feeding habits:* Ruddy Ducks dive for wild celery and other plants that grow in estuaries. When diving, Ruddies may flip forward like other river ducks or submerge vertically like a grebe.

*Description:* Both sexes have a black cap and white cheeks. Their long tail is fan-shaped and often uptilted. In taking flight Ruddy Ducks, like all divers, must patter along the surface of the water for a short distance. On land Ruddies, like grebes, are almost helpless.

SUBFAMILY MERGINAE: MERGANSERS

## Hooded Merganser
*Lophodytes cucullatus*
16–19 in. (40–48 cm)

*Range:* A locally fairly common winter resident, the Hooded Merganser is most numerous along the coast where it is found on both fresh and brackish waters. Hooded Mergansers breed at least very rarely southward to Charleston and inland to Orangeburg, S.C., Wake County, N.C., and

*Hooded Merganser, male*
Michael P. Schultz

probably to North Wilkesboro, N.C.

*Nesting habits:* A hole-nesting species, the Hooded Merganser may occupy Wood Duck boxes or old Pileated Woodpecker cavities. The 8 to 12 eggs are almost round and glossy white in color. Young apparently leave nests in the Carolinas in April or May.

*Feeding habits:* Mergansers dive for fish.

*Description:* Mergansers have long slender serrated bills. The male Hooded has a black head with a fanlike white crest that is bordered with black. The female has a brownish head with a bushy crest.

## Common Merganser
(American Merganser)
*Mergus merganser*
21–27 in. (53–68 cm)

*Range:* A rare to uncommon winter visitor from November to April, the Common Merganser is found primarily on fresh water in

the northern half of North Carolina. A pair once nested successfully in a stump at Bennett's Pond in Chowan County, N.C.

*Feeding habits:* Mergansers dive for fish.

*Description:* Mergansers have long slender serrated bills. The male Common has a green head that contrasts sharply with the white neck and breast; the crest seldom is noticeable. Females have a cinnamon head that contrasts sharply with the white of the neck and breast; the crest is more pronounced than in the male. At close range the female shows a well-defined white throat patch.

## Red-breasted Merganser
*Mergus serrator*
19–26 in. (48–66 cm)

*Range:* An abundant winter resident on salt water from late October to May, the Red-breasted Merganser is an uncommon transient and winter visitor inland. The species breeds at least locally and on rare occasions along the coast southward to Charleston. Numerous summer sightings of adults suggest that breeding may be more common than the scant evidence indicates.

*Nesting habits:* On its Canadian breeding grounds, the species normally builds its nest on the ground in a place well concealed by driftwood, a fallen tree, or low overhanging branches. Sites usually are in the borders of fresh-

*Red-breasted Merganser, female*
Edward Burroughs

water ponds or rivers, but occasionally the birds nest on the shore of the ocean.

*Feeding habits:* Mergansers dive for fish.

*Description:* Mergansers have long slender serrated bills. The male Red-breasted has a green head with a shaggy crest, and its white throat patch contrasts sharply with the reddish-brown breast patch. The female has a brown head with a shaggy crest, and the dark head and neck plumage gradually fades into the light breast.

# Order Falconiformes: Vultures, Hawks, and Falcons

Falconiformes are diurnal birds of prey that have strong feet with long claws and an opposable hind toe. Their bills are sharply hooked, and their nostrils open through a fleshy cere on the upper mandible.

Vultures feed almost exclusively on dead animals. Various hawks, like their nocturnal counterparts the owls, play a key role in controlling populations of rabbits, rats, mice, and other small animals that can become pests if they are too numerous. Because of their feeding habits, birds of prey give early warning when environmental pollutants (e.g., certain pesticides) that are harmful to people build up in the food chain. These pollutants become concentrated in the tissues of flesh-eating birds and eventually cause illness, sterility, or death.

In most species of falconiformes both parents help build the nest, incubate the eggs, and care for the young. Newly hatched birds are covered with down and have their eyes open, but they must be tended in the nest for a month or more in the large species. The soft natal down is replaced by a woolier coat of down before the first true feathers emerge. Young hawks, eagles, and kites can generally eject loose feces over the rim of the nest soon after hatching, but nests sometimes become soiled during the long nestling period. Several birds, notably the Red-tailed Hawk, have been seen adding green boughs to nests well after the eggs have hatched: This may be done to cover excrement, or perhaps to provide shade for the nestlings while the adults are away from the nest. Falconiformes generally obtain sexual maturity at the same time that they acquire adult plumage, which may be a period of several years in eagles and other large species.

## Family Cathartidae: American Vultures

### Turkey Vulture
*Cathartes aura*
26–31 in. (66–81 cm)
*Range:* Fairly common to common permanent residents throughout the Carolinas, Turkey Vultures are rare in the mountains in winter. Elsewhere, the local population is increased in winter by the arrival of migrants from the north. Although vultures breed in remote woodlands and swamps, they visit highways and farmlands in search of food. Both Turkey and Black Vultures are considerably less numerous today than they

*Turkey Vulture*
Michael Tove

*Turkey Vulture*
Chris Marsh

abandoned buildings may select a spot with an accumulation of debris, though sometimes eggs are deposited on perfectly bare surfaces. The large eggs are white, splotched with brown and purplish markings. Incubation requires slightly more than a month, and nestlings are ready for flight in about 10 to 11 weeks. If the downy white young are disturbed, they will regurgitate their most recent meal of semidigested carrion.

*Feeding habits:* Turkey Vultures feed almost exclusively on dead animals, which they locate by sight and by scent. They are frequently seen along highways where animals have been killed by motor vehicles.

*Description:* These large brownish-black birds are often seen soaring on rising air currents with wings held motionless, angling upward from their bodies in a shallow V. Adults have red skin on a head bare of feathers. Immatures have a black head. Look for the two-toned under-wing pattern, dark on the leading edge and light on the trailing edge. Wingspan is about 6 feet (2 m).

were before the disposal of garbage in sanitary landfills and the burial of dead stock became widespread practices.

*Nesting habits:* Two, rarely three, eggs are laid in early April, though eggs also have been found in February and March. Birds nesting in natural cavities in large living or dead trees may pull some rotten wood from inside the hollow, but no real attempt is made to build a nest. Birds nesting on rocky ledges, in caves, or in

## Black Vulture
*Coragyps atratus*
23–27 in. (58–68 cm)

*Range:* Common in the lower coastal plain of the Carolinas but uncommon in the piedmont, Black Vultures tend to be rare in

*Black Vultures*
Michael Tove

*Black Vulture*
Chris Marsh

the mountains and most numerous in southeastern South Carolina. Locally the species is called "Carrion Crow" or "South Carolina Buzzard."

*Nesting habits:* Black Vultures have essentially the same nesting habits as the Turkey Vulture. Egg laying usually begins a little earlier, and Black Vulture eggs are greenish-white with brown markings.

*Feeding habits:* More gregarious than Turkey Vultures, Blacks usually gather around large carcasses and ignore small dead animals. Both vultures frequent cattle farms.

*Description:* The Black Vulture has a bare black head, a short tail, and a conspicuous white patch at the tip of each under-wing surface. Smaller than the Turkey Vulture, the Black has a wingspan of 4½ to 5 feet (about 1.5 m). In flight the Black flaps more frequently and rapidly than does the Turkey, and it holds its wings straight out from the body while soaring.

# Family Accipitridae: Hawks, Eagles, and Kites

## White-tailed Kite
*Elanus leucurus*
15–17 in. (38–43 cm)
*Range:* The White-tailed Kite is a very rare accidental in the grasslands and marshes of the Carolinas.

*Feeding habits:* Kites hunt by hovering and slipping downward feet first to seize their prey. After the capture they swoop, or kite, upward. The White-tailed Kite's diet consists chiefly of rodents and insects.

*Description:* Adults have a white head, tail, and underparts; gray back; and gray wings marked with a large black patch at the bend. The long white tail and pointed wings identify the brownish immatures. White-tailed Kites are gull-like in flight.

## Swallow-tailed Kite
*Elanoides forficatus*
19–26 in. (48–66 cm)

*Range:* In the heavy woodlands, river bottoms, and cypress lagoons of coastal South Carolina from the Santee River southward, the Swallow-tailed Kite is an uncommon breeding summer resident. Usually arriving in mid-March and departing by late August, the birds are sometimes present from early March into November. Many spring and summer sightings in eastern North Carolina, particularly on the Outer Banks, suggest the possibility of breeding; but as yet no nests or young birds have been found in this state. The Francis Marion National Forest appears to be the northernmost point on the East Coast at which one can expect to see Swallow-tailed Kites regularly during the breeding season.

The Swallow-tailed Kite was a regular fall migrant in the North Carolina mountains prior to 1900. At that time the species still bred in the upper Mississippi Valley.

*Nesting habits:* Swallow-tailed Kites usually form colonies of three to six pairs with nests in the tops of tall trees that stand within about 300 feet (90 m) of each other. The birds repair and use old nests, which are platforms of twigs and bark mixed with Spanish moss. Eggs number two, or sometimes three, and are white splashed with brown and black markings. The incubation period is 3 to 4 weeks, and young remain in the nest 36 to 41 days.

*Feeding habits:* Swallow-tailed Kites eat mostly insects (particularly dragonflies), reptiles, and amphibians. See White-tailed Kite for hunting method.

*Description:* The Swallow-tailed Kite is a black-and-white hawk with a long, deeply forked black tail.

## Mississippi Kite
*Ictinia mississippiensis*
13–15 in. (33–38 cm)

*Range:* The Mississippi Kite is a fairly common summer resident of riverbottom forests and adjacent farmlands in the coastal plain of South Carolina from March to October. It is very rare farther inland, throughout North Carolina in all seasons, and along the South Carolina coast in winter. Numerous sightings along the Roanoke River downstream from Roanoke Rapids suggest the possibility of local nesting, but as yet no nests or preflight young have been found.

*Nesting habits:* Mississippi Kites usually reach the South Carolina breeding grounds in late April and begin laying about a month later. Made of twigs, leaves, and moss, nests are placed in a fork or crotch of a tree and are usually more than 100 feet (30 m) above ground. The same nest may be used in successive years. The one, two, or rarely three whitish eggs require about 31 or 32 days for incubation. Young leave the nest when about 5 weeks old and are fed on the wing for several weeks.

*Feeding habits:* Mississippi Kites often feed in flocks. Their diet is composed almost entirely of insects, which are captured and consumed while the birds are on the wing.

*Description:* Adults have a plain gray head and underparts, dark back and wings, and notched black tail. Immatures are brownish with a notched black tail that is barred with white below.

## Goshawk
*Accipiter gentilis*
Male about 22 in. (56 cm)
Female about 25 in. (63 cm)

*Range:* The status of the Goshawk in the Carolinas is uncertain. The species appears to be a rare permanent resident in the North Carolina mountains. Elsewhere in our region Goshawks are very rare accidental transients. The first North Carolina record occurred in Macon County in 1969 and the first South Carolina record at

Carolina Sandhills National Wildlife Refuge in 1973. These and other early Carolina sightings, including one report of possible nesting in Avery County, N.C., coincided with an unprecedented southward movement of the species that could result in a major range extension.

*Feeding habits:* The Goshawk eats small birds and mammals, and it is capable of capturing grouse and squirrels.

*Description:* Larger than a crow, the Goshawk is a robust, barrel-chested hawk with an extremely long rounded tail and longer, more tapered wings than characteristic of our other accipiters. Adults are dark gray above and light gray below. Immatures are brown with a streaked breast. Look for the conspicuous white eye stripe and fluffy under-tail coverts.

## Sharp-shinned Hawk
*Accipiter striatus*
10–14 in. (25–35 cm)

*Range:* The Sharp-shinned Hawk is a fairly common fall migrant, an uncommon winter resident, and a rare to absent breeding species throughout the Carolinas. Although it will hunt in any kind of woods, it prefers conifers for nesting.

*Nesting habits:* The nest is built of small sticks and twigs in a crotch against the main trunk from 10 to 60 feet (3–18 m) above ground. Breeding apparently

*Sharp-shinned Hawk, immature*
E. Wayne Irvin

*Sharp-shinned Hawk, immature*
Michael Tove

begins in late April. Eggs usually number three to five, rarely seven, and are nearly spherical, being white splashed with brown. Incubation requires about a month and young remain in the nest about 23 days.

*Feeding habits:* The Sharp-shinned Hawk dodges through woodlands in swift pursuit of the small birds that compose the major portion of its diet. Although the species normally takes birds no larger than thrushes, individuals have been known to capture, or at least pursue, Common Flickers, Bobwhites, Wood Ducks, and small herons.

*Description:* Adults are slate-blue above and barred with rusty brown below. Immatures are dark brown above and streaked with brown below. Wings are short and rounded. The long slender tail is squared off when folded, but it

may look slightly rounded when fanned. Size overlaps with that of the Cooper's Hawk, which is generally similar in appearance but has a proportionately larger head and a wider tail that is noticeably rounded even when folded. Cooper's Hawks fly with deep, deliberate wing strokes, often with three flaps and a glide. The Sharp-shinned has a comparatively shallow and irregular wing beat.

## Cooper's Hawk
*Accipiter cooperii*
Male 14–18 in. (35–45 cm)
Female 16–20 in. (40–51 cm)

*Range:* An inhabitant of dense woods and adjacent edges, the Cooper's Hawk is an uncommon winter resident throughout the Carolinas and a rare summer resident found chiefly in the mountains.

*Nesting habits:* The nest is made of sticks and twigs with a lining of bark strips. Usually, it is placed 20 to 60 feet (6–18 m) above ground in the main fork of a tree. The three to six pale bluish-white eggs usually are laid in April and require 35 to 36 days for incubation. Food for nestlings appears to consist entirely of birds, which are picked bare of feathers before being brought to the young. Although they may leave the nest when about a month old, young are not fully independent until they are about 8 weeks old.

*Feeding habits:* The Cooper's Hawk is a bold hunter that frequently visits farmyards to carry away young poultry, thus deserving more than any other of our hawks the name "Chicken Hawk." This accipiter is sometimes destructive to the Bobwhite. It also eats rats, mice, grasshoppers, and birds that may be considered pests (e.g., Rock Doves, blackbirds).

*Description:* The slate-blue back of adult Cooper's and Sharp-shinned Hawks gives these two species the local name of "Blue Darter." See Sharp-shinned Hawk for a comparative description.

*Red-tailed Hawk*
Robert F. Soots Jr.

---

# Red-tailed Hawk
(Harlan's Hawk)
*Buteo jamaicensis*
19–25 in. (48–63 cm)

*Range:* The Red-tailed Hawk is a fairly common permanent resident throughout the Carolinas. The influx of migrants from the north makes the species more numerous in fall and winter than during the breeding season. Red-taileds frequently perch on tall poles or snags along busy highways.

*Nesting habits:* The nest is a bulky structure of sticks lined with finer materials and placed 30 to 60 feet (9–18 m) above ground in the crotch of a large tree near the edge of a patch of heavy timber. Although Red-tailed Hawks prefer to feed in upland habitats, they frequently nest in flood plains. Eggs usually are laid in April, number two to four, and are dull white blotched with varying shades of brown. Incubation takes about 28 days with the male feeding the female on the nest and perhaps relieving her from time to time. Both parents feed the young, which remain in the nest about 6 weeks.

*Feeding habits:* Buteos are soaring hawks that circle overhead and drop (stoop) upon their prey in a steep dive. As a group they are extremely beneficial to man, consuming huge quantities of rats, mice, and other rodents but rarely taking poultry. Other items of diet include rabbits, reptiles, amphibians, and destructive insects such as grasshoppers.

*Description:* Buteos are large-bodied hawks with broad rounded wings and broad fanned tails. Look for the uniformly red tail of the adult Red-tailed Hawk and for the brown belly band that is conspicuous in both adult and immature birds. The species is highly variable, having light phases, dark phases, and many subspecies. One uncommon form that winters in the southern Great Plains, the Harlan's Hawk (*B. j. harlani*), occurred once in late January at the Savannah River National Wildlife Refuge in South Carolina. Now classified as a race of the Red-tailed Hawk, this form has a predominantly white tail.

*Red-shouldered Hawk*
Chris Marsh

## Red-shouldered Hawk
*Buteo lineatus*
17–20 in. (43–51 cm)

*Range:* The Red-shouldered Hawk is a fairly common permanent resident of wet woodlands and nearby farmlands in the coastal plain, uncommon in the piedmont, and rare in the mountains, where its scarcity is attributed to the lack of suitable habitat. In recent years the Red-shouldered Hawk population has declined until this species is less numerous than the Red-tailed Hawk, which seems to be increasing in numbers.

*Nesting habits:* This species has essentially the same nesting habits as the Red-tailed Hawk except that the male Red-shouldered incubates the eggs to a much greater extent.

*Feeding habits:* The Red-shouldered Hawk preys mostly on rats and mice but also takes squirrels, frogs, crayfish, and snakes as well as an occasional bird.

*Description:* This hawk has reddish-brown underparts and wing coverts, and its tail is boldly banded with black. Overhead, the Red-shouldered has translucent patches at the base of the primaries and lacks a belly band.

## Broad-winged Hawk
*Buteo platypterus*
13–19 in. (33–48 cm)

*Range:* Fairly common summer residents in the mountains, becoming uncommon to absent toward the coast, Broad-winged Hawks migrate southward in flocks, often in company with falcons and accipiters. The peak of fall movement usually occurs during the last week of September when many flocks of 50 or more Broad-winged Hawks pass over the mountains. A few Broad-wingeds may linger into winter, but southern Florida is normally the northern limit of winter range.

*Nesting habits:* The nest of sticks and twigs is placed 24 to 40 feet (7.5–12 m) above ground in the crotch of a woodland tree. The two or three eggs, usually laid in April, are whitish with beautiful brown and lilac markings. Incubation, mostly by the female, takes 21 to 25 days, and young may remain in the nest up to 6 weeks.

*Feeding habits:* This small woodland hawk habitually hunts from a perch for insects and small mammals and reptiles.

*Description:* Wings of this species have whitish linings and are extremely wide in proportion to their length. The adult Broad-winged has reddish-brown underparts, and its tail is broadly banded with black and white.

## Swainson's Hawk
*Buteo swainsoni*
19–22 in. (48–56 cm)

*Range:* Swainson's Hawks appear to be very rare accidentals on the Carolina coast in late fall. These brown-chested Western birds often perch near the ground in open country. They feed mostly on small to medium-sized rodents but sometimes eat grasshoppers. (hypothetical status)

## Rough-legged Hawk
*Buteo lagopus*
19–24 in. (48–61 cm)

*Range:* This far-northern hawk is a rare and erratic winter visitor in the Carolinas, occurring most frequently in the northern half of North Carolina. Several of these birds may be seen one winter and none at all the next. An open-country species, the Rough-legged Hawk flies low over fields, often hovering. It frequently perches on fence posts when at rest. Our other buteos tend to prefer tall poles and treetops as perches.

*Feeding habits:* Rodents compose the bulk of the species' diet.

*Description:* The Rough-legged is our only buteo that has a white tail broadly tipped with black. See field guides for illustrations of dark and light phases.

## Golden Eagle
*Aquila chrysaetos*
31–41 in. (78–104 cm)

*Range:* The Golden Eagle appears to be a rare but regular year-round resident in the southern Appalachians, but no evidence of breeding can be cited. The species is a rare fall transient and winter visitor elsewhere in the Carolinas. A good place to look for Golden Eagles is in the vicinity of Graveyard Fields along the Blue Ridge Parkway in Haywood County, N.C.

*Feeding habits:* Golden Eagles feed mostly on mammals such as

*Golden Eagle*
Bill Duyck

rabbits, but on occasion they will take game birds up to the size of a Turkey. Although in some parts of the country Golden Eagles undoubtedly present a problem for ranchers at calving and lambing time, they probably consume enough rabbits and rodents to be more beneficial than harmful in the long run.

*Description:* This massive bird has a wingspan of about 78 inches (2 m). The adult is dark brown with faint light bands on the tail and golden neck plumes that can be seen only at close range. The immature is similar but has white patches at the base of the tail and near the tip of each wing; it lacks the golden neck plumes. The legs are feathered nearly to the toes.

## Bald Eagle

*Haliaeetus leucocephalus*
32–43 in. (81–109 cm)

*Range:* Bald Eagles are rare transients found at lakes throughout the inland portions of the Carolinas as well as along the coast, where a few birds may appear at any month. A few pairs still breed in the region, most of them in southeastern South Carolina.

*Nesting habits:* The nest, which may be used for many years, is placed in the top of a tall tree and may measure 6 feet (2 m) across and is often just as deep. Boat-tailed Grackles and Great Horned Owls may take apartments in the sides of the massive structure. Breeding begins in December or January, incubation of the two white eggs requires 35 days, and

*Bald Eagle*
Elizabeth Conrad

*Bald Eagles at nest*
Dan Guravich

young remain in the nest at least 10 weeks after hatching. Young birds require several years to reach maturity.

*Feeding habits:* Bald Eagles eat mostly fish picked up dead on the shore or robbed from Ospreys.

They can capture coots, herons, small mammals, and wounded ducks; but they almost never take poultry, healthy game species, or fish of commercial value. Bald Eagles and all other birds of prey are fully protected by law in the hope that the end of senseless shooting will enable these magnificent birds to recover from the adverse effects of pesticide pollution.

*Description:* This eagle has a wingspan of more than 6 feet (2 m). Adults are dark brown except for the white head and tail. Immatures are brown and irregularly marked with white until their fourth year. The lower part of the leg is not feathered. Eagles soar with their wings held straight out from the body.

## Marsh Hawk
(Harrier)
*Circus cyaneus*
17–24 in. (43–61 cm)

*Range:* A winter resident throughout the Carolinas, the Marsh Hawk is uncommon over most of the inland counties, common over coastal marshes, and most numerous during migrations. On very rare occasions Marsh Hawks may breed in northeastern North Carolina.

*Nesting habits:* The Marsh Hawk nests and roosts on or near the ground. The species is almost silent except during its spectacular courtship flights. The nuptial flight is a series of nose dives with the bird almost stalling at the peak of each upward swoop before plunging downward again. Made mostly of sticks and straws and sometimes well lined with grasses, the nest may be flimsy or substantial depending upon its

susceptibility to flooding. The four to six dull white or pale bluish-white eggs are generally unmarked. Laying probably begins by mid-April. Incubation is mostly by the female and requires about a month. Young are ready to fly when 5 or 6 weeks old. The family group remains together for quite a while, and parents often drop prey for the young hawks to catch in midair.

*Feeding habits:* Marsh Hawks hunt by sailing low over fields, meadows, and marshlands. They eat frogs, insects, and small snakes and birds in addition to mice, rats, and other small mammals. They perch on low stumps or posts to consume their prey.

*Description:* Both the gray male and the brown female have a long banded tail with a prominent white rump patch.

# Family Pandionidae: Osprey

## Osprey
*Pandion haliaetus*
21–25 in. (53–63 cm)

*Range:* Ospreys breed on or near the Carolina coast in good numbers, but they become rare in winter. During migrations the birds occur regularly around lakes inland to the mountains.

*Nesting habits:* "Fish Hawks" build bulky nests of sticks in tall

dead trees, on stumps in water, or on man-made platforms such as channel markers. In areas of suitable habitat, breeding populations appear loosely colonial. Returning to the same nest year after year, usually by early March, the birds repair and enlarge the structure each season before the female lays two to four buffy eggs splotched with reddish brown. The eggshells absorb an

*Osprey*
James F. Parnell

oily odor from the adults' plumage during the 4 to 5 weeks of incubation. The female does most of the incubating, being relieved by the male only when she is off feeding. Young remain in the nest about 8 weeks.

*Feeding habits:* Ospreys feed almost entirely on fish obtained by hovering over water and diving headlong upon the prey, impaling it with the claws. In addition to sharply curved nails, their feet have pads with short stiff spicules that help them hold their slippery prey. When flying to a feeding perch or carrying food to young in the nest, the Osprey holds the head of its catch facing forward, thus reducing wind resistance.

During the 1960s, Osprey populations were threatened because many of the fish used for food had high levels of pesticide residues that caused eggshell thinning or sterility in adult birds. Recent studies indicate that the species is making a good recovery now that the use of persistent pesticides is strictly controlled in the United States.

*Description:* A dark bird with white underparts, the Osprey has a white head with a black eye stripe. Watch for the arched position of the wings in flight and for the black spot underneath at the bend of each wing.

# Family Falconidae: Caracaras and Falcons

## Caracara
(Audubon's Caracara)
*Caracara cheriway*
20–25 in. (51–63 cm)

*Range:* Normally not found north of the Kissimmee Prairie region of Florida, the Caracara is accidental in the Carolinas. Because the species is often kept in captivity, all extralimital records are questionable. The one South Carolina sighting in Charleston County on May 1, 1943, appears to be valid; but the North Carolina bird was remarkably tame and appeared in the northeastern part of the state a few days after a Caracara is known to have escaped from a zoological garden in Norfolk, Virginia. (hypothetical status)

## Prairie Falcon
*Falco mexicanus*
16–21 in. (40–53 cm)

*Range:* Although there is no reason to doubt the careful

identification of the bird seen in Carteret County, N.C., on May 23, 1968, all extralimital records of falcons are subject to question because captive birds frequently escape. (hypothetical status)

## Peregrine Falcon
(Duck Hawk)
*Falco peregrinus*
15–20 in. (38–51 cm)

*Range:* Although the Peregrine Falcon visits all parts of the Carolinas and is known to have bred on certain rocky crags in the southern Appalachians, the species is most likely to be seen as an uncommon fall transient and rare winter resident along the coast. It is not presently known as a nesting species in our region.

*Peregrine Falcon, immature*
Richard A. Rowlett

*Peregrine Falcon, adult*
Charles E. Newell

*Feeding habits:* Peregrines feed almost entirely on birds, with waterfowl, shorebirds, and pigeons being among those taken most frequently. Watching a Peregrine put several hundred teal to flight and capture its prey while passing through the flock at a speed possibly in excess of 165 miles (265 km) an hour is one of the supreme thrills of bird-watching. Being near the top of the food chain, the Peregrine Falcon is extremely sensitive to the use of persistent pesticides in any part of its range. Populations that winter where DDT is still used decline even though its use is banned on the breeding grounds.

*Description:* Adults have blue-gray upperparts, barred underparts, a dark cap and wide sideburns that sharply contrast with the white throat, long pointed wings, and a tapered tail that is faintly barred. Immatures are brown with prominent sideburns and a streaked breast.

## Merlin
(Pigeon Hawk)
*Falco columbarius*
10–14 in. (25–35 cm)

*Range:* The Merlin is seen in the Carolinas most frequently as a fall migrant, rare inland and uncommon to fairly common along the coast where a few spend the winter.

*Feeding habits:* Merlins capture many birds, including some

*Merlin, female or immature*
James F. Parnell

species larger than themselves, but they rarely molest poultry. They also consume many insects and occasional small mammals.

*Description:* The adult male Merlin is blue-gray above and streaked below with no sideburns. The female is brown with a streaked breast. Both sexes have long pointed wings and a tapered tail that is boldly barred. Young males resemble females.

## American Kestrel
(Sparrow Hawk)
*Falco sparverius*
9–12 in. (22–30 cm)

*Range:* In the Carolinas, the American Kestrel is fairly common to common in winter, rare to absent in the breeding season, and most abundant during migrations. The "Killy Hawk" or "Kitty Hawk" is seen most frequently perched on wires along the roadside, wagging its tail as it watches for prey.

*American Kestrel, male*
E. Wayne Irvin

four or five eggs are nearly spherical in shape with a buffy ground color that is more or less marked with reddish brown. Nesting is somewhat irregular, but most clutches probably are laid in April or May. Incubation requires about a month, with the female assuming most of the responsibility. Both adults feed the preflight young.

*Feeding habits:* If this bird were named for its most common prey, it would be called "Grasshopper Hawk." Kestrels hunt from a perch and take mice, lizards, small birds, and a variety of insects.

*Description:* The American Kestrel is the smallest, most colorful, and best known of our falcons. The male has a reddish-brown back and tail, blue wings, and prominent sideburns. The female is similar but has brown wings and a barred tail. Both sexes have the long pointed wings and tapered tail typical of falcons. This is our only hawk that regularly sits on roadside wires and wags its tail.

The American Kestrel was formerly a fairly common nesting species in the piedmont and mountains of North Carolina.

*Nesting habits:* Nesting in natural or man-made cavities, the American Kestrel often appropriates old Pileated Woodpecker nest holes or occupies crevices in church steeples or office buildings. The

# Order Galliformes: Fowl-like Birds

All members of this order of fowl-like scratching birds—including the many varieties of domestic chickens, supposedly developed from an Asian jungle fowl—are highly esteemed at the dinner table. They are good runners and fly well for short distances.

# Family Tetraonidae: Grouse

## Ruffed Grouse
*Bonasa umbellus*
16–19 in. (40–48 cm)

*Range:* The Ruffed Grouse lives in the heavy woodlands of the mountains and extreme western piedmont of the Carolinas, where it is a fairly common but very secretive permanent resident.

*Nesting habits:* Male Ruffed Grouse are famous for their drumming performances, which may be heard throughout the year, although they are most frequent in spring and fall. The sound may carry up to a mile (1.6 km) away in calm weather. Each cock has a favorite elevated place, usually a log or stump, where he stands while rapidly beating his wings, both to attract a mate and to warn other males to stay out of his territory. The 8 to 14 creamy or buffy eggs are laid in May or June in a leaf-lined depression sheltered by a log or stump or concealed in dense brush. Eggs hatch in 3 weeks, or perhaps a little longer in cold weather. The female has complete responsibility for incubation of eggs and care of the precocial young, which have their eyes open at hatching and leave the nest as soon as their protectively colored down is dry. Although the chicks quickly learn to scratch for food, the hen must keep them warm and dry at night and in wet weather. Young birds can fly when 10 to 12 days old.

*Feeding habits:* Ruffed Grouse prefer vegetable food such as berries, nuts, acorns, and various seeds; but they consume many grasshoppers and crickets, sometimes searching for them along roadsides and in fields.

*Description:* This grayish- or reddish-brown bird has a heavy body, a slightly crested head, and a wide tail that is barred and broadly tipped with black. The name, often mistakenly given as "Ruffled Grouse," is derived from tufts of black feathers the bird can erect on each side of the neck. The ruff is greatly reduced or absent in the female. Displaying males erect the ruff and point the fanned tail upward. Flight is rapid and evasive.

# Family Phasianidae: Quails and Pheasants

## Bobwhite
*Colinus virginianus*
8–11 in. (20–28 cm)

*Range:* A common permanent resident in all parts of the Carolinas, the "Quail" or "Partridge" may be greatly reduced locally by excessive hunting, habitat destruction, or heavy rains during the nesting season; but the Bobwhite's high reproductive rate soon restores the population to adequate numbers if suitable habitat remains available.

Bobwhite, male
James F. Parnell

*Nesting habits:* In spring the male's clearly whistled *bob-white* can be heard wherever hedgerows, overgrown fields, and open woods offer suitable habitat. The female responds with a lovely four-syllable whistle. Clutches of 12 to 20 pure white eggs are generally completed by late May. The eggs are sharply pointed at one end so they can fit snugly under the body of the incubating bird during the 23 or 24 days required for hatching. Both adults share in nest construction and in the care of eggs and young. The nest is difficult to find because the incubating bird flushes very reluctantly. Always on the ground, the nest is a hollow lined with dead grass and usually protected by overhanging vegetation or a fence. If eggs are taken by predators, a hen will lay again and again until at least one chick survives. This explains reports of young birds seen in November.

Bobwhite chicks are precocial and ready to travel almost as soon as they are dry. In the event of danger, they will scatter and freeze while chicks and adults simultaneously utter the piping "scatter" call to confuse the intruder. Once the chicks have hidden, the parents give a monotonous alarm note with mechanical regularity until the threat has passed. Other special calls can be detected by the careful listener. Winter coveys of perhaps as many as 30 birds are based upon the family group. At night the covey roosts on the ground positioned in a circle with heads pointed outward. When disturbed, quail take off in all directions at once with a whir of wings almost as startling as an explosion.

*Feeding habits:* The Bobwhite eats a great deal of vegetable matter, including various weed seeds; but approximately 17% of its food is insects such as grasshoppers, boll weevils, cutworms, and potato beetles. Many farmers plant lespedeza to provide an abundance of wholesome food for these economically valuable birds.

*Description:* The Bobwhite is a short-tailed chunky brown bird. The male has a white throat and a white stripe above the eye. The female has a buffy throat and eye stripe.

*Introduced game birds:* From time to time game management personnel have attempted to improve hunting opportunities by introducing game birds from other parts of the world. These include smaller races of Bobwhite often called "Mexican Quail," the Japanese Quail (*Coturnix coturnix japonica*), and the Chukar (*Alectoris chukar*), a large European partridge that has become established in the western United States. No evidence exists that these introduced birds have begun breeding in the Carolinas, although some of the smaller Bobwhites may have interbred with the resident race.

## Ring-necked Pheasant
*Phasianus colchicus*
Male 30 in. (76 cm)
Female 20–24 in. (51–61 cm)

*Range:* Many attempts have been made to introduce this handsome long-tailed Asian game bird in various parts of the United States. Introductions in the Northern and Western States generally have been successful, but one of the few breeding populations known in the Southeast is on Hatteras Island in North Carolina. The birds were found breeding near Cape Hatteras in the 1930s and now appear to be well established as far north as Pea Island. They frequent fields with tall grass and the margins of thickets and marshes, normally nesting and roosting on the ground. Pen-raised pheasants sometimes escape and may be seen at scattered locations.

*Nesting habits:* Pheasants usually are polygamous, but some males have monogamous tendencies. The female deposits her 10 to 12 olive-buff eggs in a natural depression in the ground or hollows out a site for herself. The nest is lined with leaves, grasses, or weed stems and often is concealed by overhanging grass or weeds. Laying probably begins by mid-April, and the incubation period is 23 to 27 days. Although the young are brooded and remain with the female for 6 or 7 weeks, they are able to follow the hen in search of food as soon as their down is dry and can fly at 2 weeks. The male assumes no role in incubation of eggs or care of young. Crowing is most frequent in spring when males proclaim their territories, but cocks sometimes are heard in autumn and on pleasant days in winter.

*Feeding habits:* Pheasants eat insects, weed seeds, and wild fruits and berries. In some situations they become very destructive to cultivated crops, but at other times they destroy many mice and harmful insects.

*Description:* The Ring-necked Pheasant is our only large, brown, and heavy-bodied bird with a very long and slender pointed tail. The male has an iridescent head and a white neck band. Colorful head markings are absent in the female.

# Family Meleagrididae: Turkeys

## Turkey
*Meleagris gallopavo*
48–50 in. (122–127 cm)

*Range:* Formerly permanent residents throughout the Carolinas from the mountains to the sea, the wild Turkey is now greatly reduced in numbers and thrives only in widely scattered places where large tracts of swamps and mature forests remain.

*Nesting habits:* When a hen is ready to lay, usually about mid-April, she slips away from the cock and his harem to deposit her

*Turkey*
John Trott

8 to 15 eggs on the ground in a sheltered depression lined with leaves or grass. The whitish or light buff eggs are heavily speckled with reddish brown. The hen alone incubates the eggs for 28 days and cares for her single annual brood of precocial chicks. Turkeys seldom fly and prefer to run from danger. They do fly to roosts in trees at night. Young birds can fly to a low perch when they are about 2 weeks old.

*Feeding habits:* Wild Turkeys feed on insects, berries, and seeds, with acorns at times making up 60% of their diet.

*Description:* Although they sound just like the domestic birds, wild Turkeys are more slender and long-legged, with chestnut-tipped tail feathers and a brilliant metallic bronze sheen to the plumage. The gobbler wears a beard of coarse hairlike tufts protruding from the breast, a characteristic sometimes found in the hen. Weights of adult birds generally range from 12 to 25 pounds (5.5–11.4 kg), and gobblers very rarely reach a maximum of about 40 pounds (18 kg).

# Order Gruiformes: Cranes, Rails, and Allies

Birds of this order are rather diversified in outward appearance, being classified together primarily on the basis of skeletal and muscular structures. In flight they extend the neck straight forward, and their feet usually trail conspicuously behind. The characteristics of rails and their allies are given under the family heading.

## Family Gruidae: Cranes

### Whooping Crane
*Grus americana*
about 45 in. (114 cm)

*Range:* Although a few Whooping Cranes continue to migrate from the breeding grounds in Canada to the wintering grounds on the Texas Gulf Coast, no sighting of this extremely rare and endangered species has been reported in the Carolinas for well over a century. The last known record is a specimen taken about 1850 on the Waccamaw River in South Carolina. North Carolina has no documented record, but the species may have visited the state in colonial times.

*Feeding habits:* Cranes have feeding habits similar to those of herons and egrets.

*Description:* The adult Whooping Crane is a very large white long-legged wader with black wing tips, black legs, a black facial mask, and a red crown. Immatures have a brownish head and upperparts with white underparts.

### Sandhill Crane
*Grus canadensis*
33–48 in. (83–122 cm)

*Range:* Sandhill Cranes are rare transients and winter visitors in South Carolina, and very rare transients in North Carolina. Found somewhat erratically from late July to May, mostly in marshes along the coast, cranes sometimes wander inland. A few records suggest a migratory route across extreme western North Carolina and piedmont South Carolina, but the regularity of

Sandhill Crane
Paul W. Sykes Jr.

*Limpkin*
Paul W. Sykes Jr.

such passage has not been established.

*Feeding habits:* Sandhill Cranes wade in marshes and wet fields where they take small rodents, frogs, and insects.

*Description:* The uniformly gray adult has white cheeks, red crown, dark bill, and dark legs. Immatures are uniformly brownish with dark bill and legs. Similar to Great Blue Herons, which fly with the neck doubled back on the shoulders, cranes fly with the neck extended.

# Family Aramidae: Limpkins

## Limpkin
*Aramus guarauna*
25–28 in. (63–71 cm)

*Range:* The Limpkin occurs very rarely in southern South Carolina inland to Aiken and northward in the coastal plain to Lake Waccamaw, N.C. Most sightings take place in late summer and autumn.

*Feeding habits:* The Limpkin's chief item of food is a freshwater snail that is not known to occur north of the Altamaha River in central Georgia. In addition, Limpkins eat other mollusks, small reptiles, amphibians, insects, crayfish, and worms found in swamps and marshlands.

*Description:* This brown long-legged wader has white crescent-shaped spots on the body plumage, a long slender bill that is slightly decurved, and dark legs. Immature night-herons are sometimes mistaken for Limpkins.

# Family Rallidae: Rails, Gallinules, and Coots

Rails are the birds some people are as thin as. Their laterally compressed bodies enable them to slip through densely tangled marsh vegetation, rarely taking flight and rarely being seen by anyone except hunters and bird-watchers. Rails, gallinules, and coots have long legs, long toes, and short pointed tails. Rails and gallinules normally carry their tails cocked upward, flicking them up and down when agitated.

## King Rail
*Rallus elegans*
15–19 in. (38–48 cm)

*Range:* The King Rail is found in freshwater marshes throughout the Carolinas in summer. The species winters here, mostly near the coast where it occurs in fresh and brackish marshes. Listen for the King Rail's grunting *bup-bup-bup* wherever you find good stands of cattails and rushes.

*Nesting habits:* Breeding extends from March to July. The nest is a platform of grasses, rushes, and other vegetation placed 6 to 18 inches (15–45 cm) above shallow water in buttonwood bushes or tussocks of grass, sedges, or rushes. The 8 to 12 eggs are buffy with a few brown specks, and incubation takes about 3 weeks. The precocial young are covered with black down. Both parents incubate eggs and care for young, as is the case with all our rails.

*King Rail at nest*
Morris D. Williams

*Feeding habits:* King Rails eat small aquatic animals.

*Description:* This large brown rail has a long, slightly decurved bill. Look for the rusty patch at the bend of the wing and for the prominent barring on the flanks. The Clapper Rail is slightly smaller and grayer with less distinct barring on the flanks. Clappers prefer salt marshes, but habitat is not reliable for separating the two species because during migration each may visit the habitat preferred by the other.

*Clapper Rail*
Jack Potter

## Clapper Rail
*Rallus longirostris*
12–16 in. (30–40 cm)

*Range:* Clapper Rails are very common permanent residents of salt marshes the entire length of coastal Carolina. Populations increase in autumn with the arrival of migrants from the north. During migrations Clapper Rails may occur inland, but sightings are very rare.

*Nesting habits:* Nests are depressed platforms of marsh grass or sedges usually placed in a clump of grass or attached to a marsh plant over shallow water. In either case the eggs are less than 2 feet (61 cm) above water or wet sod. The 8 to 12 eggs are creamy buff marked with lilac and brown spots, the incubation period is about 3 weeks, and the black downy chicks are precocial. Both adults incubate eggs and care for the young. The nesting season may begin as early as March and extend into late summer if eggs are lost repeatedly to predators and high tides. The small, dark race (*R. l. waynei*) breeding from Brunswick County, N.C., southward to east-central Florida, is said to be double-brooded.

*Feeding habits:* At low tide these secretive birds may venture from cover to feed on fiddler crabs and other small aquatic animals found on exposed banks and mudflats.

*Description:* The "Marsh Hen" utters a remarkable variety of clacks, grunts, groans, and shrieks. If silence prevails, the birder need only clap his hands together smartly to get some idea how many Clappers are lurking in the marsh. See King Rail for a comparative description.

*Virginia Rail*
John Trott

## Virginia Rail
*Rallus limicola*
8–11 in. (20–28 cm)

*Range:* The Virginia Rail migrates across inland portions of the Carolinas to winter along the coast, arriving in August and lingering into early May. Though infrequently reported inland, the species is fairly common to common in the fresh and brackish coastal marshes. Virginia Rails breed sparingly in Dare County, N.C., along the Savannah River, and perhaps elsewhere in our region.

*Nesting habits:* Nests are built in clumps of rushes and may contain from four to eight pale buff eggs that are lightly spotted with brown, chiefly around the large end. Incubation is shared by both sexes and lasts approximately 19

days. The precocial chicks have black down, and the first to hatch often leave the nest while the rest of the eggs are still being incubated.

*Feeding habits:* Virginia Rails eat seeds, berries, insects, snails, and small crustaceans.

*Description:* A small, dark reddish-brown rail with heavily barred flanks and large rusty patches in the wing, the Virginia Rail has gray cheeks and a long, slightly decurved bill.

## Sora
*Porzana carolina*
8–10 in. (20–25 cm)

*Range:* The Sora is a spring and fall transient found in most parts of the Carolinas from April

*Sora*
James F. Parnell

through May and from August through October. Common in marshes along the coast, it is generally uncommon inland where it nevertheless is the rail most frequently seen. Soras are winter residents in southern South Carolina and northward along the entire Carolina coast. They are seen throughout the summer in coastal North and South Carolina, but no evidence of breeding has been found.

*Feeding habits:* Soras feed on seeds (especially wild rice), small mollusks (snails), and insects.

*Description:* This predominantly gray rail has a streaked back and barred sides. The adult has a black throat, a short and thick yellow bill, and yellow legs. Green-legged immature Soras are similar but do not have the black throat.

## Yellow Rail
*Coturnicops noveboracensis*
6–8 in. (15–20 cm)

*Range:* The Yellow Rail is a fall and spring migrant throughout the Carolinas, and it winters along the coast to an undetermined extent. Records place this small, secretive bird in the marsh edges, wet meadows, and grain fields of our region from late September to mid-April. Many individuals are sometimes flushed by winter grass fires, indicating that the species may be locally common along the coast. Because the Yellow Rail is seldom flushed by bird-watchers and, unlike our other rail species, is generally silent in winter, its distribution and abundance in the Carolinas may never be fully understood.

*Feeding habits:* The Yellow Rail's

*Yellow Rail*
James F. Parnell

diet appears to be mostly insects and small freshwater snails.

*Description:* This rail has a short yellow bill and yellowish-brown plumage that is heavily streaked on the back and barred on the sides. In flight the bird flashes a prominent white patch on the trailing edge of each wing near the body.

## Black Rail

*Laterallus jamaicensis*
5–6 in. (12–15 cm)

*Range:* The Black Rail lives in salt and brackish marshes amid juncus and cordgrasses, and inland it frequents freshwater marshes, meadows, and grain fields. Nests have been found as far inland as Buncombe County, N.C., but the species' range is not well known. Most records of these extremely secretive birds are for the spring and fall seasons, when they probably are fairly common along the coast. Black Rails appear to be abundant at Cedar Island National Wildlife Refuge in Carteret County, N.C., where at least 80 were heard calling around midnight in late May of 1973. The birds arrive in March or early April and remain until October or November, with small numbers apparently spending the winter along the coast.

*Nesting habits:* The 6 to 10 white or buffy eggs are heavily speckled with brown and lilac. Incubation requires 12 to 14 days. Downy chicks are black and precocial.

*Black Rail*
Richard A. Rowlett

*Feeding habits:* Black Rails probably eat insects and seeds more than anything else.

*Description:* Our smallest rail is predominantly black with yellow legs; rusty shoulders; and white barring on the back, wings, and flanks.

## Purple Gallinule
*Porphyrula martinica*
12–14 in. (30–35 cm)

*Range:* The Purple Gallinule breeds in the lower coastal plain at least as far north as southern Craven County, N.C. During migration birds turn up surprisingly far inland, and a few individuals may spend the winter in southern South Carolina. Although rare in most parts of the Carolinas, Purple Gallinules tend to become locally fairly common at suitable nesting sites, usually in fresh water with an abundance of tall grasses and floating vegetation along the margins.

*Nesting habits:* Nest building begins in early May, and several incomplete nests usually can be found near the one in which the eggs finally are laid. The nest is a depressed platform of rushes and grass attached to stems of aquatic plants such as pickerelweed or settled into floating islands of dead vegetation. The six to eight elongated creamy eggs are finely dotted with lilac and reddish brown. Clutches usually are completed by late May, and incubation requires about 24 days. The precocial young have black down,

*Purple Gallinule*
David S. Lee

yellow feet, and bills mottled with yellow and black.

*Feeding habits:* Food is primarily the seeds and fruits of aquatic plants, but snails and other animal matter are taken.

*Description:* The adult Purple Gallinule has an iridescent bluish-purple body, brownish wings, and yellow legs; and its short, stout bill is red with a yellow tip and a white frontal shield. Brown immatures lack the white lateral stripe of the young Common Gallinule. Gallinules nod the head while swimming and, like rails, flick the short pointed tail when agitated.

## Common Gallinule
(Florida Gallinule)
*Gallinula chloropus*
12–15 in. (30–38 cm)

*Range:* More numerous in summer than in winter, the Common Gallinule is a permanent resident on and near the Carolina coast, being locally common in southern South Carolina and becoming uncommon toward northeastern North Carolina. Although a popular field guide indicates that the species is found throughout the Carolinas during the nesting season, the absence of definite breeding records indicates it is only a rare transient in the piedmont and mountains.

*Nesting habits:* Beginning in early May, Common Gallinules build their nests in freshwater ponds,

*Common Gallinule*
James F. Parnell

rice fields, and backwaters, often placing them in clumps of rushes or grass, or in willows, buttonwood bushes, or climbing vines. The 10 to 12 buffy eggs are heavily marked with brown and gray. Shared by both sexes, incubation requires about 3 weeks. The precocial young have black down, black feet, and red bills.

*Feeding habits:* Common Gallinules eat snails, insect matter, and seeds from aquatic plants.

*Description:* The black body of the adult Common Gallinule has a white stripe along the side, a mark also found on the grayish immature. Adults have long slender toes, long yellow legs with red "garters," and a short stout bill that is red with a yellow tip. Gallinules nod the head while swimming and flick the short pointed tail.

## American Coot
*Fulica americana*
13–16 in. (33–40 cm)

*Range:* In winter the American Coot is one of the most abundant water birds in the Carolinas. Once considered only a transient in the inland portions of the two states, this species now winters in large numbers on some of the major reservoirs. Coots have bred in Barnwell, Colleton, and Charleston Counties in South Carolina and in Pamlico County in North Carolina. They are permanent residents at several other places along our coast, but their breeding status is uncertain.

*American Coot*
Haskell Hart

*Nesting habits:* Built by the female, the nest may be placed on a floating platform of vegetation or built like that of a rail. The 8 to 12 buffy eggs are finely dotted with dark brown. Incubation requires 21 to 22 days with both parents in attendance. The precocial chicks have dark down on the body but are reddish-orange about the bill and head. They have very large feet for their size and can swim and dive very well from the first day.

*Feeding habits:* Coots take most of their food, primarily various parts of aquatic plants, from the surface of the water.

*Description:* Like gallinules, coots nod the head while swimming and must patter along the surface of the water for a considerable distance before becoming airborne. Unlike gallinules, coots have lobed toes and waddle awkwardly when they walk. The adult American Coot has a dark gray body and a black head. Its short stout bill has a frontal shield and is white with a dark band near the tip.

# Order Charadriiformes: Shorebirds, Gulls, Auks, and Allies

Shorebirds are predominantly white and gray or brown wading birds with pointed wings and long toes that may be partially webbed. They usually inhabit beaches, mudflats, and other shorelines. Many species, particularly the smaller sandpipers, nest in the Arctic tundra. Shorebirds, including the several species that nest in the Carolinas, lay their protectively colored eggs in depressions in the ground and hatch out precocial chicks with sand-colored down.

Shorebirds generally eat mollusks, crustaceans, and other small aquatic animals, which they usually obtain by probing into mud or wet sand with long slender bills. Some species eat insects and a significant amount of vegetable matter. Shorebirds may use their feet to stir the water or pat the sand to induce hidden animals to expose themselves. A few species feed primarily by snatching from the surface and rarely probe.

During the middle years of the nineteenth century, great flocks of relatively tame shorebirds provided easy targets for market hunters who supplied meat for the tables of rapidly growing cities. By 1880 many species had been gunned to the verge of extinction. Following protection from hunting, most shorebirds were able to make good recoveries; however, no species appears to have reached its former level of abundance.

Characteristics of jaegers and skuas, gulls and terns, skimmers, and alcids are discussed under their respective family headings.

## Family Haematopidae: Oystercatchers

### American Oystercatcher
*Haematopus palliatus*
17–21 in. (43–53 cm)

*Range:* The American Oystercatcher is a fairly common permanent resident on the Carolina coast, and apparently more birds of this species winter at Cape Romain than anywhere else on the Atlantic seaboard. Inland records are accidental and extremely rare.

*Nesting habits:* The two or three buffy eggs are heavily splotched with dark brown and lavender, making them difficult to see against the sand. Clutches usually are laid in April and May. Incubation is by both sexes and takes about 27 days. The precocial chicks can swim and dive, as well as run with great agility.

*Feeding habits:* The American Oystercatcher feeds primarily on

*American Oystercatcher at nest*
Randy Lennon

mollusks, especially oysters. The majority of the shellfish taken, however, are raccoon oysters, which are not commercially valuable.

*Description:* One of our largest shorebirds, the American

Oystercatcher is black above and white below with a wide white wing stripe, a white rump, a long orange-red bill, and flesh-colored legs.

# Family Recurvirostridae: Stilts and Avocets

## Black-necked Stilt
*Himantopus himantopus*
13–15½ in. (33–39 cm)

*Range:* Generally rare along the Carolina coast, the Black-necked Stilt is locally common from April through August near established nesting sites such as Bodie Island, Pea Island, and Cape Romain.

*Nesting habits:* Nesting in loose colonies, Black-necked Stilts

display in groups with much running about and loud calling. Individuals halt, crouch, and call with extended wings aquiver; or they may stand and call with outstretched wings. Lined with bits of shell and dried grass, the nest depression is usually made in a slightly elevated mound of mud that is surrounded by shallow water, but dry sites may be used. Both adults sit upon the eggs,

*American Avocet, breeding plumage*
Robert H. Lewis

*Black-necked Stilt*
James F. Parnell

which number four or sometimes only three. Incubation takes about 21 to 28 days, and both parents tend the precocial young.

*Feeding habits:* Stilts feed primarily in shallow fresh and brackish ponds and impoundments.

*Description:* Black above and white below with a white tail and rump, the Black-necked Stilt has a long neck, long and thin straight black bill, and very long red legs.

# American Avocet
*Recurvirostra americana*
15–20 in. (38–51 cm)

*Range:* Along most of the Carolina coast this Western shorebird is merely a rare accidental, but it is a permanent resident of coastal Dare County, N.C. Sixty or more American Avocets frequently visit the shallow pond at Bodie Island Lighthouse and the roadside impoundments on Pea Island. A single brood of downy chicks provides evidence of nesting on Pea Island. The very few inland records are for the fall season.

*Nesting habits:* Nesting in colonies, the birds display in groups, bowing, crouching, and calling with the wings held extended. Scattered nests vary from scantily lined depressions to sizable mounds of debris. They may be placed on a sun-baked mudflat or among plants growing near water. Sites usually are subject to flooding. Both parents incubate the four dark-spotted olive-buff eggs and tend the precocial chicks, which swim readily. The incubation period is 22 to 24 days, and the young become independent in about 6 weeks.

*Feeding habits:* The avocet feeds by walking through shallow water with its bill, and often its head, completely submerged. Sweeping the long recurved bill from side to side, it stirs up and consumes a wide variety of aquatic insects and seeds from marsh plants.

*Description:* This predominantly white bird has a black stripe running the length of the wing and a black bar across the wing where it meets the body. The head and long neck are gray in winter and cinnamon in summer; the long legs are blue-gray; and the long bill is dark and thin, curving upward at the tip. The avocet strikingly exhibits the shorebird habit of resting by standing on one leg and tucking the head beneath a wing.

# Family Charadriidae: Plovers

## Lapwing
*Vanellus vanellus*
12 in. (30 cm)

*Range:* This rare accidental from Europe is most often found in eastern North America on the coast north of the Carolinas. One Lapwing was collected inland at Siler City, N.C., on November 12, 1926, and another appeared near Charleston, S.C., on December 3, 1940.

*Feeding habits:* The Lapwing feeds in farmlands, grasslands with short turf, and marshy fields, as well as at freshwater margins and coastal mudflats.

*Description:* Dark above and white below with a long thin crest, the Lapwing has rusty under-tail coverts, a white tail with a black tip, and wings rounded at the tips. This is the only crested shorebird known to occur in our region.

---

## Semipalmated Plover
*Charadrius semipalmatus*
7–8 in. (17–20 cm)

*Range:* The Semipalmated Plover is an abundant migrant and fairly common winter resident along the Carolina coast. Although present every month of the year, it does not breed here. For this and many other species of shorebirds, the spring and fall migrations cover an extended period of time. Thus, the last northbound birds may be seen here in June, and the earliest southbound birds of the same species may arrive in early July. Semipalmated Plovers occur rather frequently on inland

Semipalmated Plover, nonbreeding
plumage
Robert Schmitt

Wilson's Plover, female shading eggs
Robert Schmitt

mudflats, usually in April and May and from August to October.

*Feeding habits:* See comments on order.

*Description:* Dark above and white below with one narrow black neck band, the Semipalmated Plover has a white wing stripe, yellowish legs, and a very small light-colored bill with a dark tip. The species is named for its half-webbed toes. In winter the neck band is dark gray.

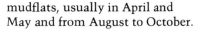

## Wilson's Plover
*Charadrius wilsonia*
7–9 in. (17–22 cm)

*Range:* The Wilson's Plover is a fairly common summer resident along most of the Carolina coast from March through October, but it is uncommon along the Outer Banks. A few individuals may linger into winter. Inland sightings are very rare and accidental.

*Nesting habits:* Wilson's Plovers nest on sparsely vegetated beaches or on islands in sounds or bays. The three eggs usually are laid in May or June, are buffy splotched with black, and hatch in 24 or 25 days. Both sexes incubate eggs and help care for the precocial young.

*Feeding habits:* See comments on order.

*Description:* The male Wilson's Plover is dark above and white below with one wide black neck band, a white wing stripe, and flesh-colored legs. The female is similar, but the dark parts are gray. In both sexes the bill is black and relatively long and thick in comparison to that of the smaller Semipalmated Plover.

*Killdeer*
James F. Parnell

# Killdeer
*Charadrius vociferus*
10–11 in. (25–28 cm)

*Range:* The Killdeer is a common permanent resident throughout the Carolinas, but it is considerably less numerous during the breeding season than at other times of the year. Killdeer may visit almost any open ground such as a pasture, mudflat, or golf course.

*Nesting habits:* Nesting takes place in open habitats from March through June. The four buffy eggs are heavily speckled with blackish brown, and the nest scrape is sometimes lined with a few leaves, grasses, pebbles, or bits of shell. The eggs are large for the size of the bird and conical in shape, lying in the nest with the points toward the center, thus affording maximum efficiency during the 24 to 25 days of incubation. Both sexes incubate eggs and care for the precocial young. Like many other shorebirds, the Killdeer distracts intruders from its eggs or young by fluttering along the ground as if it has broken a wing.

*Feeding habits:* The Killdeer consumes a great number of harmful grubs and insects, often searching for them in soil freshly turned by the farmer's plow.

*Description:* Dark above and white below with two black neck bands, the Killdeer has a reddish-orange tail, black bill, and flesh-colored legs. Downy young have only one neck band. The heartbroken cry of *kil-dee, kil-dee* is diagnostic.

# Piping Plover
*Charadrius melodus*
6–8 in. (15–20 cm)

*Range:* The Piping Plover is a fairly common winter resident along the Carolina coast from early August to late May. Migrating birds seldom wander inland. Piping Plovers usually remain singly or in small flocks on the drier portions of beaches and mudflats. The species formerly nested on Pea Island, but the breeding birds apparently did not survive the arrival of domestic cats in 1908. Recent summer records indicate that Piping Plovers are reestablishing their breeding range in North Carolina and now nest sparingly southward along the coast to Shackleford Banks near Morehead City.

*Nesting habits:* Eggs are buffy and lightly marked with fine black, blackish-brown, and purplish-gray dots. Sets usually number four, but replacement clutches may be smaller. The shallow scrape may contain bits of shell. Incubation requires 27 days with both adults sitting upon the eggs and tending the precocial preflight young. Nesting probably begins in late April, but a nest with three eggs was found on Ocracoke in July.

*Feeding habits:* See comments on order.

*Description:* White below and gray above with a white rump, the Piping Plover has yellow legs. Its bill is yellow in summer and dark in winter. Summer birds have a narrow black neck band (often incomplete) and a black band extending across the top of the head from eye to eye. The similar Snowy Plover, which has dark legs and rump, has not been recorded in the Carolinas.

American Golden Plover, breeding plumage
Heathcote Kimball

---

## American Golden Plover
*Pluvialis dominica*
10–11 in. (25–28 cm)

*Range:* The American Golden Plover is an uncommon to rare but regular spring and fall migrant occurring inland as well as along the coast between early March and early May and from mid-August to mid-January. The species is often reported from the Wright Brothers Memorial grounds and the Bodie–Pea Island

area in late summer and early fall when tropical storms drive offshore migrants landward. Although it occurs on mudflats with other shorebirds, it is more likely to be found in short-grass habitats such as pastures, golf courses, and airports.

*Feeding habits:* This plover takes the usual shorebird fare, but apparently favors grasshoppers in spring and crickets in fall.

*Description:* Similar to the Black-bellied Plover, the American Golden Plover has a golden hue to the upperparts. Look for the dark rump, gray axillars, and the absence of a wing stripe.

---

## Black-bellied Plover
*Pluvialis squatarola*
11–12 in. (28–30 cm)

*Range:* The Black-bellied Plover can be found along the Carolina coast every month of the year,

*Black-bellied Plover*
James F. Parnell

*Black-bellied Plover, nonbreeding plumage*
James F. Parnell

being common in winter and during migrations but scarce in summer. It does not breed here. As with many other shorebirds, the last northbound birds have just departed from the Carolinas when the earliest nesters leave their precocial young in the Arctic and return to the wintering grounds. The birds of the year follow their parents southward a month or more later. Inland sightings of the Black-bellied Plover are rare in the Carolinas and usually occur in fall.

*Feeding habits:* See order.

*Description:* This gray plover has a thick black bill, a white wing stripe, white rump, barred tail, and black legs. Summer birds have black underparts extending from a facial mask to the belly. In flight the Black-bellied Plover flashes black axillars. Winter birds have a white stripe above the eye and a dark stripe through the eye. The American Golden Plover has a thinner bill, a dark rump, gray axillars, and no wing stripe.

# Family Scolopacidae: Sandpipers and Allies

## Hudsonian Godwit
*Limosa haemastica*
14–17 in. (35–43 cm)

*Range:* One of the least abundant of North American shorebirds, the

Hudsonian Godwit is very rare inland and along most of the Carolina coast; but it appears to be a regular though uncommon autumn visitor in the Bodie–Pea

*Hudsonian Godwits, nonbreeding plumage*
Richard A. Rowlett

Island area between early August and mid-November. Some autumn flocks of this species migrate from Labrador directly across the Atlantic Ocean to South America, and the majority of the birds seen in the Carolinas probably have been forced off course by storms. Hudsonian Godwits have been seen in late February at Pea Island and Cape Romain, but the species is very rare in spring because the northward movement is across the central United States.

*Feeding habits:* The Hudsonian Godwit has a long thin recurved bill that is flexible at the tip. The species shows a preference for feeding in water of a depth about equal to the length of the bill, which is immersed "to the hilt."

*Description:* Brown with a barred breast in summer and gray in winter, the Hudsonian Godwit has a white rump and a black tail narrowly tipped with white. The long thin recurved bill has a dark tip. Legs are long and dark. In flight, the wing linings are dark and the axillars black.

## Bar-tailed Godwit
*Limosa lapponica*
15 in. (38 cm)

*Range:* This Eurasian godwit has been found twice at Pea Island, once from late August to early September of 1971 and again in mid-October of 1974. Similar to the Hudsonian Godwit, the Bar-tailed has the entire length of its tail narrowly barred with black and white. (hypothetical status)

## Marbled Godwit
*Limosa fedoa*
16–20 in. (40–51 cm)

*Range:* Although recorded on the Carolina coast during every month of the year, the Marbled Godwit does not breed here. Apparently having made a good recovery from nineteenth century overhunting, the species is now a fairly common fall migrant; and it winters in good numbers around Charleston, S.C., and Wilmington, N.C. The Marbled Godwit has yet to be recorded inland.

*Marbled Godwits*
John Trott

*Feeding habits:* This species feeds in groups, frequently in shallow water.

*Description:* Predominantly brown, the Marbled Godwit is mottled above and barred below. Its extremely long bill is dark and recurved at the tip. Look for the dark rump and cinnamon wing linings.

## Eskimo Curlew
*Numenius borealis*
12–15 in. (30–38 cm)

*Range:* Formerly a very rare transient along the South Carolina coast, this smallest of our curlews was believed to be extinct when two were seen in the spring of 1945 on Galveston Island, Texas. Migrants have occurred there with encouraging regularity from 1959 to the present. In modern times two birds thought to be this very rare species have been sighted in Charleston County, S.C., one in flight at Cape Romain in 1946 and another at rest on Folly Island in 1956. Unfortunately, the wing linings are not mentioned in the published accounts of these two sight records. Historically, Eskimo Curlews migrated northward across the central part of our continent. The fall migration was mostly over the open ocean from the Atlantic Maritime Provinces to the Lesser Antilles and South America.

*Feeding habits:* The Eskimo Curlew feeds on berries, snails, insects, and various small invertebrates.

*Description:* The Eskimo Curlew is smaller than a Whimbrel, has a comparatively shorter and more slender bill, and has cinnamon wing linings.

## Whimbrel
(Hudsonian Curlew)
*Numenius phaeopus*
15–19 in. (38–48 cm)

*Range:* Although the Whimbrel may be found along the Carolina coast during any month of the year, it is primarily a fairly common to common spring and fall migrant. The species winters sparingly from the vicinity of Charleston, S.C., southward. Inland records are very rare.

*Feeding habits:* The Whimbrel eats berries, fiddler crabs, crayfish, and worms.

*Whimbrel*
Thad Monroe

*Description:* A gray-brown bird with a striped crown, the Whimbrel has long legs and a long decurved bill. The Long-billed Curlew has cinnamon wing linings and a much longer bill in proportion to its head size.

## Long-billed Curlew
*Numenius americanus*
22–26 in. (56–66 cm)

*Range:* The Carolina coast once swarmed with this largest of our North American shorebirds, but by 1879 the species had been overhunted almost to the point of extinction. Although still considered a rare species, the Long-billed Curlew now occurs regularly at Cape Romain from late July through March and occasionally appears elsewhere along the coast.

*Feeding habits:* The Long-billed Curlew probes in wet sand or mud, either exposed or covered by shallow water, for worms and various invertebrates. Fiddler crabs are a favored item, and berries are taken in upland habitats.

*Description:* A large brown curlew with long legs, the Long-billed Curlew has an extremely long decurved bill that accounts for about 6 to 8 inches (15–20 cm) of its total length. Its bill is approximately four times as long as the head. Look for the unstriped crown and cinnamon wing linings.

## Upland Sandpiper
(Upland Plover)
*Bartramia longicauda*
11–13 in. (28–33 cm)

*Range:* The Upland Sandpiper is an uncommon spring and fall transient from mid-March through early May and from mid-

Long-billed Curlew
Michael P. Schultz

Upland Sandpiper
John Trott

July through October. It is seen most frequently near the coast in early fall. This bîrd prefers grassy meadows and airports to shorelines.

*Feeding habits:* Insects predominate in a diet that also includes some seeds and berries.

*Description:* Upland Sandpipers have yellow legs and a distinctive silhouette: short bill, small head, long neck, and a longer tail than our other shorebirds. Uplands fly stiffly, much like a Spotted Sandpiper, and hold the wings erect briefly after landing.

*Yellowlegs (see Greater Yellowlegs description)*
William G. Cobey

## Greater Yellowlegs
*Tringa melanoleuca*
12–15 in. (30–38 cm)

*Range:* Like many other shorebirds, the Greater Yellowlegs can be found on mudflats along the Carolina coast throughout the year, but it is common only during migrations and does not breed here. The species is fairly common in winter and rare in summer. Inland the Greater Yellowlegs is an uncommon to fairly common spring and fall transient, March to May and August to November, and a rare winter visitor.

*Feeding habits:* The Greater Yellowlegs feeds on insects and their larvae, snails, crabs, worms, and small fish.

*Description:* This tall gray sandpiper has bright yellow legs, a white rump, and a barred tail. It is distinguished from the Lesser Yellowlegs by the sharp three- to five-note whistle and the relatively long bill that may turn upward very slightly toward the tip. Lesser has a soft one- to three-note whistle and a bill that is relatively short and slender.

## Lesser Yellowlegs
*Tringa flavipes*
9–11 in. (22–28 cm)

*Range:* Generally less widespread than the Greater Yellowlegs, the Lesser Yellowlegs is a fairly common spring and fall migrant and uncommon winter resident along the coast. Migrants occur inland more often in fall than in spring. This species generally avoids saltwater mudflats, and it migrates later in spring and earlier in fall than does the Greater Yellowlegs.

*Feeding habits:* The Lesser Yellowlegs is similar to the Greater Yellowlegs in feeding habits.

*Description:* See Greater Yellowlegs for a comparative description.

## Solitary Sandpiper
*Tringa solitaria*
8–9 in. (20–22 cm)

*Range:* The Solitary Sandpiper is a fairly common spring and fall migrant from late March to early June and from early July to October. It occurs throughout the Carolinas, and like the Spotted Sandpiper it frequents the margins of ponds and streams. Solitary Sandpipers often visit pig pens during migration.

*Feeding habits:* Although the Solitary Sandpiper sometimes probes in water or soft mud, it usually feeds by catching insects, their larvae, and various other small invertebrates.

*Description:* This gray sandpiper has its back and wings dotted with white. Look for the black bill and legs, prominent white eye ring, and barred outer tail feathers. The Solitary Sandpiper often teeters in the manner of a Spotted Sandpiper. The Spotted flies stiffly and has a white wing stripe. The Solitary lacks the wing stripe, and its flight is graceful, almost like that of a swallow.

## Willet
*Catoptrophorus semipalmatus*
14–16 in. (35–40 cm)

*Range:* The Willet is a permanent resident of coastal Carolina, common in summer, less numerous in winter, and very rarely found inland.

*Nesting habits:* Located in sparse to rather dense grasses, often just behind the beach, the nest is a grass-lined hollow in the ground more or less sheltered by surrounding clumps of grass. The conical eggs usually number four, are pale olive splotched with dark brown, and require 21 to 23 days for incubation. Males apparently assist females in incubating eggs and feeding the precocial young. Adults become greatly agitated at the approach of an intruder, hovering over and diving at his head and giving piercing cries that surely must be avian profanity.

*Solitary Sandpiper*
James F. Parnell

*Willet*
David DuMond

*Willets, nonbreeding plumage*
James F. Parnell

*Feeding habits:* Willets feed on small aquatic animals obtained by probing or snatching.

*Description:* This large sandpiper, gray in winter and brown in summer, has black legs and bill. A prominent white stripe runs the length of its wings, which it often holds erect briefly after flight. Its tail is white except for a dark tip. The Willet's loud cry of *pilly-will-willet* is easily learned.

## Spotted Sandpiper
*Actitis macularia*
7–8 in. (17–20 cm)

*Range:* The Spotted Sandpiper is present in the Carolinas in all seasons, common and widespread during migrations, scarce in winter, and possibly breeding to a greater extent than the few published records indicate. This most characteristic inland sandpiper is a bird of the margins of inland ponds and streams as well as coastal shorelines.

*Spotted Sandpiper, breeding plumage*
Heathcote Kimball

*Nesting habits:* The breeding season appears to be from May through July. The female is the dominant partner in courtship displays. Usually located among grasses, the nest is a depression in the ground litter, but it may be lined with grass. Clutches almost invariably consist of four buffy eggs that are irregularly spotted with various shades of brown. Incubation requires about 20 days and is frequently performed by the male, who also assumes responsibility for the precocial young. A female often lays for more than one male, and she may help incubate a late clutch. Even as a newly hatched chick, the Spotted Sandpiper constantly teeters up and down.

*Feeding habits:* The Spotted Sandpiper forages in mud and shallow water for insects and various other invertebrates.

*Description:* Mud-colored upperparts contrast with underparts that are white in winter and spotted in summer. Look for the white wing stripe and grayish legs. The Spotted Sandpiper teeters almost constantly while standing or walking. In flight the bird holds its wings stiffly bent downward, alternating a few rapid wing beats with periods of sailing. This behavior makes the species easy to recognize even in its unspotted winter plumage.

## Ruddy Turnstone
*Arenaria interpres*
8–10 in. (20–25 cm)

*Range:* A nonbreeding year-round resident of the Carolina coast, the Ruddy Turnstone is fairly common to common except in summer. It rarely occurs inland. Turnstones are often seen on jetties and around rocks as well as on beaches and mudflats.

*Ruddy Turnstone*
James F. Parnell

## Wilson's Phalarope
*Phalaropus tricolor*
8–10 in. (20–25 cm)

*Range:* Wilson's Phalaropes normally migrate across the western United States, but a few transients visit the Carolinas every year. They are found sparingly along the coast from late March to early June and from mid-July through September, occurring regularly each fall on the ponds in the Bodie–Pea Island area. Inland the species is a very rare migrant.

*Feeding habits:* The Ruddy Turnstone has a slender bill that is slightly upturned at the tip and well adapted for flipping over stones, shells, and other debris in search of mollusks, crustaceans, and worms. The bill is also used to dig in sand and to crack mollusk shells with woodpecker-like blows.

*Description:* Winter birds have gray backs and yellowish legs; summer birds, brown backs and red-orange legs. In both seasons a wide breast band gives the impression that the bird wears a black vest. Watch for the short up-turned bill. In flight, upperparts present a striking black, white, and brown pattern—the most elaborate of all shorebirds in our region.

*Feeding habits:* A somewhat terrestrial freshwater species, the Wilson's Phalarope may forage on wet or dry land or wade into water, even submerging the head and neck to feed below the surface. It also spins on the surface like other phalaropes. Its diet includes insects, crustaceans, and seeds of marsh plants.

*Description:* This phalarope's very thin, straight bill is much longer than its head. Winter birds are gray above and white below. Summer birds are brownish above with a bold stripe running down the side of the neck. In flight, this species can be separated from our other phalaropes by the white rump and the absence of a wing stripe. Breeding females are more colorful than males. Toes are lobed.

Northern Phalarope, female in breeding plumage
Richard A. Rowlett

Northern Phalarope, nonbreeding plumage
Gilbert S. Grant

## Northern Phalarope
*Phalaropus lobatus*
7–8 in. (17–20 cm)

*Range:* Although Northern Phalaropes are common spring and fall migrants over the ocean well off the Carolina coast, they rarely visit our coastline, probably doing so only as a result of storms. The species is most likely to be seen in May or in September and October. It is a very rare visitor to inland lakes.

*Feeding habits:* In fresh water Northern Phalaropes eat insect larvae more than anything else. At sea they feed on the tiny invertebrates that eat plankton. Phalaropes spin on the surface of water to stir up food.

*Description:* The Northern Phalarope is dark above and white below with a thin black bill that is shorter than that of the Wilson's Phalarope. Summer birds have golden-brown streaks on the back, a white throat, and a rusty neck. Toes are lobed.

## Red Phalarope
*Phalaropus fulicarius*
8–9 in. (20–22 cm)

*Range:* Each spring and fall, large numbers of Red Phalaropes pass the Carolina coast well offshore, usually from mid-March to mid-May and from mid-August to early December. Storm-blown birds are sometimes found on beaches and very rarely as far inland as the Great Smoky Mountains. One report of large flocks of Red Phalaropes offshore in late December suggests that this species may winter in Carolina waters.

*Feeding habits:* Feeding habits of the Red Phalarope are similar to those of the Northern Phalarope.

*Description:* The Red Phalarope is our only phalarope with a yellow bill, but some immature birds have dark bills. Winter birds are dark above and white below.

152

Summer birds are brownish above and robin's-breast red below with a white face. Toes are lobed.

---

## American Woodcock
*Scolopax minor*
10–12 in. (25–30 cm)

*Range:* The American Woodcock is a fairly common permanent resident throughout the Carolinas, being more numerous in the coastal plain during the winter months than in summer. It is the only member of the sandpiper group that lives in damp woods as well as the only one that is predominantly crepuscular and nocturnal in habits.

*Nesting habits:* Following a series of *peent* calls that sound much like a Bronx cheer, the male woodcock makes a spectacular courtship flight. Rising from an opening in the woods to a height of perhaps 300 feet (90 m), twittering all the way, he then zig-zags downward, uttering a series of descending bell-like notes accompanied by some twittering. Returning to the same small plot of ground, he almost immediately begins calling again. This performance may be repeated many times in a single night, most often in the hour following sunset or the one preceding dawn, but on occasions throughout the night, particularly when the moon is full. Courtship may begin in January and nesting as early as February. The four buffy eggs are blotched with brown. The nest is

*American Woodcock*
E. Wayne Irvin

an unconcealed leaf-lined depression in the ground in low, wet woods. The female incubates the eggs 20 to 21 days and cares for the precocial young.

*Feeding habits:* The American Woodcock's extremely long bill has an upper mandible that is flexible near the tip and remarkably well adapted for probing in soft mud for earthworms and other animal matter.

*Description:* This long-billed stocky bird offers an outstanding example of protective coloration. The cinnamon-brown plumage is marked above with black, brown, and gray, giving the impression of dead leaves dappled with sunlight. The woodcock will remain

motionless on the woodland floor until the intruder almost steps on it, at the last moment bursting into flight with the wings making a peculiar whistling noise. Dodging behind trees, it soon drops to the ground, once more to become virtually invisible among the fallen leaves. The American Woodcock is a highly prized game bird both in the field and on the dinner table.

## Common Snipe
(Wilson's Snipe)
*Gallinago gallinago*
10–12 in. (25–30 cm)

*Range:* The Common Snipe is a winter resident throughout the Carolinas, being uncommon in the mountains and becoming

*Common Snipe*
James F. Parnell

common toward the coast. From late August into May, snipe frequent damp open areas such as meadows, bogs, grassy fields, and the edges of marshes, ponds, and streams.

*Feeding habits:* Snipe eat earthworms, cutworms, grasshoppers, and other insects.

*Description:* Like the American Woodcock, the Common Snipe has a very long bill, is protectively colored, and will remain motionless until it flushes almost under foot. Once flushed, it takes off in a swift, erratic, twisting flight, flashing a russet tail and giving a characteristic explosive *scaipe* note. Although the snipe and woodcock have similar silhouettes, the snipe has comparatively long yellowish legs and predominantly white underparts. Its streaked back and russet tail separate the snipe from the dowitchers.

# Short-billed Dowitcher
*Limnodromus griseus*
10–11 in. (25–28 cm)

*Range:* Although the Short-billed Dowitcher occurs in coastal Carolina throughout the year, it does not breed here. The species is abundant during spring and fall migration, but only fairly common in winter, often being scarce or locally absent in South Carolina. Inland sightings occur only rarely during migration, mostly between late August and mid-October.

*Feeding habits:* The Short-billed Dowitcher eats insects, marine worms, mollusks, and small crustaceans.

*Description:* Predominantly brown in summer and predominantly gray in winter, dowitchers have long greenish-yellow legs and a long heavy black bill. The tail is white barred with black, and the white of the rump extends

*Dowitchers, partial breeding plumage*
James F. Parnell

into a triangular white patch that comes to a point about half-way up the bird's back. Short-billed and Long-billed Dowitchers are more easily separated by voice than by appearance. The Short-billed's call is a low mellow rapid whistle, *too-too* or *too-too-too*. The Long-billed's is a single thin *keet* or a series of the same. While feeding, dowitchers often wade belly-deep in water and immerse the long bill full-length with mechanical regularity.

## Long-billed Dowitcher
*Limnodromus scolopaceus*
10–12½ in. (25–31 cm)

*Range:* The Long-billed Dowitcher is a regular but un-common fall migrant along the Carolina coast and a rare winter resident and spring migrant. Southbound birds of this species pass our way mostly from mid-September through January, an unusually late time of year for a shorebird. By comparison, the Short-billed Dowitcher's fall migration reaches its peak in July and August. The Long-billed Dowitcher is seldom seen on saltwater mudflats, but it fre-quents shallow fresh and brackish ponds and mudflats, especially in the Bodie–Pea Island area. It is extremely rare inland.

*Feeding habits:* The Long-billed's feeding habits are similar to those of the Short-billed, but with insects constituting a greater pro-portion of the diet.

*Description:* See Short-billed Dowitcher for a comparative description.

## Red Knot
*Calidris canutus*
10–11 in. (25–28 cm)

*Range:* Found on beaches and flats along the Carolina coast through-

*Dowitcher, nonbreeding plumage (see Short-billed Dowitcher description)*
James F. Parnell

Red Knot
Richard A. Rowlett

Red Knot, nonbreeding plumage
Chris Marsh

out the year, the Red Knot is fairly common to common during migrations, mid-April through May and July to mid-October; but it is uncommon in summer and winter. The species does not breed here and rarely occurs inland.

*Feeding habits:* The Red Knot's diet includes small mollusks, insects, and crustaceans as well as some vegetable matter. Knots forage from the surface or by probing.

*Description:* This species is sometimes called "Robin Snipe" because in breeding plumage it has a gray back and a rusty breast. A stocky medium-sized sandpiper, the winter knot is gray with a white rump and white wing stripe. The white of the rump does not extend up the back as in the larger, longer-billed dowitchers.

## Sanderling
*Calidris alba*
7–8¾ in. (17–22 cm)

*Range:* Although the Sanderling is a common to abundant resident of our ocean beaches all year, it is least numerous in summer and does not breed here. Spring and fall migrants occasionally occur inland.

*Feeding habits:* This is the funny little bird that runs back and forth on the beach like a mechanical toy, following each retreating

Sanderlings, nonbreeding plumage
James F. Parnell

wave and retreating before each advancing one. Sanderlings probe in wet sand for tiny animals and snatch those exposed by the washing of the waves.

*Description:* Gray above and white below, the Sanderling has black legs and bill. In flight it displays a wide white wing stripe and a black patch at the bend of each wing. Watch for the feeding behavior described above.

---

## Semipalmated Sandpiper
*Calidris pusilla*
5½–6¼ in. (14–16 cm)

*Range:* The Semipalmated Sandpiper is primarily a common to abundant spring and fall migrant found on the mudflats and beaches of coastal Carolina from early April to early June and from early August through October. The species is an uncommon migrant inland, more frequently seen in fall than in spring.

*Feeding habits:* Semipalmated Sandpipers feed mostly on aquatic

*Semipalmated Sandpiper, nonbreeding plumage*
Richard A. Rowlett

insects or crustaceans obtained both by snatching and by probing.

*Description:* Five very small peep sandpipers occur in our region. They are the Semipalmated, Western, Least, White-rumped, and Baird's Sandpipers. They are often seen in large mixed flocks. Separation of the peep sandpipers in the field requires reference to field guides, and even then accurate identification of some individuals may be impossible. Semipalmateds have a relatively short black bill and black legs. Westerns have a relatively long bill that droops toward the tip. Leasts have a dark bill and yellow legs. White-rumpeds have a white rump. Baird's Sandpipers have a streaked back, and the folded wings extend beyond the tip of the tail. Bill length, leg color, and wing length are variable characteristics that may be misleading in individual birds. When in doubt, just call them "peeps."

---

## Western Sandpiper
*Calidris mauri*
5¾–7 in. (14.5–17.5 cm)

*Range:* Despite its name, this species occurs regularly on the East Coast. Found along the Carolina coast throughout the year, the Western Sandpiper does not breed here. Common to abundant in fall migration, the species is much less common in spring. Western Sandpipers winter in good numbers from Charleston southward, but they are only fairly common

*Western Sandpiper, nonbreeding plumage*
Robert H. Lewis

northward. Inland transients are rare, occurring mainly in fall.

*Feeding habits:* Western and Semipalmated Sandpipers feed together on both freshwater and saltwater mudflats along the coast.

*Description:* See Semipalmated Sandpiper. Western and Semipalmated Sandpipers are so similar in appearance that even experts often call them "peeps."

## Least Sandpiper

*Calidris minutilla*
5–6¾ in. (12.5–17 cm)

*Range:* Least Sandpipers occur in the Carolinas every month of the year, but they do not breed here.

They are very common in May and from August through October when large flocks are likely to be seen along the coast in company with flocks of larger shorebirds. Least Sandpipers are generally uncommon in midwinter. Inland the species is an uncommon to fairly common spring and fall transient.

*Feeding habits:* When feeding on coastal mudflats with other peep sandpipers, Leasts feed close to the marsh grasses and frequent the muddy channels that wind through the grass.

*Description:* See Semipalmated Sandpiper.

*Least Sandpiper*
James F. Parnell

## White-rumped Sandpiper
*Calidris fuscicollis*
7–8 in. (17.5–20 cm)

*Range:* The White-rumped Sandpiper is an uncommon transient along the coast and a rare one inland. Occurring from late April to mid-October, the species prefers freshwater mudflats, particularly around impoundments.

*Feeding habits:* The White-rumped Sandpiper may pick animal matter from the surface or probe for it in mud that is exposed or covered by very shallow water. When probing, this species tends to insert the bill very deeply and rapidly several times in one spot, then run forward and repeat the action.

*Description:* See Semipalmated Sandpiper.

*White-rumped Sandpiper, nonbreeding plumage*
Richard A. Rowlett

*Baird's Sandpiper*
Richard A. Rowlett

## Baird's Sandpiper
*Calidris bairdii*
7–7½ in. (17.5–19 cm)

*Range:* Baird's Sandpiper is a very rare spring and rare fall migrant along the Carolina coast, very rarely occurring inland in fall. Although sometimes found on shores and mudflats, it seems to prefer slightly boggy short-grass habitats. The species has been recorded in the Carolinas from late March to early June and from late July to mid-December. In fall the Bodie–Pea Island area is a good place to look for this difficult to identify Western species.

*Feeding habits:* Baird's Sandpiper snatches up insects, spiders, and small aquatic invertebrates.

*Description:* See Semipalmated Sandpiper.

## Pectoral Sandpiper
*Calidris melanotos*
8–9½ in. (20–24 cm)

*Range:* Along the Carolina coast the Pectoral Sandpiper is a fairly common spring and fall transient, late March to early May and mid-July through October, and a very rare winter visitor. Inland occurrences are uncommon in spring and fairly common in fall. Hunters call this species "Grass Snipe" because of its fondness for boggy places and the similarity between its flight and that of the Common Snipe. Pectoral Sandpipers are seldom seen near salt water, preferring freshwater impoundments when along the coast.

*Feeding habits:* Pectorals eat a wide variety of animal matter, but insects predominate.

*Description:* The Pectoral Sandpiper has a white belly, dark breast and upperparts, dark bill, and greenish legs. A sharp line

*Pectoral Sandpiper*
James F. Parnell

where the streaking of the breast meets the white of the other underparts is a good field mark. Snipe-like flight and absence of a wing stripe should be noted.

## Purple Sandpiper
*Calidris maritima*
8–10 in. (20–25 cm)

*Range:* From October through April watch for the Purple Sandpiper along the Carolina coast wherever rock jetties are splashed by salt water. First recorded in the Carolinas in 1929, this species is now a regular winter resident; but it is seldom numerous and is almost entirely restricted to the jetties scattered along the coastline. It frequently associates with Ruddy Turnstones and Sanderlings.

*Feeding habits:* The Purple Sandpiper feeds on the various invertebrates that live in the crevices of intertidal rocks or among the plants growing on such rocks.

*Description:* This small dark gray sandpiper has yellow legs and a

thin bill that is yellow at the base and dark at the tip.

## Dunlin
(Red-backed Sandpiper)
*Calidris alpina*
8–9 in. (20–22 cm)

*Range:* The Dunlin is an abundant winter resident along the Carolina coast from late August to late May. Stragglers are present the other months of the year, but the species does not breed here. Inland sightings are rare and occur mostly during fall migration. The Dunlin frequents tidal mudflats, oysterbanks, and beaches—often in flocks of several hundred.

*Dunlin*
Heathcote Kimball

*Purple Sandpipers, nonbreeding plumage*
James F. Parnell

*Dunlin, nonbreeding plumage*
James F. Parnell

*Feeding habits:* Food is almost entirely animal matter obtained by snatching or probing.

*Description:* Winter birds are predominantly gray with black legs and a long black bill that droops near the tip. Summer birds are gray with a reddish-brown back and a black belly patch.

Stilt Sandpiper
Richard A. Rowlett

## Curlew Sandpiper
*Calidris ferruginea*
7–9 in. (17.5–22.5 cm)

*Range:* This Old World species is rare in fall on the East Coast north of the Carolinas. First found in North Carolina near Morehead City on June 29, 1971, the Curlew Sandpiper appears to be a very rare visitor along the Carolina coast between mid-May and mid-August.

*Feeding habits:* General habits are similar to those of the Dunlin, its frequent associate and look-alike in winter plumage.

*Description:* Summer birds are rusty brown with a white eye ring, a white rump, dark legs, and a dark bill that is long and decurved throughout its length. Gray winter birds are best recognized by the distinctive bill and the white rump.

## Stilt Sandpiper
*Micropalama himantopus*
7½–9¼ in. (19–23 cm)

*Range:* Rare in spring and uncommon in fall, the Stilt Sand-piper usually migrates along the Carolina coast rather than inland. It is known to occur from mid-March to mid-May and from early August to mid-October, sometimes becoming quite numerous in the Bodie–Pea Island area. Like the White-rumped Sandpiper and Long-billed Dowitcher, it usually shuns salt water, preferring fresh and brackish flats and pools.

*Feeding habits:* This very deliberate feeder takes a wide variety of small animal matter by snatching and probing. Stilt Sandpipers have been seen swinging the immersed bill from side to side in shallow water, a strategy also used on occasions by yellowlegs.

*Description:* This is a tall slender sandpiper with long greenish legs and a long slender dark bill. Summer birds are brown, heavily barred underneath, and adorned with a distinctive rusty cheek patch. Winter birds are gray. The clear white rump and the dark trailing edge of the unstriped wing are good field marks for birds in flight. The dowitcher is a larger, chunkier bird with white on its back and white on the trailing edge of its wing.

## Buff-breasted Sandpiper
*Tryngites subruficollis*
7–9 in. (17–22 cm)

*Range:* The Buff-breasted Sandpiper normally migrates across the Central Plains, but in recent years small flocks have been sighted along the Carolina coast almost annually between July and early November, most frequently in September. A few birds have been seen inland to Forsyth County, N.C., and Clemson, S.C. The only spring record for our region is a bird taken in South Carolina on May 5, 1844, but the increased number of fall sightings may presage the regular arrival of spring migrants.

*Feeding habits:* These remarkably tame birds feed in short grass and other sparse vegetation. A flock feeding amid glasswort on a dry

Buff-breasted Sandpiper
Michael P. Schulz

flat just north of North Pond on Pea Island remained in the same general area for an entire weekend even though they were stalked repeatedly by crowds of curious bird-watchers.

*Description:* This is our only sandpiper with buffy underparts, pale legs, white eye ring, dark bill, and white wing linings. When flushed, it flies like a snipe.

## Ruff
(female, Reeve)
*Philomachus pugnax*
10–12½ in. (25–31 cm)

*Range:* This rare visitor from Eurasia was first recorded in the Carolinas when a female was collected in Wake County, N.C., on May 6, 1892. The second sighting did not occur until 1959. The first South Carolina sighting took place in 1961. The modern occurrences, including several from the Bodie–Pea Island area, suggest that the species is very rare along the coast from mid-July to late May.

*Feeding habits:* The Ruff feeds in grassy or marshy places.

*Description:* Similar to a Lesser Yellowlegs, the Ruff has browner plumage and dull yellowish legs. In flight, the Ruff flashes oval white patches on each side at the base of the tail. The species gets its name from the male's enormous nuptial neck plumes that are raised during mock combats on the breeding grounds.

# Family Stercorariidae: Jaegers and Skuas

Jaegers and skuas are dark gull-like birds with elongated central tail feathers, sharply curved claws, and bills hooked at the tip. They are birds of the ocean and rarely come ashore except at their Arctic or Antarctic breeding grounds. They habitually raid nests of other species and rob other sea birds of their fishy prey.

## Pomarine Jaeger
*Stercorarius pomarinus*
20–23 in. (51–58 cm)

*Range:* The Pomarine Jaeger probably occurs off the Carolina coast throughout the year except for a brief absence at midsummer. Although it is generally uncommon, the species is seen regularly in fall and early winter from the shore along the Outer Banks and occasionally elsewhere along the coast.

Pomarine Jaeger
Richard A. Rowlett

*Feeding habits:* See comments on family.

*Description:* Jaegers are easy to recognize (see comments on family) but hard to identify by species. The Pomarine is the largest of our jaegers and the one most often seen in our region. Consult field guides and books on pelagic birds for details on plumages of the various species of jaegers, their color phases, and age classes.

## Parasitic Jaeger
*Stercorarius parasiticus*
15–21 in. (38–51 cm)

*Range:* The Parasitic Jaeger is found off the Carolina coast from early August to early June, but sightings are most frequent from mid-May to early June and from mid-September through October. This species occurs inland very rarely during migration, and it is sighted fairly often from the beaches along the Outer Banks.

*Feeding habits:* See comments on family.

*Description:* See Pomarine Jaeger.

## Long-tailed Jaeger
*Stercorarius longicaudus*
20–23 in. (51–58 cm)

*Range:* The Long-tailed Jaeger appears to be a rare spring and fall transient in Carolina offshore waters, and it is very rarely seen along the beaches. On very rare occasions it may visit the South Carolina coast in winter. The scarcity of published records can be attributed to the great difficulty of identifying immature birds.

*Feeding habits:* See comments on family.

*Description:* Adults wearing the extremely long central tail feathers are unmistakable. Immatures and molting adults are another matter. See Pomarine Jaeger.

---

## Great Skua
*Catharacta skua*
20–22 in. (51–55 cm)

## South Polar Skua
*Catharacta maccormicki*
about 21 in. (53 cm)

*Range:* Skuas are rare transients in our offshore waters, and they are very rarely seen from the beaches. They have been reported off North Carolina in all seasons, with the Great Skua apparently occurring mostly in fall and winter and the South Polar Skua probably found mostly in spring and summer. However, nonbreeding birds may visit our waters during the species' nesting season. A Great Skua banded on the nesting grounds in Iceland was found dead at Cape Lookout in December of 1975, its year of hatching. A South Polar Skua was found injured at Cape Hatteras in May 1976, and another bird apparently of this species was photographed off Cape Hatteras the following May. Several other North Carolina sightings cannot be reliably attributed to either species.

*Feeding habits:* See comments on family. Although they habitually force other birds to disgorge their prey, skuas act more often as scavengers than do jaegers.

*Description:* Skuas look like dark, short-tailed immature Herring Gulls with very slightly elongated central tail feathers and prominent white patches at the base of the primaries. In flight they look more like hawks than gulls, and they sometimes soar when not feeding. Separating the different species in the field is always difficult and often impossible. Characters and color phases of the six commonly recognized forms, three of which are known to occur in the Atlantic Ocean, are given in *Auk* 94:417–429.

# Family Laridae: Gulls and Terns

Gulls are heavy-bodied birds with webbed toes, long pointed wings, and a stout bill that is hooked at the tip. They eat small fish, assorted mollusks and crustaceans, and other animal matter. The larger gulls tend to be scavengers, and at times thousands may be seen at garbage dumps or fish docks. Adults generally have white bodies and predominantly gray or black mantles (back and upper-wing surfaces). Immature gulls are brownish, and in some of the larger species they do not acquire adult plumage until several years old. Gulls build substantial nests, and their downy chicks are precocial. At feeding time the adults simply regurgitate the catch on the ground, and the young help themselves.

More slender and graceful in flight than gulls, terns have webbed toes, pointed bills, long narrow wings, and forked tails. They feed by diving from the air upon insects and small fish. Tern nests usually are simple depressions in the sand, but sometimes they are lined with shells or grasses. Both parents incubate eggs and care for the precocial young. They also shelter eggs and chicks from the hot sun. Adult terns feed the offspring by poking fish into their gullets. Gulls and terns are colonial nesters.

---

## Glaucous Gull
*Larus hyperboreus*
26–32 in. (66–81 cm)

*Range:* The Glaucous Gull is a rare winter visitor along the Carolina coast, mainly along the Outer Banks, from mid-November to late May. One lingered at Roanoke Rapids Lake in North Carolina for about a week in late May of 1972.

*Feeding habits:* See comments on family.

*Description:* The adult Glaucous Gull is larger than a Herring Gull and nearly all white; its feet are pinkish; and its bill is yellow with

*Glaucous Gull, immature*
Richard A. Rowlett

a red spot on the lower mandible. Second-winter Glaucous is similar, but the bill is flesh-colored with a dark tip. First-winter Glaucous is mottled with gray and has a dark-tipped flesh-colored bill. Iceland Gulls are similar but are generally smaller than a Herring Gull and have a relatively small head and bill. First-winter Iceland has a completely dark bill. The relative length of the tail and the folded wings is not a reliable field character. Some individuals apparently cannot be separated in the field.

## Iceland Gull
*Larus glaucoides*
23–25 in. (58–63 cm)

*Range:* The Iceland Gull is an extremely rare winter visitor along the Carolina coast. It has

*Iceland Gull, immature*
Richard A. Rowlett

been reported inland near Clemson, S.C. (hypothetical status)

## Great Black-backed Gull
*Larus marinus*
28–31 in. (71–78 cm)

*Range:* The Great Black-backed Gull is an abundant winter resident in the vicinity of Oregon Inlet. Southward along the Carolina coast it becomes a fairly common to uncommon winter visitor. It also occurs regularly in tidewater North Carolina and at Lake Mattamuskeet. It is a very rare transient inland. A few Great Black-backed Gulls nest among Herring Gulls on dredged material islands in Pamlico Sound near Oregon Inlet. Two nests were found in the summer of 1973, and by 1977 the number had grown to 10. At present this is the southernmost breeding site known on the East Coast.

*Nesting habits:* Great Black-backed Gulls build bulky, well-cupped nests of dry grasses placed directly on the sand. The two or three pale olive-buff eggs are blotched with dark brown and black. Incubation takes about 26 days. Although the precocial downy gull chicks may stay in or near the nest for a day or two, they are soon able to run about. Both parents incubate eggs and care for the young, sheltering chicks from the hot sun until they are well feathered and feeding them until they are old enough to fly.

*Great Black-backed Gull*
James F. Parnell

*Great Black-backed Gull, immature*
James F. Parnell

*Feeding habits:* See comments on family.

*Description:* Adults are white with a black mantle, a yellow bill, and pink feet. Immatures are separated from young Herring and Ring-billed Gulls by their large size, whitish head, and completely black bill.

## Lesser Black-backed Gull

*Larus fuscus*
21–22 in. (53–56 cm)

*Range:* This Eurasian species is a very rare winter visitor on the Carolina coast between October and early April.

*Feeding habits:* See comments on family.

*Description:* Slightly smaller than a Herring Gull, the Lesser Black-backed is almost identical to the Great Black-backed except for size and leg color, which is yellow instead of pink.

## Herring Gull

*Larus argentatus*
22–26 in. (56–66 cm)

*Range:* A permanent resident of coastal and tidewater Carolina, the Herring Gull is abundant except during the summer. It was first discovered nesting in North Carolina's Pamlico Sound in 1962. The species now breeds, often in close association with Laughing Gulls, at several sites from Oregon Inlet to the lower Cape Fear River. In 1977 about 500 pairs

nested in North Carolina. No nesting has been discovered in South Carolina, but a recent marked increase in summer residents suggests that breeding range extension will continue southward. Most of the Herring Gulls seen in the Carolinas in summer are nonbreeding immature birds. In winter Herring Gulls are uncommon to locally fairly common on large inland lakes.

*Nesting habits:* Although in other parts of the country Herring Gulls sometimes build nests in trees, the North Carolina nests have been well-cupped mounds of grass and other vegetation placed directly on the ground. Eggs number two or three and are highly variable with ground colors ranging from blue to gray to light brown and with specks, blotches, and streaks of brown, black, and lilac. Incubation varies from 24 to 28 days, chicks are precocial, and both adults incubate eggs and care for young. The species is single-brooded.

*Feeding habits:* See comments on family.

*Herring Gull, immature*
David S. Lee

*Herring Gull*
James F. Parnell

*Description:* The adult Herring Gull is white with a gray mantle and black wing tips; it has pink feet and a yellow bill with a red spot on the lower mandible. Immatures are brownish and have no white band on the tip of the tail.

## Thayer's Gull
*Larus thayeri*

*Range:* A bird apparently of this species was seen on the beach near Kill Devil Hills, N.C., on October 26, 1971. Thayer's Gull normally winters on the western coast of North America. A dark-eyed version of the Herring Gull, Thayer's Gull has a brown iris, a medium-gray mantle, and flesh-pink legs and feet. The Herring Gull has yellow eyes, but it too

has pink feet. The two forms are very difficult to separate under field conditions. (hypothetical status)

## Ring-billed Gull
*Larus delawarensis*
18–20 in. (45–51 cm)

*Range:* An extremely abundant winter resident of coastal and tidewater Carolina, the Ring-billed Gull is found inland more frequently and in larger numbers than are our other gulls. The species is present along the coast all year, but it is not known to breed in the Carolinas.

*Feeding habits:* In the coastal plain Ring-billed Gulls often feed on waste grain and hunt insects behind farm tractors. Otherwise

*Ring-billed Gull*
William G. Cobey

their feeding habits are like those of the other gulls.

*Description:* The adult Ring-billed is a white gull with a gray mantle and black wing tips; it has yellow feet and a yellow bill with a dark band encircling it near the tip. The immature is mottled with gray and has pinkish feet and a dark-tipped flesh-colored bill; its tail is white with a black band next to the narrow white tip.

## Black-headed Gull
*Larus ridibundus*
14–15 in. (35–38 cm)

*Range:* A very rare transient and winter visitor, this Eurasian gull has been found on or near the Caro-

lina coast between early August and late April.

*Feeding habits:* See comments on family.

*Description:* Similar in general appearance to the Bonaparte's Gull, the adult Black-headed is a slightly larger bird with a larger, dark red bill and with primaries that are dark underneath. In breeding plumage the head is very dark brown. Consult field guides for further information.

## Laughing Gull
*Larus atricilla*
15–17 in. (38–43 cm)

*Range:* The Laughing Gull is the only common black-headed gull

*Laughing Gull, breeding adult*
James F. Parnell

*Laughing Gulls, adults in fall molt*
David S. Lee

in the Carolinas. It is a permanent resident in coastal and tidewater Carolina, abundant in summer and uncommon to locally absent in midwinter. Inland sightings occur at lakes and are rare.

*Nesting habits:* Partly or completely concealed, the substantial nests of seaweeds, grasses, and sedges are raised a little off the sand or mud of grassy islands or high marshes that may be partially covered with shallow water at high tide. Eggs usually number three and are dark olive, splotched and scrawled with black. Laid in May or early June, they require about 20 days for incubation. Both sexes incubate eggs and care for the precocial downy chicks, which remain in the nest a few days.

*Feeding habits:* See comments on family. Laughing Gulls regularly follow our coastal ferries hoping for handouts from the passengers.

*Description:* The adult Laughing

Gull has a white body and tail, dark gray mantle with a white border on the trailing edge of the wing, and dark feet and bill; its black head molts to become predominantly white in winter. See a field guide for illustrations of the immature plumages. The name of the species is derived from its call, a sound like high-pitched cackling laughter.

*Bonaparte's Gull, immature*
James F. Parnell

## Franklin's Gull
*Larus pipixcan*
13½–15½ in. (34–39 cm)

*Range:* A bird of the prairies, Franklin's Gull rarely occurs east of the Appalachian Mountains. In October 1952, an individual of this species was shot on the Catawba River just north of the South Carolina line. On May 8, 1975, one was found following a tractor near Townville in Anderson County, S.C. Another was seen at Huntington Beach State Park in Georgetown County, S.C., on September 26, 1976; and a third South Carolina record occurred April 2, 1978, when a Franklin's Gull was seen on Lake Greenwood.

*Feeding habits:* This gull eats insects more than anything else. It often follows the plow and is adept at catching insects in flight.

*Description:* Although similar to the adult Laughing Gull, the adult Franklin's in flight has a white band separating the gray wing from the black wing tip.

## Bonaparte's Gull
*Larus philadelphia*
12–14 in. (30–35 cm)

*Range:* Bonaparte's Gulls are somewhat erratic winter residents along the Carolina coast from late August to early June, generally being fairly common to common but occasionally abundant for short periods. This species visits large inland lakes from November through early May, but it is scarce in midwinter.

*Feeding habits:* Although the Bonaparte's Gull eats much insect matter, it also takes small fish, crustaceans, and other small aquatic animals. It often plucks food from the surface of the water while on the wing.

*Description:* Similar to the Laughing Gull, Bonaparte's has a large white triangular patch extending from the bend of the wing toward its tip. The white of the primaries is visible underneath as well as from above. See a field guide for illustrations of the differences between Bonaparte's and the very rare Black-headed Gull.

# Little Gull
*Larus minutus*
11 in. (28 cm)

*Range:* A European species that now breeds in Canada near Toronto, in the Niagara area, and at Lake St. Clair, the Little Gull has been seen several times in northeastern North Carolina. The species was first recorded on August 29, 1971, at Roanoke Rapids Lake following the passage of a tropical storm. Since then, one to three birds have appeared occasionally from late August to early March along the Outer Banks southward to Cape Hatteras.

*Feeding habits:* Less a scavenger than the larger gulls, the Little Gull takes insects, small fish, and other small aquatic animals.

*Description:* Watch for the small size, rounded wings, and ternlike flight of the Little Gull. The adult has a gray mantle and a black under wing. Its head is black in summer but mostly white in winter. Consult a field guide for the immature and winter plumages.

*Black-legged Kittiwake*
Michael Tove

*Black-legged Kittiwake, immature*
Richard A. Rowlett

# Black-legged Kittiwake
*Rissa tridactyla*
16–18 in. (40–45 cm)

*Range:* A bird of the open sea, the Black-legged Kittiwake occurs mostly out of sight of land, but occasionally it visits the North Carolina coast between October and May. First recorded off Cape Hatteras in February 1940, the species is now known to be a fairly regular, though still uncommon, winter visitor along the Outer Banks. The species has not yet been recorded in South Carolina.

*Feeding habits:* Less a scavenger than the larger gulls, the kittiwake snatches small fish, crustaceans, and other animal matter from the surface of the sea.

*Description:* The adult Black-legged Kittiwake has a white

body, a gray mantle with sharply defined solid black wing tips, a yellow bill, and black feet and legs. Immatures have a somewhat mottled mantle, a black bill, a black band across the back of the neck, and a black tip on the very slightly forked tail.

## Sabine's Gull
*Xema sabini*
13 in. (33 cm)

*Range:* A Sabine's Gull was sighted from the beach just north of Oregon Inlet, N.C., on May 27, 1972. In early October of 1976, an adult bird still in breeding plumage spent at least 5 days on Salem Lake, Forsyth County, N.C. Excellent photographs added the species to the state list. Sabine's Gull is a very rare transient along the East Coast in late spring and early fall when it normally migrates along the Pacific Coast between the Arctic breeding grounds and a

*Sabine's Gull, adult beginning fall molt*
E. Wayne Irvin

wintering territory south of the equator.

*Feeding habits:* Sabine's Gull eats small fish and other suitable animal matter.

*Description:* The adult Sabine's Gull has a black bill tipped with yellow; a dark head in summer; a white body; a white tail that is very slightly forked; and a mantle boldly marked with triangular patches of black, white, and gray. The immature is similar; but its forked tail has a black band at the tip, and its bill is completely dark.

## Gull-billed Tern
*Gelochelidon nilotica*
13–15 in. (33–38 cm)

*Range:* A fairly common summer resident along the Carolina coast, the Gull-billed Tern is usually present from mid-April to September. Inland occurrences are accidental.

*Nesting habits:* Laying begins in May, and the two or three brown-spotted greenish-buff eggs hatch in 22 to 23 days. Only one brood is raised each season. The small breeding colonies of Gull-billed Terns are often associated with those of Common Terns or Black Skimmers. The Gull-billed colony at Cape Romain is unusually large, numbering about 700 pairs in some seasons.

*Feeding habits:* Gull-billed Terns feed extensively over marshes and consume more insects than most

Gull-billed Tern at nest
James F. Parnell

of their relatives except the Black Tern.

Description: This predominantly white tern has a slightly forked tail and a very thick black bill.

## Forster's Tern
*Sterna forsteri*
14–15 in. (35–38 cm)

Range: Forster's Tern is a common winter resident along the Carolina coast. Occasionally it appears inland, particularly after coastal storms in late summer and early autumn. The species breeds fairly commonly in Pamlico and Core Sounds in northeastern North Carolina.

Nesting habits: Nests found recently along the Outer Banks indicate that the birds lay their

two to four well-splotched olive eggs on drifts of dried vegetation in salt marshes or on low sandy islands rarely visited by human beings. The incubation period is 23 days, and the young remain in

Forster's Tern, winter
James F. Parnell

Forster's Terns, winter
Richard A. Rowlett

Common Tern
James F. Parnell

the nest a few days. The species is single-brooded.

*Feeding habits:* See comments on family.

*Description:* Although similar to the Common Tern, Forster's has more white in the primaries and its deeply forked tail is mostly pale gray.

---

## Common Tern
*Sterna hirundo*
13–16 in. (33–40 cm)

Common Tern at nest
James F. Parnell

*Range:* Common Terns are found along the Carolina coast during all seasons of the year. They are common to abundant during migrations but uncommon as winter residents along the South Carolina coast. This species occasionally visits large inland lakes, usually in April and May and from July to mid-October. Many Common Terns breed in colonies on the Outer Banks and on small sandy islands in Pamlico Sound. Nests become less numerous southward along the coast to Charleston, S.C., the present southern limit of known breeding on the Atlantic Coast.

*Nesting habits:* The two or three blotched eggs are laid in a depression in the sand that may have a lining of shell fragments or dry grass. Incubation requires about 23 to 26 days in this single-brooded species.

*Feeding habits:* See comments on family.

*Description:* In summer the adult Common Tern has a black cap, a bright red-orange bill that is more or less dusky at the tip, a deeply forked tail that is mostly white, and a gray mantle that becomes noticeably darker toward the outer primaries. Consult a field guide for identification of immatures and winter adults.

## Arctic Tern
*Sterna paradisaea*
14–17 in. (35–43 cm)

*Range:* Apparently Arctic Terns migrate well offshore and are rarely seen in North Carolina waters. Our only records are from May and September.

*Feeding habits:* See comments on family.

*Description:* Similar to a Common Tern, the adult Arctic Tern has grayish underparts and a blood-red bill without a dusky tip. In flying birds, watch for a translucent spot near the tip of each wing. The one North Carolina specimen is an immature bird, which has a dark bill and an incomplete cap.

## Roseate Tern
*Sterna dougallii*
14–17 in. (35–43 cm)

*Range:* Mostly a rare coastal transient from late March to mid-May and from late July to October, the Roseate Tern became known as a breeding species in North Carolina in the summer of 1973 when one pair nested near Core Banks in Carteret County.

*Nesting habits:* See comments on family.

*Feeding habits:* See comments on family.

*Description:* The summer adult has a black bill and cap, a light gray mantle, and a very long and very deeply forked tail that is completely white.

## Sooty Tern
*Sterna fuscata*
15–17 in. (38–43 cm)

*Range:* Storm-blown Sooty Terns may appear anywhere in the Carolinas at any season, but most of the records are coastal and are concentrated in the June through September period when the species appears to be an uncommon but probably regular summer visitor. A nest was discovered at Morgan Island, Carteret County, N.C., in June 1978, apparently a rare case of extralimital breeding.

Sooty Tern
Douglas Pratt

*Feeding habits:* The Sooty Tern snatches fish from the surface of the water without diving.

*Description:* Black above and white below, the Sooty Tern has a black bill, a white forehead above the black eye line, and a deeply forked black tail that is narrowly edged with white on the sides. The immature is mottled dark brown and has a moderately deep fork in the tail.

## Bridled Tern
*Sterna anaethetus*
14–15 in. (35–38 cm)

*Range:* The Bridled Tern has been recorded in the Carolinas from mid-April to early October. The species appears to be a fairly common summer visitor offshore from late June to late September. This and other pelagic terns often rest on floating wooden crates and boards.

*Feeding habits:* See comments on family.

*Description:* Similar to the Sooty Tern, the Bridled has a dark gray mantle and tail. Note the light streak across the back of the neck.

## Least Tern
*Sterna albifrons*
8½–9¾ in. (21–24 cm)

*Range:* Once nearly extirpated by plume hunters, the Least Tern is a fairly common summer resident along the Carolina coast from April to October, with a few stragglers remaining until late December. Inland the species is mostly a very rare accidental, usually following tropical storms in August, September, or October. Nevertheless, nesting colonies have been found at Lakes Marion and Murray, 65 to 110 miles (105–175 km) from the South Carolina coast.

*Least Tern at nest*
Robert Schmitt

*Nesting habits:* Least Terns usually begin nesting in May. The two or three eggs are laid in a scrape on a beach, a shell bank, or a sand bank formed by channel dredging. In the Charleston area some nesting colonies are located on the flat gravel-topped roofs of large buildings. The eggshells are so mottled and splotched that they are almost invisible among the pebbles, debris, or fragments of seashells around the nesting site. Incubation requires about 3 weeks, and the young can fly when about 24 days old. Second broods may be attempted in the southern part of the species' range, but one is the usual number on the Carolina coast. Least Tern nesting is often disrupted by adverse weather conditions, sometimes resulting in several nesting attempts in a single season. Considered an endangered species on the West Coast, the Least Tern appears to be having difficulty maintaining its population on the East Coast.

*Feeding habits:* See comments on family.

*Description:* Noticeably smaller than our other terns, the Least has a predominantly yellow bill in summer.

---

# Royal Tern
*Sterna maxima*
18–21 in. (45–53 cm)

*Range:* The Royal Tern is a permanent resident of coastal and tidewater Carolina, abundant most of the year but only fairly common from late December to late March. Inland sightings are very rare.

*Nesting habits:* The nesting season starts in May; but if eggs are destroyed by high tides, the birds will lay a second, third, or rarely a fourth time. Sometimes several thousand pairs of Royal Terns breed in a single colony on a small sandy island. Nests may be placed so close together that the distance between centers is only 12 to 14 inches (30–35 cm). Each scrape usually contains a single egg, although clutches of two or three eggs do occur. Incubation requires 3 to 4 weeks, which means that Royal Terns nesting on low sandflats must lay eggs within a week after lunar high tide in order to hatch successfully before the passing of a lunar month. Soon after hatching, the precocial young flock together near the nesting site but at a safe distance from the bills of adults still incubating eggs.

*Feeding habits:* See comments on family.

*Description:* This is our most abundant tern with a shaggy black crest. Note the orange bill, white forehead, and well-forked tail. The similar Caspian Tern is a larger bird with a blood-red bill, darker wings, and a slightly forked tail. Royals have the black cap extending all the way to the bill only for a very short time during the nest-

*Royal Tern*
William G. Cobey

*Royal Terns with downy young*
James F. Parnell

ing season, but Caspians have some dark feathers on the forehead even in winter.

## Sandwich Tern
(Cabot's Tern)
*Sterna sandvicensis*
14–16 in. (35–40 cm)

*Range:* A fairly common, but very local, summer resident of coastal Carolina, the Sandwich Tern is usually present from April to October. Stragglers occur until late December, and on very rare occasions a few linger throughout the winter. Oregon Inlet appears to be the northernmost area along the Atlantic Coast where this mostly subtropical species breeds in appreciable numbers.

*Nesting habits:* Sandwich Terns nest in colonies with Royal Terns, laying in early June two or three slightly smaller eggs in scrapes that tend to be clustered among those of the larger and more abundant Royals. Incubation requires about 21 days, and the species is single-brooded. Young Sandwich Terns mature rapidly and are ready for prolonged flight by the time they are only 6 or 7 weeks old.

*Feeding habits:* See comments on family. Sandwich Terns tend to feed offshore.

*Description:* Similar to the Royal Tern but smaller, the Sandwich is our only tern with a yellow-tipped black bill.

## Caspian Tern
*Sterna caspia*
19–23 in. (48–58 cm)

*Range:* Fairly common along the Carolina coast from mid-April to

*Sandwich Terns*
James F. Parnell

*Caspian Tern*
Chris Marsh

late May and from August to early November, the Caspian Tern winters regularly in South Carolina and southeastern North Carolina, and stragglers may be found farther north along the North Carolina coast until early January. Inland, the species occurs as a spring and fall transient, usually around large lakes in late April or early May and from August through early October. Small numbers of Caspian Terns occur in Carolina coastal waters in summer, and recently a few nests have been found at Oregon Inlet, Hatteras Inlet, and Cape Romain.

*Nesting habits:* The 1970 Cape Island nest contained two eggs and was situated in a colony with Black Skimmers and Gull-billed Terns. The nest was an unlined depression in the sand, and the incubation period was apparently no less than 28 days. (In some regions the Caspian Tern builds a fairly elaborate nest, and the incubation period is reported as being only 20 days.) Each year from 1972 through 1977, one to ten Caspian Tern nests were found on the bare or nearly bare sandy ' domes of dredged material islands in North Carolina. Scrapes lined with small shell fragments, the nests contained one or two eggs or chicks. Caspian Terns breeding in North Carolina were associated with colonies of Black Skimmers, Common Terns, or Royal Terns.

*Feeding habits:* See comments on family.

*Description:* See Royal Tern.

---

## Black Tern
*Chlidonias niger*
9–10 in. (22–25 cm)

*Range:* Along the coast the Black Tern is an uncommon spring transient from late April to early June, but it is a common southbound migrant from July through September. A few stragglers may linger into early winter. Inland sightings are uncommon, occurring mainly during the fall migration. Although they are seen most frequently over coastal marshes, many Black Terns migrate well offshore.

*Feeding habits:* Black Terns hawk for insects and dive much less often than our other terns.

*Description:* The adult Black Tern is almost completely dark above and below, and it has a slightly

*Black Tern, fall*
James F. Parnell

forked tail. Immatures are predominantly plain gray with a white head, but the head and underparts are blotched with black and gray.

## Brown Noddy Tern (Noddy)
*Anous stolidus*
13–16 in. (33–40 cm)

*Range:* A very rare accidental occurring from mid-June to mid-September, the Brown Noddy Tern has been recorded along the Carolina coast northward to the vicinity of Oregon Inlet. In most cases, the sighting of this tropical tern was directly related to the passage of a hurricane.

*Feeding habits:* This highly pelagic tern feeds without diving.

*Description:* The Brown Noddy Tern has dark wings and body, a white cap, and a dark wedge-shaped tail.

# Family Rynchopidae: Skimmers

Skimmers have bills that are laterally compressed into knife-like blades, the upper mandible being short and having a single cutting edge that fits snugly into the double-edged lower mandible.

## Black Skimmer
*Rynchops niger*
16–20 in. (40–51 cm)

*Range:* Permanent residents of coastal Carolina, Black Skimmers are abundant in summer, and they remain fairly common in winter north to Cape Lookout. Although the species normally occurs only along the coast, storm-blown birds are occasionally found inland.

*Nesting habits:* Skimmers nest on remote coastal islands or beaches, laying clutches of three to five eggs in bare scrapes in the sand during June or July. The creamy eggs are blotched and scrawled with dark brown. Although single-brooded, the females will lay again if clutches are destroyed by high tides, storms, or predators. Incubation requires 21 to 23 days. Adults will feign injury if the nest is disturbed. Precocial chicks are covered with buffy down and have bills of equal length. When newly hatched, they will scratch a hole in the sand and freeze at the approach of danger, remaining

*Black Skimmer at nest*
James F. Parnell

motionless even when picked up;
but very soon they can outrun the
curious naturalist.

*Feeding habits:* Skimmers feed by
flying along just above the water
with the tip of the long lower
mandible shearing the surface.
When a shrimp or small fish
strikes the bill, the upper mandible snaps shut. Then the bird can
carry its prey to the nestlings or
simply flip it out of the water and
swallow it while still skimming
the shallows. Black Skimmers
feed mostly when the water is
calm in early evening and at
night. Their nocturnal habits
often startle people taking moon-
light strolls along the beach.

*Description:* Predominantly black
above and white below, the Black

*Black Skimmer*
Mark L. Hintsa

Skimmer has a long orange bill
that is tipped with black, and its
lower mandible is longer than the
upper (see comments on family).

# Family Alcidae: Auks, Murres, and Puffins

Alcids are the northern counterparts of the Antarctic penguins. Web-footed, heavy-bodied, short-winged, and awkward on land, alcids nevertheless are strong fliers as well as excellent swimmers and divers. They use their wings for "flying" underwater in active pursuit of small fish and crustaceans.

The extinct Great Auk (*Pinguinus impennis*), last positively recorded alive in 1844, reportedly wintered in the Atlantic Ocean as far south as South Carolina. Although it was flightless, the Great Auk, unlike penguins, had well-developed flight feathers.

## Razorbill
(Razor-billed Auk)
*Alca torda*
15–18 in. (38–45 cm)

*Range:* The Razorbill is a rare to very rare winter visitor from mid-November to mid-March on the Carolina coast. Most of the onshore sightings involve sick, injured, or oil-soaked birds. This species normally remains at sea except during the breeding season.

*Feeding habits:* See comments on family.

*Description:* Our only alcid with an extremely thick black bill, the Razorbill has a white line extending from the eye forward to the bill and downward across it.

## Thick-billed Murre
(Brünnich's Murre)
*Uria lomvia*
17–20 in. (43–51 cm)

*Range:* The Thick-billed Murre is an extremely rare winter visitor on the Carolina coast. The species has been found in our region only in December, January, and February. During the great winter flight of 1896–1897, a Thick-billed Murre was taken at Anderson, S.C., but all modern records are coastal.

*Feeding habits:* See comments on family.

*Description:* On the water, Thick-billed Murres in winter plumage strongly resemble Common Loons. Look for a white streak at the base of the bill. The similar Common Murre, which is not known from the Carolinas, has a thinner bill and lacks the white streak at the base of the bill.

## Dovekie
*Alle alle*
7–9 in. (17–22 cm)

*Range:* An offshore winter visitor along the Carolina coast from late October through February, the Dovekie may be fairly common some years and go unreported in others. If a storm coincides with a major southward movement, Dovekies may be found surprisingly far inland, as was the case in Decem-

*Thick-billed Murre, winter*
M. M. Browne

ber 1950 when they occurred inland to Raleigh, N.C.

*Feeding habits:* Dovekies feed on shrimp, crabs, and other small crustaceans.

*Description:* This small alcid has a stubby bill and several short white streaks on its black back.

## Black Guillemot
*Cepphus grylle*
12–14 in. (30–35 cm)

*Range:* A sickly bird of this species was seen at the mouth of Charleston Harbor on September 21, 1958. Five people saw an apparently healthy Black Guillemot about 500 feet (150 m) offshore from Huntington Beach State Park, S.C., on April 17, 1975. This is the only Atlantic alcid with a large white wing patch. (hypothetical status)

# Order Columbiformes: Pigeons and Allies

Doves and pigeons are small-headed, swift-flying birds that bob their heads while walking. They consume a wide variety of vegetable matter, and they are able to suck up water without raising their heads as other birds must do when swallowing.

# Family Columbidae: Pigeons and Doves

### Rock Dove
(Domestic Pigeon)
*Columba livia*
about 11 in. (28 cm)

*Range:* This introduced species has become thoroughly naturalized in all but the most remote regions of the Carolinas. Pigeons avoid woodlands and are most numerous in urban habitats.

*Nesting habits:* Rock Dove nests are crude platforms of twigs and straws placed in the eaves and crannies of large buildings wherever caves and cliffs are not available. Pigeons in urban habitats may nest throughout the year in the Carolinas, and two or more broods are raised annually. Reproduction is generally limited by the food supply. The two white eggs hatch in about 17 days. Both sexes incubate, the male usually by day and the female by night. Young pigeons and doves are altricial, and they are brooded and fed by both parents until ready to leave the nest at 2 or 3 weeks of age. During incubation the linings of the adults' crops thicken. This tissue sloughs off into a cheesy curd that is regurgitated to provide the first food for the nestlings. Pigeons' milk has about the same food value as mammals' milk. Later the young poke their beaks into the throats of the parents to obtain regurgitated semidigested grain. Young, unfledged pigeons (squab) are a table delicacy, and historically pigeons have served as message carriers and ornamental birds for parks. Pigeons are also particularly useful as laboratory animals.

*Feeding habits:* See comments on order.

*Description:* Rock Doves may be gray, brown, or pure white, often mottled and touched with iridescence. The white rump readily separates the Rock Dove from all our other doves.

### White-winged Dove
*Zenaida asiatica*
11–12½ in. (28–31 cm)

*Range:* A rare accidental from Mexico and the southwestern United States, the White-winged Dove is more likely to occur along the Carolina coast than inland.

*White-winged Dove*
James F. Parnell

All records are from early October through December except for a single bird seen at Pea Island on June 23, 1942.

*Feeding habits:* See comments on order.

*Description:* Our only dove with large white wing patches, the White-winged Dove has a dark rump that readily separates it from the Rock Dove. White-winged's rounded tail separates it from the Mourning Dove.

## Mourning Dove
*Zenaida macroura*
11–13 in. (28–33 cm)

*Range:* An abundant permanent resident throughout the Carolinas, the Mourning Dove is valuable not only as a game species but also as a consumer of weed seeds. It occurs in open country habitats such as fields, woodland margins, and suburban neighborhoods, but it is scarce in dense woods.

*Nesting habits:* Although limited nesting occurs during every month of the year in the warmer portions of our region, Mourning

*Mourning Dove*
Edward Burroughs

Doves normally lay the first of their two or three annual clutches in March. The male gathers nesting materials, and the female does the building. The nest usually is a frail platform of twigs and pine needles built on the ground, in vines or bushes, or on a horizontal limb of a tree 15 to 30 feet (4.5–9 m) above ground. Sometimes doves take over old robins' nests. Mourning Doves lay two pure white eggs that hatch in 12 to 14 days. Care of young, which fledge at 13 to 15 days, is essentially the same as for the Rock Dove. Formation of large autumn and winter flocks makes the Mourning Dove subject to great hunting pressure, but the species seems to have no trouble maintaining its numbers.

*Feeding habits:* See comments on order.

*Description:* A buffy gray-brown bird with a small head and a long pointed tail that is edged in white, the Mourning Dove often perches on roadside wires where its distinctive silhouette is easily seen.

## Passenger Pigeon
*Ectopistes migratorius*
15–18 in. (38–45 cm)

*Extinct:* Once an extremely abundant transient in the mountain and piedmont regions of North Carolina and a winter resident in South Carolina, the Passenger Pigeon was last reliably reported in the two states in 1894 and 1895, respectively. Excessive hunting and habitat destruction are thought to have caused the extinction of the species.

## Ringed Turtle Dove
*Streptopelia risoria*
about 11 in. (28 cm)

*Range:* This introduced species is breeding in the wild at Winston-Salem, N.C., near Charleston, S.C., and possibly at other places in the Carolinas where domesticated birds have been released.

*Nesting habits:* See Rock Dove.

*Feeding habits:* See comments on order.

*Description:* This pale dove has a narrow black band across the back of the neck.

## Ground Dove
*Columbina passerina*
6–7 in. (15–17 cm)

*Range:* A fairly common permanent resident in southeastern South Carolina, the Ground Dove becomes uncommon to rare northward along the coast to Onslow County, N.C. The species is known to breed in North Carolina only in Brunswick, New Hanover, and Pender Counties; however, recent sightings indicate that it is a year-round resident northward to Carteret County. Usually it occurs in sandy and grassy habitats near shrubs and woodland margins, but it can be found in some towns along the South Caro-

*Ground Doves*
Heathcote Kimball

lina coast. Inland the Ground Dove occurs very rarely from early September to late May westward and northward to Richland County, S.C., and to Buncombe and Guilford Counties in North Carolina.

*Nesting habits:* Nesting usually begins about mid-April and lasts into fall with as many as four broods sometimes being raised. The flimsy nests of twigs, grasses, and pine needles may be placed on the ground, on a stump, on a cross-rail of a grape arbor, or in a bush, waxmyrtle being a popular choice. The two white eggs hatch in 12 to 14 days, and care of the young is essentially the same as for other doves.

*Feeding habits:* See comments on order.

*Description:* The Ground Dove looks like a House Sparrow-sized Mourning Dove with a short rounded tail and rufous wing patches.

# Order Psittaciformes: Parrots and Allies

This distinctive group of colorful and essentially arboreal birds includes many species that are popular as caged birds. Parrots and their allies have large heads and short necks; large, strongly down-curved, hooked bills; and strong, grasping feet with two toes turned forward and two behind. Some species have patches of bare skin around the eyes, and all have sparse plumage with powder-down scattered through it.

# Family Psittacidae:
# Lories, Parrots, and Macaws

### Monk Parakeet
*Myiopsitta monachus*

*Range:* This popular cage bird, a fruit-eating native of Argentina, has been positively reported from Asheville, N.C., Georgetown County, S.C., and Charleston, S.C. At present the Monk Parakeet is known to have bred successfully in the wild at only one place in the Carolinas, in the Asheville area. Power transformers appear to be favored nesting sites. It is too early to tell whether or not this introduced species has become established in our region. (hypothetical status)

*Monk Parakeets*
Michael Tove

# Budgerigar

*Melopsittacus undulatus*
7 in. (17.5 cm)

*Range:* Escaped Budgies can survive in the wild in the Carolinas and may even breed successfully from time to time. There is, however, no evidence of an established wild population in our region. (hypothetical status)

# Carolina Parakeet

*Conuropsis carolinensis*

*Extinct:* Formerly an abundant permanent resident over much of our region, the species was last positively found in the Carolinas during the mid-1800s; but a flock reportedly survived in the Santee Swamp until the late 1930s. Carolina Parakeets were persecuted by fruit growers and shot for the millinery trade as well as for the collectors of bird skins. Egg collectors also helped push the species into oblivion.

# Order Cuculiformes: Cuckoos and Allies

Cuckoos and their allies are long-tailed birds that have slightly hooked beaks and feet with two toes in front and two behind.

# Family Cuculidae: Cuckoos, Roadrunners, and Anis

## Yellow-billed Cuckoo
*Coccyzus americanus*
11–13 in. (28–33 cm)

*Range:* A fairly common to common summer resident of deciduous woodlands throughout the Carolinas, the Yellow-billed Cuckoo arrives about mid-April and departs about mid-October with a few stragglers remaining into November or December.

*Nesting habits:* During the May to August or September breeding season, cuckoos can be heard calling to each other by day and by night; but after the young are on the wing, the birds are mostly silent. The cuckoo's resonant *kuk-kuk-kuk, keow-keow-keow* call is thought by many to foretell the coming of rain, hence the local name "Rain Crow." There may be some scientific basis for this bit of folklore, because cuckoos apparently adjust the timing of their nesting effort to the temporary local abundance of suitable prey, which in many cases coincides with periods of rainfall.

Occasionally, North American

*Yellow-billed Cuckoo feeding young*
Bill Duyck

cuckoos lay in alien nests of their own or other species, behavior similar to that of their European relatives, which are notorious brood parasites. Normally, the Yellow-billed Cuckoo builds a shallow nest of twigs lined with a few skeletonized dry leaves and adorned with pine needles on the rim. Placed 4 to 20 feet (1.2–6 m) above ground in a bush or low tree, the nest is built by both adults and may still be under construction when the female lays the first of her two to four greenish-blue eggs. Incubation begins with the laying of the first egg. During the first day or two of incubation, the male may continue to bring twigs and pine needles for the female to add to the nest, and he may rearrange the nest materials while he is incubating. In one North Carolina nest, four eggs were laid on four successive days, and each of the four eggs hatched on the ninth day after laying. The normal incubation period appears to be 9 to 11 days, which is very short for a bird the size of a Yellow-billed Cuckoo. Apparently both parents share more or less equally in the care of eggs and young.

At hatching the black-skinned chick is blind and nearly naked. Pinfeathers begin to appear on the second day, and by the fifth day the nestling is covered with long sheathed quills. On the palate and tongue nestlings have several soft whitish spots (papillae) that enable them to grasp the bill of the adult during feeding. At first they receive semidigested food regurgitated by the adults; but within 24 hours after hatching, they are fed whole caterpillars, butterflies, and katydids, some of the caterpillars being so large that the parent must give them a couple of pokes before the chick can close its beak.

Young cuckoos develop rapidly and are able to stand on the rim of the nest by the third or fourth day. Parents swallow or carry away fecal sacs until the chicks begin expelling feces over the side of the nest when about 6 days old. On the sixth day after hatching, the sheaths burst, within several hours transforming the nestling into a dark-billed, bob-tailed version of the adult Yellow-billed Cuckoo. Young may leave the nest at 7 days of age or remain up to several days longer. The period of 16 or 17 days between onset of incubation and freedom from the nest is one of the shortest known for any bird, precocial or altricial. Although records of adults incubating eggs as late as September 22 in the Carolinas suggest the possibility of second clutches, there is no positive evidence that Yellow-billed Cuckoos are double-brooded.

*Feeding habits:* The Yellow-billed Cuckoo is a useful species, being among the few birds that will eat tent caterpillars.

*Description:* Brown above and white below, the Yellow-billed

Cuckoo has a decurved bill that is mostly yellow near the base. The wings are marked with rufous patches near the tips, and the long tail has large white spots underneath.

## Black-billed Cuckoo
*Coccyzus erythropthalmus*
11–12 in. (28–30 cm)

*Range:* The Black-billed Cuckoo is a rare to uncommon summer resident of extensive deciduous woodlands in the North Carolina mountains. Although the species has bred at least sparingly in the piedmont and coastal plain of North Carolina, it is primarily a transient in these regions and throughout South Carolina. Normally present in the Carolinas from April through October, the

Black-billed Cuckoo once was found in Yancey County, N.C., in December.

*Nesting habits:* The Black-billed Cuckoo is not known to differ significantly from the Yellow-billed in nesting habits. The incubation period is 10 to 11 days.

*Description:* Similar to the Yellow-billed Cuckoo, the Black-billed has a completely black bill and much smaller tail spots. The adult Black-billed has a red eye ring; the immature, a white one. The immature Yellow-billed Cuckoo has a dark bill at first, but the part that becomes yellow is gray rather than black.

# Order Strigiformes: Owls

Owls have soft fluffy plumage that enables them to fly silently in pursuit of rodents and other small animals, which they catch with their hooked beaks and strong feet. The indigestible portions of their prey are coughed up in elongated pellets that can be found scattered about the roost and examined to determine the diet of each species.

Although owls appear to be short-necked, their necks actually are rather long, allowing them to twist their heads a full 180 degrees to right or left. Owls have large forward-looking eyes set in a pronounced facial disk. Contrary to folklore, they are not blind in the daytime. Their nictitating membrane, or third eyelid, is well developed to protect the sensitive retina from bright light. Owls also have highly developed ears concealed by the facial disk, which functions to absorb sound waves and direct them to the ears. Many species, including the Barn Owl, hunt by sound rather than by sight.

Most owls build little or no nest, preferring to lay their eggs in a natural cavity or in the vacant nest of another species. Owl eggs are pure white and almost spherical. Newly hatched owlets are blind and helpless, but they are covered with white down. Both parents care for the young until they are ready to fly, which in some of the larger species may be 8 to 10 weeks.

# Family Tytonidae: Barn Owls

## Barn Owl
*Tyto alba*
15–21 in. (38–53 cm)

*Range:* Rare to uncommon at most localities, the Barn Owl is a permanent resident everywhere in the Carolinas except on the higher mountains. The population is increased slightly in winter by the arrival of a few migrants from the north. The species is seen most frequently over coastal marshes at dusk during the winter months.

*Nesting habits:* Barn Owls appear to mate for life, nesting year after year in the same hollow tree, barn loft, church steeple, or abandoned building. No nest is built by the Barn Owl, and laying may take place at any time of year. The four to nine eggs are deposited at intervals, making it possible to find unhatched eggs and young from the same clutch at several stages of development. The female incubates each egg for 21 to 24 days. She is fed regularly by her mate.

*Feeding habits:* Birds living in cities make long flights to hunt in

*Young Barn Owls*
Morris D. Williams

rural fields and marshes, but never in woodlands.

*Description:* Golden brown above and very light below, the Barn Owl has a heart-shaped face resembling that of a monkey. The unbirdlike screams, chuckles, and snores of Barn Owls undoubtedly have given many an old building the reputation for being haunted.

# Family Strigidae: Typical Owls

## Screech Owl
*Otus asio*
8–10 in. (20–25 cm)

*Range:* The Screech Owl is a fairly common or common permanent resident of woodlands, preferably conifers, throughout the Carolinas.

*Nesting habits:* The Screech Owl nests in natural cavities, old woodpecker holes, unused chimneys, and nest boxes from 3 to 50 feet (1–15 m) above ground. The two to six eggs usually are laid in April and require about 26 days for incubation. The species is single-brooded.

*Feeding habits:* See comments on order.

*Description:* The Screech Owl is our only small owl with ear tufts. Despite its name, the bird calls in a plaintive, tremulous whistle that is musical and not at all

*Screech Owl, red phase*
Michael Tove

unpleasing. This owl, like others, will snap its bill menacingly when disturbed. Both nestlings and adults exhibit two color phases, one red and the other gray, which bear no relationship to age, sex, or season. The red phase, however, seems to predominate in the race that breeds in the western counties, while the gray phase appears to predominate in the east.

## Great Horned Owl
*Bubo virginianus*
18–25 in. (45–63 cm)

*Range:* Uncommon to fairly common, the Great Horned Owl is a permanent resident of dry woodlands throughout the Carolinas.

*Nesting habits:* Although capable of building a skimpy nest, the

*Great Horned Owl*
Robert F. Soots Jr.

Great Horned Owl almost always takes over one built by a hawk or crow, uses and vacates an Osprey nest before the return of the owner, or takes an apartment in a Bald Eagle nest with both species incubating at the same time only a few feet apart. The two, or sometimes three, eggs are laid very early, from late December to March, and require about a month for incubation.

*Feeding habits:* See comments on order. Although Great Horned Owls occasionally consume poultry and game birds, they are fully protected along with all other birds of prey.

*Description:* The Great Horned Owl is a large brown owl with large yellow eyes and with ear tufts set wide apart. This is the "Hoot Owl" whose deep, resonant call is a series of four to seven hoots, perhaps *hoo-hoo, hoo-hoo-o-o* with a final rising inflection, or more commonly *hoo-hoo, hoo-hoo-hoo, hoo, hoo.*

## Snowy Owl
*Nyctea scandiaca*
20–27 in. (51–68 cm)

*Range:* This bird of the Arctic tundra is a rare and irregular winter visitor in the Carolinas, having been found from the mountains to the coast between late October and early February. Occurrences probably are related to the shortage of rodents in the far north and the arrival of unusually cold weather in our region.

*Feeding habits:* See comments on order.

*Description:* The Snowy is our only predominantly white owl. Adults are almost pure white, but the immatures have dark spots on most of the feathers.

---

## Burrowing Owl
*Athene cunicularia*
9–11 in. (22–28 cm)

*Range:* The Burrowing Owl is a very rare accidental along the Carolina coast. Single birds were found at Beaufort, S.C., in December 1943; on Hatteras Island, N.C., in February 1967; near Morehead City, N.C., from June to early September 1972; at Charleston, S.C., on December 30, 1975; and at Huntington Beach

Burrowing Owl
Michael Tove

State Park, S.C., on June 24, 1976. Two of the birds were roosting beneath unused boats on the shore, and another was using an old dredge pipe. One bird apparently had enlarged a sand crab tunnel some distance from its boat and divided its time between the two sites. The Hatteras bird was collected and proved to be of the Florida race, *A. c. floridana.*

*Feeding habits:* Burrowing Owls hunt by day, hovering on the wing in pursuit of small mammals and insects, especially locusts, crickets, and grasshoppers.

*Description:* The Burrowing Owl is a small, long-legged, sandy-colored owl that frequently bobs up and down.

---

## Barred Owl
*Strix varia*
18–24 in. (45–61 cm)

*Range:* Barred Owls are fairly common permanent residents of swamps, river bottoms, and moist woodlands throughout the Carolinas.

*Nesting habits:* Nesting begins early, often in January or February, with the two or three eggs usually being laid in a natural tree cavity, but occasionally in the abandoned nest of a hawk or crow. Incubation requires about 28 days.

*Feeding habits:* Barred Owls eat rodents, insects, small birds, frogs, and sometimes fish. They rarely molest poultry.

*Barred Owl*
John L. Tveten

*Description:* The Barred Owl is a large gray-brown bird with dark eyes and no ear tufts. Its clearly accented raspy hoots are typically given in two consecutive groups of four or five syllables each and end with a distinctive, descending *aww.*

---

## Long-eared Owl
*Asio otus*
13–16 in. (33–40 cm)

*Range:* A rare winter resident from late October to mid-March, the Long-eared Owl frequents dense growths of cedars and other evergreen trees. It probably occurs throughout the Carolinas and may be considerably more numerous than the few published records indicate. Because the Long-eared Owl is mostly silent on the wintering grounds, it is seldom recorded.

*Feeding habits:* See comments on order.

*Description:* The Long-eared Owl is similar to the larger Great Horned Owl, but the slender ear tufts stick up directly above the relatively small yellow eyes. The "ears" of the Long- and Short-eared Owls, like the "horns" of the Great Horned Owl, actually are tufts of feathers.

---

## Short-eared Owl
*Asio flammeus*
13–17 in. (33–43 cm)

*Range:* The Short-eared Owl is a bird of the open prairies, mead-ows, and salt marshes. On the barrier islands it frequents the dunes and shrubbery adjacent to marshes, hunting at twilight and on overcast days. The species is an uncommon visitor along the Carolina coast from late October to late April. Inland sightings were not rare during the early 1900s, but in recent years the Short-eared Owl has become very rare away from the coast.

*Feeding habits:* Although somewhat diurnal, the Short-eared Owl is much like our other owls in feeding behavior.

*Description:* The Short-eared Owl frequently perches on the ground in open grassy habitats. When flushed, it looks like a completely brown Marsh Hawk with dark spots near the bend of each wing. The ear tufts are so small that they can be seen only at very close range.

---

## Saw-whet Owl
*Aegolius acadicus*
7½–8 in. (19–20 cm)

*Range:* Breeding in the Canadian zone forests of the North Carolina mountains and wintering in dense pines and cedars at least to a limited extent throughout the Carolinas, the Saw-whet Owl is one of the rarest owls found in our region. The species occurs most frequently in the transition habitat where spruce-fir stands meet hardwoods. Evidence of breeding in the southern Appalachians rests primarily on the sighting of immature birds at Richland Balsam on July 10, 1965, and at Mount Mitchell State Park on September 2, 1965. No nests or preflight young have been found in North Carolina. Further evidence of breeding is the location of numerous calling stations in the Great Smoky Mountains National Park and along the Blue Ridge Parkway in Jackson, Haywood, and Transylvania Counties. Saw-whet Owls call most often from the first week in April through the middle of June. The song consists of a series of resonant, bell-like cooing notes repeated at the rate of one or two per second and often continuing for several hours without interruption. The bird's voice is not likely to be heard, however, except on nights when winds are calm.

*Nesting habits:* According to reports from other states, Saw-whet Owls lay their four to seven eggs in April, nesting 14 to 60 feet (4.3–18.4 m) above ground in old woodpecker holes, preferably those of the Common Flicker. Rapping on the tree trunk usually causes the incubating bird to poke its head out the entrance, behavior that is in keeping with the species' general reputation for tameness.

*Feeding habits:* See comments on order.

*Description:* The Saw-whet Owl is smaller than a Screech Owl and has no ear tufts. Fledglings are plain brown with a white forehead. The call sounds remarkably like someone sharpening a saw. Fledgling Screech Owls lack ear tufts and are easily mistaken for Saw-whets.

*Saw-whet Owl*
Michael P. Schultz

# Order Caprimulgiformes: Nightjars and Allies

Nightjars, like all other nocturnal birds, wear somber plumage. Predominantly brown and black with spots of white, the North American nightjars—often referred to by the misnomer "goatsuckers"—look like sun-dappled dead leaves by day as they rest motionless on the ground or perch lengthwise on a tree limb with lids covering their large eyes. They can shuffle a few steps on their small feet, but they seldom do, preferring to fly even short distances. The underside of the middle toenail bears serrated notches similar to those found in herons. Although the function is unknown, the comb is assumed to be used in grooming. Nightjars feed on the wing, capturing night-flying insects with their extremely wide mouths, gaping up to 2 inches (5 cm) in the Chuck-will's-widow, which occasionally swallows small birds such as wrens, warblers, and sparrows. Both Chuck-will's-widows and Whip-poor-wills have long forward-pointing facial bristles thought by some ornithologists to increase the effective span of their mouths and by others to protect their eyes and nostrils during feeding flights. Although Common Nighthawks, swifts, and swallows have similar feeding habits, these species have rictal bristles that are poorly developed, or none at all—a fact that only compounds the puzzle.

## Family Caprimulgidae: Nightjars

### Chuck-will's-widow
*Caprimulgus carolinensis*
11–12 in. (28–30 cm)

*Range:* The Chuck-will's-widow is a common summer resident of thick woodlands adjacent to fields throughout most of South Carolina and in the eastern and central counties of North Carolina. It becomes uncommon toward the mountains where it is known only as a transient. Males return to the breeding grounds from late March to mid-April, soon to be followed by the females. Chuck-will's-widows depart for the tropics and subtropics by late September.

*Nesting habits:* Nests can be found year after year in virtually the same location. Eggs are laid

*Chuck-will's-widow*
F. S. Barkalow Jr.

directly upon the leaf-carpeted ground, usually from mid-April to early June. The two deep cream eggs are variously marbled and spotted with colors ranging from pale blue to dark brown. Incubation requires about 20 days, and calling ceases when the young emerge from their shells. Chicks are covered with silky, protectively colored down. Young remain in or near the nest and require parental care until they can fly well enough to capture their own food. If eggs are taken, the female will lay again and again. The sitting bird will feign injury and lead intruders from the nest. Reports of goatsuckers' removing eggs or chicks from a disturbed nest apparently have a basis in fact.

*Feeding habits:* See comments on order.

*Description:* The Chuck-will's-widow is larger and more brownish than the Whip-poor-will. The throat patch is reddish-brown in the male Chuck, buffy in the female Chuck, and dark gray in Whips. Goatsuckers are best identified by their loud and persistent calls, often given hundreds of times in succession. The Chuck may seem to have three, four, or five syllables according to the distance between the bird and the listener. The soft initial *cluck* is not heard at a great distance. Some people hear only four syllables as in the common name, but others hear the bird saying *kiss William's widow.* The Whip-poor-will says its name.

---

## Whip-poor-will
*Caprimulgus vociferus*
9–10 in. (22–25 cm)

*Range:* A fairly common to common summer resident of woodlands in the mountains, piedmont, and inner coastal plain, the Whip-poor-will becomes uncommon to absent toward the coast during the breeding season. In winter the species is uncommon to fairly common in central and eastern South Carolina, and a few individuals winter in coastal North Carolina.

*Nesting habits:* The Whip-poor-will and the Chuck-will's-widow have similar nesting habits.

*Description:* See Chuck-will's-widow for a comparative description.

---

## Common Nighthawk
*Chordeiles minor*
9–10 in. (22–25 cm)

*Range:* A common transient in the western counties and an uncommon to fairly common summer resident across the Carolinas, the Common Nighthawk is present from mid-April to October; but earlier and later sightings occur frequently. During migration, particularly in fall, nighthawks are sometimes found in dense flocks numbering into the thousands.

*Nesting habits:* Usually laid in May or early June, the two grayish-white eggs are thickly spotted with various drab colors. Nesting in open situations, the female lays her eggs directly upon a sand dune, the ground between rows of field crops, or the flat gravel-topped roof of a building. In the inland portions of the Carolinas, urban rooftops now appear to be the preferred nesting sites. Incubation requires about 19 days, and the adult will distract an intruder by feigning injury. Almost always returning to the eggs from the same direction, incubating nighthawks sometimes gradually and unintentionally move a clutch as much as 50 feet (15 m) before the downy young emerge from the shells. Young require some degree of parental care for about 4 weeks.

*Feeding habits:* Nighthawks constantly give buzzing nasal calls while on the wing. More diurnal than our other nightjars, Common Nighthawks can be seen wheeling and diving high above marshes, pastures, and business districts by day in pursuit of insects. After dark, "Bullbats" often feed around street lights and lighted signs.

*Description:* This gray bird has long slender pointed wings and a slightly forked tail. Its throat is white, and there is a white bar across each wing as well as across the tail near the tip.

*Common Nighthawk*
John L. Tveten

# Order Apodiformes:
# Swifts and Hummingbirds

Although superficially quite different in appearance, swifts and hummingbirds share the characteristic of having very short bones in the section of the wing before the final bend. They also have weak legs and feet.

## Family Apodidae: Swifts

### Chimney Swift
*Chaetura pelagica*
4¾–5½ in. (12–14 cm)

*Range:* Abundant summer residents from April through October, Chimney Swifts begin arriving in the Carolinas in March, and some may linger into early November. They appear to migrate by day.

*Nesting habits:* Although a few Chimney Swifts still nest in large hollow trees, the great majority nest and roost, as their name implies, in chimneys. Both sexes help build the nest. Late in May they can be seen hovering at the tips of limbs while breaking off dead twigs. With saliva they fasten the twigs to each other and to the inside of the chimney, fashioning an unlined semicircular basket that may be attached almost anywhere between the top and the bottom of the flue. Our species is related to the Asian swift whose entirely glutinous nest is the basis for bird's-nest soup. The three to six pure white eggs usually are laid before mid-June, and incubation requires about 18 days. Both adults incubate eggs and care for the altricial young, which stay in or near the nest for a relatively long time, 24 days or longer. The nestlings' eyes do not open fully until the fourteenth day. Using their short stiff tails to brace themselves against the vertical walls, they exercise their wings while preparing to emerge from the chimney fully capable of extended flight. After the nesting season, swifts flock together, and a thousand or more may roost in a single large chimney.

*Feeding habits:* Chimney Swifts wheel about the sky in pursuit of insects. They usually fly high above the trees, but on cloudy days they sometimes swoop almost to the ground.

*Description:* The Chimney Swift is a dark gray bird with a short wide beak, a short bristle-tipped tail, and slender curved-back wings. It has been aptly described as a "flying cigar." In our region this species can be confused only with the swallows, most of which have distinctly forked tails.

# Family Trochilidae: Hummingbirds

## Ruby-throated Hummingbird
*Archilochus colubris*
3½ in. (8.85 cm)

*Range:* Arriving from late March to early April, the Ruby-throated Hummingbird is a fairly common summer resident of woodlands and flower gardens until late September or early October. Adult males leave the breeding grounds by mid-September, but females and young of the year may linger a month or more, occasionally into December.

*Nesting habits:* The nest, usually built by the female alone, is a tiny cup of wadded plant down, tightly pressed together and plastered with lichens bound on with spider webs. About 1 to 2 inches (2.5–5 cm) high and 1½ inches (3.8 cm) wide, it is saddled on a small down-sloping limb 4 to 60 feet (1.2–18 m) above ground and often placed in a pine, oak, or dogwood tree. Males perform a courtship flight that makes them appear to be swinging in geometric arcs as if suspended by an invisible string. They may linger about the nest a few days; but soon after the eggs have been laid, they seem to lose interest in family life. Males may be polygamous. The two pure white eggs are laid in late April or early May for the first brood and in late June or early July for the second. Incubation requires about 11 to 16 days. The altricial young are fed

*Ruby-throated Hummingbird, nesting female*
Hollis J. Rogers

by regurgitation and may remain in the nest 3 weeks or longer. Apparently air temperature greatly alters the time required for incubation of the tiny eggs and for development of the young, which, because of their feeding habits, must be able to fly well immediately upon leaving the nest. Highly pugnacious, hummers will drive an intruder from the nest area and attack much larger birds without hesitation.

*Feeding habits:* Hovering on the wing, hummingbirds feed on nectar and very small insects gathered from brightly colored blossoms having a tubular structure. Indigestible parts of the insects are ejected in minute balls, like owl pellets.

*Description:* The tiny Ruby-throated Hummingbird is an iridescent green bird with a long slender bill and a short, slightly forked tail. The adult male has a gleaming red throat patch that is absent in the female and immature birds. The humming noise is made by wings beating so fast that they are almost invisible in flight.

# Rufous Hummingbird

*Selasphorus rufus*

3½–4 in. (8.8–10.1 cm)

*Range:* A specimen of the Rufous Hummingbird was taken at Charleston, S.C., on December 18, 1909, constituting the only positive record for the Carolinas. The species winters regularly in Mexico and rarely northward to Louisiana and Florida. Two hummers seen recently in our region in late autumn appear to have been Rufous. Certainly any hummingbird found in the Carolinas during late fall or winter should be studied with great care.

*Feeding habits:* The Rufous Hummingbird feeds on nectar from brightly colored flowers with deep throats.

*Description:* The adult male Rufous Hummingbird is a predominantly reddish-brown bird, but the female and immature birds are difficult to distinguish from the Ruby-throateds of the same age and sex. A guide illustrating all the North American hummingbirds should be consulted if the presence of a Rufous is suspected.

# Order Coraciiformes: Kingfishers and Motmots

Most coraciiformes are carnivorous tropical and sub-tropical land birds with brightly colored plumage and large, dis-tinctive bills. Birds of this order have the three front toes joined for part of their length.

## Family Alcedinidae: Kingfishers

### Belted Kingfisher
*Megaceryle alcyon*
11–14 in. (28–35 cm)

*Range:* The Belted Kingfisher is a fairly common permanent resident throughout the Carolinas, but relatively few individuals remain in the mountains all winter. Kingfishers frequently perch on telephone wires above ditches that run parallel to highways or on wires and snags overhanging lakes and streams.

*Belted Kingfisher, male*
Michael Tove

*Nesting habits:* Conspicuous and raucous-voiced most of the year, Belted Kingfishers become very quiet at nesting time. Into the faces of road cuts and natural embankments near water, pairs of kingfishers dig burrows about 4 inches (10 cm) across and 3 to 6 feet (1–2 m) deep. Early in April the female deposits five to eight glossy white eggs in an enlarged chamber at the end of the tunnel. Incubation requires about 23 or 24 days. Both adults incubate eggs and care for the young. An occupied burrow usually can be spotted by inspecting the entrance hole for tracks forming a central ridge with a furrow on each side. Fish bones, fish scales, and fragments of crustacean shells found in burrows probably are pellets expelled by the parents and young rather than an attempt to build a nest. The altricial young do not open their eyes for about 2 weeks, even though they are covered with pinfeathers in a week or less. At 17 or 18 days of age the sheaths burst, and in a single day the nestlings come to look remarkably like the adults. Sometimes fledglings newly emerged from the burrow can be seen lined up on a branch or wire, waiting for the parents to arrive with food.

*Feeding habits:* Kingfishers prefer small fish not over 6 inches (15 cm) long. Fish are sighted and caught by diving into clear open water. When weather conditions reduce suitable habitat for fishing, these birds will take other animal matter, even insects.

*Description:* This slate-blue bird has a large head, long stout bill, and shaggy crest. A white collar encircles the throat. The male has a single blue band across the upper breast, but the more colorful female has a cinnamon band below the blue one. Watch for the birds as they hover over water and dive for fish or perch on wires and snags above water. The call is a loud rattle, much like a Halloween noisemaker.

# Order Piciformes: Woodpeckers and Allies

Woodpeckers usually have an undulating flight pattern, rising during a series of flaps and falling when the wings are folded against the body. All woodpeckers found in the Carolinas have four toes with two turned forward and two backward, a short stiff tail used as a prop when climbing vertical surfaces, and a chisel-like bill used for digging into wood to expose prey or to excavate nesting or roosting cavities in trees and posts. Most woodpeckers have extensible tongues tipped with sharp barbs that are useful in spearing insects and grubs. Both sexes usually take turns working on the nest hole. Woodpecker eggs are white, often glossy, and the young are altricial. Both parents incubate eggs, feed the young, and remove fecal sacs. Most species are permanent residents and usually are found singly or in pairs.

# Family Picidae: Woodpeckers

## Common Flicker
(Yellow-shafted Flicker)
*Colaptes auratus*
10–13 in. (25–33 cm)

*Range:* The Yellow-shafted Flicker is a common permanent resident throughout the Carolinas, with the population in winter greatly increased by flocks of migrants from the north. Flickers occur in a wide variety of woodlands, especially in open woods, groves, and suburbs.

*Nesting habits:* Although flickers usually nest in natural cavities, they will occupy large birdhouses. Occasionally they lay their 5 to 10 eggs directly on the ground in open places. Laying takes place from early April to mid-May, and incubation lasts 11 to 12 days with both adults taking turns upon the nest, the male usually at night. The courtship antics of flickers involve a great deal of loud calling with pairs facing each other while weaving, bobbing, and bowing. This behavior is seen in autumn as well as in spring. While woodpeckers generally announce their presence by drumming on resonant trees and limbs, the "Yellowhammer" often prefers gutters, downspouts, garbage cans, metal roofs, or loose weather boarding, much to the consternation of the sleepy householder.

*Feeding habits:* Feeding on the ground more than most woodpeckers, flickers often raid ant colonies and feast upon peanuts, persimmons, and black gum and dogwood berries.

*Description:* The form of the Common Flicker that occurs in

*Common Flicker*
James F. Parnell

the Carolinas has a tan face, a red crescent on the nape of the neck, and yellow shafts on the primary flight feathers. When this large brown woodpecker takes flight, watch for the white rump and golden wing linings. The adult female lacks the black whisker mark of the male and immature birds, but both sexes have the black crescent on the breast.

## Pileated Woodpecker
*Dryocopus pileatus*
15–19 in. (38–48 cm)

*Range:* A fairly common permanent resident of swamps and large forests throughout the Carolinas, the Pileated Woodpecker is generally uncommon in the piedmont.

*Nesting habits:* Pileated Woodpeckers usually mate in February and spend most of the month of March digging the nesting cavity, which may be 10 to 75 feet (3–23 m) above ground in either a dead or a living tree. The three to five eggs are laid about mid-April, and incubation requires about 18 days. A single brood is raised, and the young remain with the adults for some weeks after leaving the nest. Although the birds may return to the same tree in subsequent years, they excavate a new cavity each season. Their previous efforts are not wasted, however, for other birds and small mammals take over the abandoned holes.

*Feeding habits:* Equipped with a sturdy bill about 2 inches (5 cm)

*Pileated Woodpecker*
Jack Dermid

long, Pileateds can tear away great slabs of bark and deadwood in their search for wood-boring beetles and grubs. They also feed on various fruits and wild berries, including those of the flowering magnolia, American holly, poison ivy, and pokeweed.

*Description:* The Pileated is our only crow-sized woodpecker with a red crest and white wing linings that sharply contrast with the blackish-brown flight feathers. The only similar species is the Ivory-billed Woodpecker, which is not known to occur in the Carolinas at the present time.

## Red-bellied Woodpecker
*Melanerpes carolinus*
9–10 in. (22–25 cm)

*Range:* A common permanent resident in most parts of the Carolinas, the Red-bellied Woodpecker is uncommon and rather local in the mountains where it probably is absent or only transient at the higher elevations. Having a preference for deciduous woods, the species is equally at home in swamps, dry woods, and urban parks and residential areas.

*Nesting habits:* The nest hole may be from 12 to over 100 feet (3.5–31 m) above ground, and

*Red-bellied Woodpecker, male*
Edward Burroughs

excavation begins in late March. The four or five eggs for the first clutch are laid from mid-April to early May, and incubation takes 12 to 13 days. Second broods may be raised.

*Feeding habits:* The diet is about half insects and half vegetable matter.

*Description:* The Red-bellied Woodpecker is named for the usually small patch of pale reddish-orange feathers on the abdomen. When clinging to hanging bird feeders or clusters of berries at the tips of branches, the bird may expose the underparts long enough for the colorful belly to be seen. The back is narrowly barred with black and white. The male wears a red helmet, but in the female the red is mostly confined to the nape.

## Red-headed Woodpecker
*Melanerpes erythrocephalus*
9 in. (22.5 cm)

*Range:* Found in all sections of the Carolinas at all seasons, the Red-headed Woodpecker is only a transient at the higher elevations of the mountains. It is fairly common in summer in the coastal plain, but at other seasons and inland it is uncommon to fairly common. Because it nests along city streets, in parks, around golf courses, and in open rural groves, the Red-headed Woodpecker often must defend its home from house-hunting Starlings. Its largely road-side habitat makes it susceptible

Red-headed Woodpecker
James F. Parnell

to collisions with passing cars and a tempting target for boys with guns; however, the most significant factor in the species' decline may be something less obvious, such as exposure to chemicals in wooden poles treated with preservatives.

*Nesting habits:* The nest hole is dug from 8 to 80 feet (2.5–25 m) above ground in dead timber, often a telephone pole. The four to seven eggs usually are laid in early May, and incubation takes about 14 days. Two broods may be raised in a season.

*Feeding habits:* The diet of the Red-headed Woodpecker is about two-thirds vegetable matter. Animal matter includes the eggs of other birds, but on the whole the species is more beneficial than harmful.

*Description:* This is our only woodpecker with a solid red head

and a large white wing patch. Immatures are mottled with brown, but the light and dark areas are about the same as in the adults.

---

## Yellow-bellied Sapsucker
*Sphyrapicus varius*
7½–8¾ in. (19–22 cm)

*Range:* A rather common but inconspicuous winter resident throughout the Carolinas from late September to early May, the Yellow-bellied Sapsucker breeds sparingly above 3,500 feet (1,070 m) in the mountains of North Carolina. In winter sapsuckers are found in practically every type of reasonably mature woodlands.

*Nesting habits:* Ordinarily, the nests of Yellow-bellied Sapsuckers are near openings in mature groves of deciduous trees, mainly in fire-scarred areas. The four to six or seven eggs require 12 to 13 days for incubation, with young usually leaving the nest cavity in late June or early July.

*Feeding habits:* The sapsucker is our only woodpecker that is potentially harmful to healthy trees. Its neat rows of tiny holes distort the grain of the wood, open the cambium to infection, and can kill a tree by girdling it; however, the sap and the insects attracted to it provide food for many other species of wildlife. Sapsuckers have bristle-tipped tongues especially adapted for their diet, but they also dart after flying insects

218

*Yellow-bellied Sapsucker, male*
William S. Justice

like a flycatcher and feed upon the fruits of the black gum, flowering dogwood, American holly, and pokeweed.

*Description:* The sapsucker is our only woodpecker that has a prominent lengthwise white stripe in the folded wing. The adult male has a red forehead and a red throat patch bordered in black. The adult female is similar but has a white throat. Heavily mottled immature birds have the distinctive white wing stripe.

# Hairy Woodpecker
*Picoides villosus*
7½–9 in. (19–22.5 cm)

*Range:* A fairly common permanent resident throughout the Carolinas, the Hairy Wood-

pecker is a bird of mature forests and river swamplands, only infrequently venturing near human dwellings. In the mountains the Hairy tends to be more numerous above 3,500 feet (1,070 m) than the Downy Woodpecker, but at lower elevations the reverse is true.

*Nesting habits:* Hairy Woodpeckers dig nest cavities high above ground in tall stumps or in dead limbs of trees. Nesting dates are quite variable, and young have been found in the nest as early as March 24 in southeastern South Carolina and as late as June 2 in the Great Smoky Mountains. The eggs number three or four and require 11 to 12 days for incubation. The species is single-brooded.

*Feeding habits:* The Hairy Woodpecker consumes large numbers of insects, chiefly ants and the larvae of wood-boring beetles. It also eats vegetable matter such as wild cherries, wild grapes, acorns, and corn.

*Description:* We have two small white-backed woodpeckers. The Hairy is the larger one and has a relatively long and heavy bill as well as unbarred white outer tail feathers. The smaller Downy has a relatively small bill and barred outer tail feathers. Males of both species have a patch of red on the back of the head, a spot that is black in the females. The Downy is common at bird feeders, but the Hairy also visits them on occasions.

---

## Downy Woodpecker
*Picoides pubescens*
6–7 in. (15–17.5 cm)

*Range:* A common permanent resident throughout the Carolinas, the Downy Woodpecker is a bird of suburbs, orchards, and roadside groves as well as woods and swamplands. From late summer through winter the Downy frequently travels in bands with chickadees, titmice, warblers, and other small birds. By making squeaking noises the bird-watcher can attract these flocks and sometimes find among them a rare migrant or winter visitor.

*Nesting habits:* Nesting cavities are usually dug less than 15 feet (4.5 m) above ground or water in dead trees, fence posts, or dead stubs on living trees. The four or five eggs are laid in April or May, and incubation requires about 12 days. The species is single-brooded, but its habit of excavating roosting holes might lead the casual observer to believe the nesting season is much longer than it really is.

*Hairy Woodpecker, male*
Edward Burroughs

*Downy Woodpecker, male*
Edward Burroughs

*Feeding habits:* Downy Woodpeckers usually eat insects in warm weather, supplementing their diet with wild berries in winter. At feeders they readily accept handouts of sunflower seeds and suet.

*Description:* See Hairy Woodpecker for a comparative description.

---

# Red-cockaded Woodpecker
*Picoides borealis*
7–8½ in. (17.5–21.5 cm)

*Range:* The Red-cockaded Woodpecker is a locally fairly common to rare permanent resident of open pinelands from coastal Carolina to the eastern piedmont. Nests have been found as far inland as Sumter National Forest near Clinton, S.C.; Carolina Sandhills National Wildlife Refuge, Chesterfield County, S.C.; Pee Dee Refuge, Anson County, N.C.; Uwharrie National Forest, Montgomery County, N.C.; northern Wake County, N.C.; and western Northampton County, N.C.

*Nesting habits:* Red-cockaded Woodpeckers dig their nest hole in a living pine tree, usually a longleaf or loblolly. Pine gum oozes not only from the nest hole itself but also from the many small holes the birds peck into the cambium around it. The streaking on the bark makes the nests easy to see, but apparently the sticky surface protects the eggs and young

from ants, flying squirrels, snakes, and other predators. The birds will return to the same cavity year after year as long as they can make the sap flow around the entrance hole. If a cavity must be abandoned, they will dig a new one nearby, frequently in the very same tree. The three or four, possibly five, eggs are laid most often from late April to mid-May; and incubation requires 10 to 11 days. The species is single-brooded. Offspring remain with the parents into the fall, and unmated young males may become helpers at the nest the following spring. The adults' plumage becomes matted with resin during the nesting season, but a postnuptial molt promptly restores their neat appearance.

Limited habitat and strong site attachment make Red-cockaded Woodpeckers especially vulnerable when forests are cut for timber or turned into housing developments. In some areas forest management personnel are using controlled burning to keep the understory open in the vicinity of known nesting sites. This campaign is too new for its effect upon the Red-cockaded population to be determined, but there is reason to hope that public awareness of the species' plight will make possible its survival. A primary function of the Weymouth Woods Sandhills Nature Preserve at Southern Pines, N.C., is to promote the welfare of the endangered Red-cockaded Woodpecker.

*Red-cockaded Woodpecker*
James F. Parnell

*Feeding habits:* Red-cockaded Woodpeckers feed almost exclusively on larvae of wood-boring insects, grubs, and beetles. Sometimes they visit corn fields to feast upon corn ear worms.

*Description:* This bold little woodpecker has a back barred with black and white, a black helmet, and a prominent white cheek patch. The male's tiny red cockade is just behind the eye, but it is often absent or at least very difficult to see. Red-cockadeds associate with Carolina Chickadees, Tufted Titmice, Pine Warblers, and Brown-headed Nuthatches.

---

# Ivory-billed Woodpecker
*Campephilus principalis*
19–21 in. (48–53 cm)

*Range:* Formerly a permanent resident of eastern South Carolina and southeastern North Carolina, the Ivory-billed Woodpecker today appears to have been extirpated from our region. Although a few pairs may yet survive in the South Atlantic and Gulf States or in the mountains of Cuba, there is no reason for optimism about the future of this species. The Ivory-billed declined in numbers because it was not able to adapt to a changing environment. The species apparently requires large stands of mature timber. In contrast, the similar Pileated Woodpecker thrives in cutover woodlands and may be more numerous today than it was when settlers from Europe first arrived in the Carolinas.

*Feeding habits:* Feeding principally on certain wood-boring insects that live beneath the bark of standing dead trees, the Ivory-billed Woodpecker apparently requires vast stands of undisturbed forest to support even a few pairs. Today such tracts are so rare as to be virtually nonexistent in nearly all of the species' former range.

*Description:* This crested woodpecker is larger than a crow and has a white bill. Large white patches on the folded wings separate this species from the Pileated Woodpecker. In flight the Ivory-billed has broad bands of white on the leading and trailing edges of the under wing, and the central black stripe widens at the tip. The Pileated has white wing linings and blackish-brown flight feathers. Its folded wing shows only a small white spot. The Ivory-billed has large areas of jet black plumage, whereas the Pileated Woodpecker is predominantly blackish-brown.

# Order Passeriformes: Perching Birds

The great majority of the small to medium-sized land birds are classified as passerines, or perching birds. Ranging from the elfin kinglets to big black ravens, all passerines have feet with four unwebbed toes joined at the same level with three turned forward and one, usually the strongest, turned backward.

Courtship feeding is part of the mating ritual for many passerines. This behavior apparently is the male's preparation for the responsibility of feeding the nestlings and often the incubating female as well. All passerines have altricial young that remain in the nest until they are well feathered. Nearly all passerines keep the nest scrupulously clean. The parent birds either swallow or carry away the cast-off eggshells and the fecal sacs excreted by the young before they are able to defecate over the side of the nest. The fecal sac is a clean mucous membrane encasing partly digested food that has passed rapidly through the digestive system of a newly hatched bird. By swallowing these sacs, the parents provide food for themselves and their offspring in a very efficient manner. Young passerines usually are not capable of flight when they first leave the nest, and they remain at least partly dependent upon their parents for food and protection for a period that may last several weeks.

Although ornithologists agree that passerines are the most highly developed order of birds, they find little agreement on the exact composition of families and their lineal sequence. The American school of thought considers the seedeaters and related songbirds (nine-primaried oscines) to be in the vanguard of avian evolution. Showing the greatest and most recent adaptive radiation, seedeaters are the most successful birds living today, expanding their ranges, developing new races, and generally taking advantage of the rapidly changing environment.

# Family Tyrannidae: Tyrant Flycatchers

Tyrant flycatchers are a distinctly New World family of predominantly tropical and highly insectivorous birds. Flycatchers are easily spotted when perched on roadside wires because of their characteristically upright posture. Darting from an exposed perch, the flycatcher takes insect prey on the wing in a bill that is wide at the base, hooked at the tip, and bristled at the gape. The weak feet and poorly developed voice box place flycatchers among the suboscines, or primitive songbirds. The usual pattern of breeding behavior is for both parents to participate in building the nest, for the female alone to incubate the eggs, and for the male to assist the female in rearing the young.

## Eastern Kingbird
*Tyrannus tyrannus*
8–9 in. (20–22 cm)

*Range:* Breeding throughout the Carolinas in summer, the Eastern Kingbird is common in the central counties, but uncommon in the mountains and toward the coast. Frequently seen perched on fences and telephone wires, this is a bird of rural groves, fields, and hedgerows. Spring arrival begins in March or early April, and some birds may be present a month before they begin to nest. Although an occasional straggler lingers through December, most birds depart for the tropics by mid-September.

*Nesting habits:* Kingbirds are utterly fearless in defense of their territory, attacking crows, hawks, and eagles. The rather bulky nest is well constructed of sticks, twigs, weed stems, grasses, and rootlets as well as string and Spanish moss where available. Often placed over water, the nest may be low in bushes and small cypresses or up to 100 feet (30 m) above ground near the end of a limb of a shade tree standing in the open. Occasionally Eastern Kingbirds lay in enclosures such as martin gourds, rain gauges, and old oriole nests. The three or four creamy and slightly glossy eggs are splashed and marbled with dark brown and lilac. First clutches are laid early in May, incubation requires 12 to 14 days, and the young remain in the nest about 2 weeks.

*Feeding habits:* Although economically valuable for the many harmful insects they consume, Eastern Kingbirds sometimes incur the wrath of beekeepers by feeding heavily upon inhabitants of their hives, thus earning the name often applied to them— "Bee Martin."

*Description:* Black above and white below, the Eastern Kingbird has a white tip on its black tail. The red crown patch is almost never seen.

*Eastern Kingbird*
William G. Cobey

## Gray Kingbird
*Tyrannus dominicensis*
9–10 in. (22–25 cm)

*Range:* The Gray Kingbird is a rare and irregular summer resident along the South Carolina coast. A few accidentals have occurred along the North Carolina coast northward to Pea Island. Accidentals have been found inland in April at Raleigh, N.C., and in August at North Wilkesboro, N.C. Although no nest has been found in North Carolina, Gray Kingbirds have bred successfully a number of times in South Carolina.

*Nesting habits:* Arriving from early to mid-April, Gray Kingbirds build a nest similar to that of the Eastern Kingbird but somewhat less bulky. Where mangroves are not available, as is the case in the Carolinas, they tend to place the nest near the top of a live oak, although a deciduous tree may be chosen. In late May the female lays three or four pink eggs that are blotched with dark brown. Incubation probably requires 12 to 14 days, young are thought to remain in the nest about the same length of time, and two broods may be raised in a season.

*Feeding habits:* See comments on family.

*Description:* Gray above and light below, the Gray Kingbird has a very heavy bill, a slightly crested head, and a slightly forked tail. The touch of red in the crown is very difficult to see, but the dark streak through the eye is fairly conspicuous. When perched, the kingbirds as a group have a much less upright posture than our other flycatchers.

# Western Kingbird
(Arkansas Kingbird)
*Tyrannus verticalis*
8–9½ in. (20–24 cm)

*Range:* The Western Kingbird is an uncommon but regular fall migrant on the Carolina coast from early September into November, and very rarely to mid-January. It frequently perches on roadside wires and thus is easily seen. Spring transients are rare in April and May. Inland occurrences are very rare, all to date being fall migrants seen from mid-August to mid-December.

*Feeding habits:* See comments on family.

*Description:* Greenish above and yellow below, the Western Kingbird has white outer feathers on its squared-off tail. Absence of

Western Kingbird
James F. Parnell

white in the wing prevents confusion with the Mockingbird, which also has white outer tail feathers and frequently perches on wires.

## Fork-tailed Flycatcher
*Muscivora tyrannus*
16–17 in. (40–43 cm)

*Range:* During the last week in October 1973, a Fork-tailed Flycatcher appeared on Bull's Island in the Cape Romain National Wildlife Refuge. A black-and-white photograph taken on November 1 substantiates the sight record and adds this tropical species to the South Carolina state list. Future sightings should be expected along our coast in autumn because in this season birds occur from time to time well to the north of the Carolinas.

*Feeding habits:* See comments on family.

*Description:* Having the same general shape as the Scissor-tailed Flycatcher, the Fork-tailed is slightly larger. It has white underparts and a gray back that contrasts with the black cap, wings, and tail.

## Scissor-tailed Flycatcher
*Muscivora forficata*
11½–15 in. (29–38 cm)

*Range:* The Scissor-tailed Flycatcher is a rare spring and fall transient in the Carolinas and a scarce but probably annual summer visitor, mostly along the

Scissor-tailed Flycatcher
James F. Parnell

coast. During April most Scissor-tailed Flycatchers migrate in flocks from the tropics and southern Florida to their breeding grounds in the southern Plains States. They move southward in flocks with young of the year during the latter part of September and early October. Very few birds from these flocks stray into the Carolinas. More than two-thirds of our sightings have occurred in June and July, probably as the result of eastward wandering by unmated birds. A Scissor-tailed Flycatcher seen at Hilton Head Island, S.C., on May 12, 1973, is of particular interest because this date falls within the peak laying season for the species; however, the observer found no evidence of breeding.

*Feeding habits:* See comments on family.

*Description:* Gray above and white below, the Scissor-tailed Flycatcher has pink sides and a very long, slender, and deeply forked tail. Immature birds have only a faint trace of pink on the sides and an incompletely developed tail that is still a bit on the long side. At first glance they may look like Mockingbirds.

## Great Crested Flycatcher
*Myiarchus crinitus*
8–9 in. (20–22 cm)

*Range:* A common summer resident in most parts of the Carolinas, the Great Crested Flycatcher returns to southern South Carolina in late March; but often it does not reach the mountains, where it is not common, until the latter part of April. The species usually departs before the

*Great Crested Flycatcher*
Heathcote Kimball

end of September, although occasionally a few individuals linger inland during October and along the coast until late December or early January. This is a bird of moderately open woodlands, especially in dry situations.

*Nesting habits:* The Great Crested seeks a natural or man-made cavity in which to build its nest of grass, pine needles, feathers, fur, and almost always a cast snakeskin. The deep buff eggs are heavily streaked with dark purple longitudinal lines, number four to six, and require about 14 days for incubation. Eggs are laid from mid-May to mid-June, and the species is single-brooded. Young remain in the nest at least 12 days and sometimes as long as 18 days.

*Feeding habits:* Like many other flycatchers, this highly insectivorous bird will take a small amount of vegetable matter, usually the fruits of flowering dogwood, Virginia creeper, or pokeweed.

*Description:* The Great Crested Flycatcher has gray foreparts, yellow lower breast and belly, reddish-brown primaries and tail, and a touch of yellow on the predominantly dark bill. The Ash-throated Flycatcher is similar, but it is a much smaller bird with a completely dark bill. Its pale gray and faintly creamy underparts look faded in comparison to those of the Great Crested.

## Ash-throated Flycatcher
*Myiarchus cinerascens*
7½–8½ in. (19–21.5 cm)

*Range:* An Ash-throated Flycatcher was seen and heard calling at Raleigh, N.C., on May 15, 1973. This is the first sight record for North Carolina and apparently the first spring occurrence in the eastern United States. On June 3, 1974, an individual of this Western species was reported from the Pea Island National Wildlife Refuge, but there are no published details of the sighting. See Great Crested Flycatcher for a description of the Ash-throated. (hypothetical status)

## Eastern Phoebe
*Sayornis phoebe*
6¼–7¼ in. (16–18.4 cm)

*Range:* The Eastern Phoebe is a fairly common permanent resident at the low and middle altitudes in the mountains and in the piedmont and some adjacent sections of the coastal plain. In most of the coastal plain, it is uncommon to absent during the breeding season but becomes fairly common from late September to late March. In the winter it is a bird of the open woodlands, edges of fields, and lake margins.

*Nesting habits:* The phoebe nests in sheltered places such as caves, rock ledges, atop window and door frames, and especially on the supports beneath small bridges that span woodland streams. The bulky cup of mud pellets, moss, and various plant materials often contains feathers and looks much like a Barn Swallow's nest. The four or five pure white eggs have little or no gloss and usually are unspotted. Egg dates range from early April to early June, and two

*Eastern Phoebe*
John Trott

broods may be raised in a season. The incubation period is about 15 or 16 days; young remain in the nest about the same length of time. Females may build a new nest for the second brood or merely repair the old one. Reuse often results in heavy mite infestation. A new nest may be built atop the old one, particularly if the first has been parasitized by Brown-headed Cowbirds. Another hazard facing the phoebe is flood waters that sometimes wash away nests built under bridges. Fortunately the "Bridge Pewee" is a persistent nester.

*Feeding habits:* The phoebe is highly insectivorous except in winter when berries are consumed regularly.

*Description:* Dark above and light below, the Eastern Phoebe is best recognized by its completely dark bill, sooty head, and wagging tail. Its call is a rather hoarse *fee-be.*

---

## Say's Phoebe
*Sayornis saya*
7–8 in. (17.5–20 cm)

*Range:* Single birds of this Western species were reported by competent observers from Wake County, N.C., on October 23, 1965, and from Richland County, S.C., on January 18, 1969. Say's Phoebe occurs accidentally in the eastern United States. It is a dark flycatcher with slightly rusty underparts. (hypothetical status)

## Yellow-bellied Flycatcher
*Empidonax flaviventris*
5½ in. (14 cm)

*Range:* Occurring in the mountains and piedmont more frequently than in the coastal plain, the Yellow-bellied Flycatcher is a rare spring and fall transient in the Carolinas; but it probably is more plentiful than the few published records indicate. Yellow-bellied Flycatchers apparently pass through the Carolinas from very late April to late May and from mid-August to early October. Usually they are seen in wet thickets, woodland margins, and other shrubby vegetation. Although they are generally rather quiet and inconspicuous birds, sometimes they sing during fall migration as well as in the spring.

*Feeding habits:* See comments on family.

*Description:* This is our only *Empidonax* flycatcher that has a yellow throat. Similar species, particularly their young of the year, have yellowish underparts, but their throats are whitish. Even the immature Yellow-bellied has a yellow throat.

As a group the *Empidonax* flycatchers are very difficult to identify, often being separable in the field only by voice. Frequently, even the experts cannot identify silent birds of this genus.

## Acadian Flycatcher
*Empidonax virescens*
6 in. (15.2 cm)

*Range:* A common summer resident of moist woodlands, especially deciduous floodplain forests, the Acadian Flycatcher breeds throughout the Carolinas except at the higher elevations in the mountains. The species reaches the coast in late March or early April, but usually it cannot be found inland until the latter part of April. Most Acadians migrate southward in early September, though stragglers may linger into early October.

*Nesting habits:* Often so thin that the eggs can be seen through its bottom, the saucer-shaped nest of the Acadian Flycatcher is quite durable. Typically it is suspended across the fork of a downward-hanging limb of a large tree, often over water and seldom more than 10 to 20 feet (3–6 m) high. Finely woven of plant materials, it usually is constructed of Spanish moss if near the coast, of *Usnea* lichens or hemlock twigs if in the mountains, or of fine grasses and rootlets if elsewhere. The underside may be camouflaged with faded tree blossoms or bud scales bound on with spider or caterpillar silk. Eggs usually are laid between the middle and last of May, but some clutches have been found in June and early July. Marked at the large end with a wreath of reddish-brown spots, the two to four creamy eggs

require 13 to 14 days for incubation. Young remain in the nest about 2 weeks. This shy little flycatcher will slip off its nest at the approach of an intruder. Ordinarily it perches in the shade well below the forest canopy.

*Feeding habits:* See comments on family.

*Description:* The Acadian Flycatcher is best recognized by its choice of habitat and its voice. The call cannot be rendered satisfactorily in phonetic syllables, probably because of geographically variable accents. Listen for an explosive first syllable (*psit*) that is immediately followed by a somewhat plaintive rising note (*see*).

## Willow Flycatcher
(Traill's Flycatcher)
*Empidonax traillii*
5½ in. (14 cm)

*Range:* The Willow Flycatcher breeds in the western United States and in open habitats of the eastern United States, where it has expanded its range southward in recent years. Nests of the Willow Flycatcher have been found in North Carolina at North Wilkesboro and Raleigh, and during the summer the species has been found sparingly in the North Carolina mountains south to Franklin and Brevard. Spring and fall transients occur throughout our region but apparently are more numerous inland than

*Willow Flycatcher*
Morris D. Williams

toward the coast. Although rarely seen, spring transients can be expected from late April through May. Fall migration lasts from mid-August to early October. Migrants frequent wet thickets, especially willows.

*Nesting habits:* Breeding birds establish territories in late May and lay eggs in June. Willow Flycatchers typically build very loose and deeply cupped nests from 2 to 10 feet (0.6–3 m) above ground in low, open thickets of alders, willows, elders, swamp azaleas, and saplings growing near water. Their elegant carelessness makes the nest look like a mass of plant material accidentally caught in the fork or crotch of a limb. The three or four buffy or sometimes creamy eggs are marked with a wreath of brown dots and splotches at the large end. The

incubation period is probably about 14 days. In North Carolina hatching apparently takes place in late June or early July, and young remain in the nest 12 to 15 days.

*Feeding habits:* See comments on family.

*Description:* The Traill's Flycatcher complex is divided into two species that are separable in the field only by voice. The Willow Flycatcher gives the *fitz-bew* song, and the Alder gives the *fee-bee-o* song. Both have browner backs than the very similar Acadian Flycatcher.

## Alder Flycatcher
(Traill's Flycatcher)
*Empidonax alnorum*
5½ in. (14 cm)

*Range:* The Alder Flycatcher breeds in alder swamps of the

northern forest region of Alaska, Canada, and the eastern United States. Its occurrence as a transient is essentially the same as for the Willow Flycatcher. The Alder Flycatcher was seen and heard singing during the summers of 1972 and 1974 in a bog at Price Park near Blowing Rock, N.C., and it is presumed to have been nesting. In June 1978 a small breeding colony was discovered on grassy balds at 5,600 to 6,000 feet (1,700–1,830 m) along the Appalachian Trail east of Roan Mountain. Apparently territorial males have been found in the Graveyard Fields area of southern Haywood County, N.C., amid deciduous saplings and young spruce trees at 5,800 feet (1,790 m). Previously, the Alder Flycatcher was thought to nest south only to eastern West Virginia.

*Nesting habits:* The only significant difference between the nesting habits of the Alder and Willow Flycatchers appears to be the choice of habitat.

*Feeding habits:* See comments on family.

*Description:* See the Willow Flycatcher for a comparative description.

---

## Least Flycatcher

*Empidonax minimus*
5–5½ in. (12.5–14 cm)

*Range:* The Least Flycatcher is a locally fairly common breeding species in the mountains of North Carolina. Elsewhere in our region, it is known only as a transient, uncommon in the piedmont and rare in the coastal plain. Migrants are generally seen along woodland margins and in thickets, in drier habitat than that preferred by other members of the genus. The peak of spring migration for the Least Flycatcher occurs about the first week in May; the fall movement lasts throughout September with extreme dates of August 22 and October 9. Least Flycatchers arrive on the breeding grounds in our mountains in late April and depart in early September. Nesting birds are found in open woodlands, old orchards, and woodland strips bordering rivers and fields, mostly at elevations between 3,000 and 4,500 feet (900–1,380 m). The species appears to be more numerous in the Highlands-Cashiers area and in Ashe and Alleghany Counties than elsewhere in the region.

*Nesting habits:* The nest is a compact cup of shredded bark, weed stems, grasses, and various other vegetable fibers lined with fine grasses, animal hair, plant down, or feathers. It is usually placed in an upright fork of a small tree from 5 to 20 feet (1.5–6 m) above ground. The four unmarked cream-colored eggs are said to require about 14 days for incubation, and young remain in the nest about 14 days. A second brood may be raised.

*Feeding habits:* See comments on family.

*Description:* The Least Flycatcher is best identified by its voice, a dry *che-bek* that is accented on the second syllable. This may be repeated monotonously about 50 to 70 times per minute.

---

# Eastern Wood Pewee
*Contopus virens*
6–6½ in. (15–16.5 cm)

*Range:* A common summer resident throughout the Carolinas from mid-April through October, the Eastern Wood Pewee may arrive in late March and linger, on rare occasions, through December or even January. Frequenting open woodlands, orchards, and suburban yards, the pewee is neither very shy nor very aggressive. From an exposed perch within a few yards of the bird-watcher, it will give its plaintive call and repeatedly make flying sorties to snatch insects from the air with audible clicks of the bill.

*Nesting habits:* Woven of fine grasses, rootlets, pine needles, and sometimes moss, the rather flat nest of the pewee is carefully covered with lichens. Nests may be saddled on a limb or slung across a fork from 15 to 50 feet (4.5–15 m) high in a living tree. The two to four creamy eggs are wreathed at the large end with markings of reddish brown, lilac, and dark gray. Eggs are laid from late May through early July. A second

*Eastern Wood Pewee*
Edward Burroughs

clutch tends to contain fewer eggs than the first. Incubation takes about 13 days, and young leave the nest when about 16 days of age.

*Feeding habits:* See comments on family.

*Description:* Eastern Wood Pewees resemble Eastern Phoebes, but the pewee has a light lower mandible and two wing bars. The pewee is best recognized by its plaintively whistled song, *pee-a-wee,* which slurs downward on the middle syllable and upward at the end.

## Olive-sided Flycatcher
*Nuttallornis borealis*
7–8 in. (17–20 cm)

*Range:* A rare breeding bird of the hemlock and spruce-fir forests of the mountains of North Carolina, the Olive-sided Flycatcher appears to be slightly more numerous in the Great Smoky Mountains National Park than outside its boundaries. Elsewhere in the Carolinas the species is known only as a very rare transient. It is found in the piedmont in early May and from August through October, with the peak of the fall movement about mid-September when a few individuals may be seen eastward to the coast. Because of the species' silent and solitary behavior during migration, members are seldom noticed when they visit the lowlands, even though they usually perch on bare branches of large dead trees.

*Nesting habits:* Breeding Olive-sideds reach the North Carolina mountains in late April or early May. Concealed in a cluster of twigs atop a horizontal limb of a pine, spruce, hemlock, or other conifer, the nest, sometimes composed chiefly of *Usnea* lichens, is a larger version of that built by the Eastern Kingbird. It may be placed from 7 to 100 feet (2–30 m) above ground, usually well out from the trunk. The eggs, resembling those of the Eastern Wood Pewee, are laid in June or early July and most frequently number three. Incubation requires 16 to 17 days, and young remain in the nest 2 to 3 weeks. Olive-sided Flycatchers seldom nest near human dwellings. Sometimes they are bold in defense of their territory, driving away others of their own species, larger birds, and even people by scolding and diving at the person's head. Males perch erect on dead branches or in the topmost spire of a tall tree, proclaiming possession of the territory with almost incessant dawn-to-dusk singing. As is true with many mountain species, family parties tend to wander after the young leave the nest, which probably accounts for summer records outside the mountains. On September 12, 1968, three young birds were seen begging for food at North Wilkesboro, N.C.

*Feeding habits:* See comments on family.

*Description:* This chunky, heavy-billed flycatcher resembles the

Eastern Wood Pewee. The whistled song has been rendered as *what peeves you.* The first syllable is soft and may not be heard, but the other two are emphatically accented with the final one slurring downward. The *pip-pip-pip* alarm note is given mostly by the female in the vicinity of the nest.

---

## Vermilion Flycatcher
*Pyrocephalus rubinus*
5½–6½ in. (14–16.5 cm)

*Range:* The Vermilion Flycatcher is a very rare fall transient and winter visitor in South Carolina. A bird remained at the Savannah River National Wildlife Refuge in Jasper County, S.C., from November 17, 1961, through January 28, 1962. Several other autumn and winter records from Charleston and Jasper Counties fall within the mid-November through January dates. The only spring record for the region is a bird seen inland at Columbia, S.C., on April 14, 1963.

*Feeding habits:* See comments on family.

*Description:* The adult male has dark wings, back, and tail contrasting sharply with the bright red crown and underparts. The female is light below with finely streaked sides and a pinkish wash on the lower underparts. Immatures are similar to the female, but their underparts may be washed with yellow.

# Family Alaudidae: Larks

Larks have slender bills, sing in flight, usually walk on the ground, and seldom perch in trees or shrubs.

---

## Horned Lark
*Eremophila alpestris*
6¾–8 in. (16–20 cm)

*Range:* Horned Larks are birds of barren ground, stubble fields, airports, golf courses, and other extensive areas of short vegetation and bare earth. Once confined to naturally open country such as prairies and tundra, the species moved eastward in the nineteenth century as removal of forests and cultivation of land modified the habitat to suit its needs. Traveling in flocks, Horned Larks are rather localized winter residents south to eastern North Carolina and central South Carolina, being most numerous in the piedmont from December through March. Horned Larks may be fairly common or common at one place and absent from nearby habitat that appears equally suitable. The species breeds from the mountains eastward to Rocky Mount, N.C., and Sumter, S.C. First discovered nesting in the piedmont of North Carolina in 1937 and in the piedmont of South Carolina in 1950,

*Horned Lark*
Chris Marsh

Horned Larks generally can be found year-round in the vicinity of established colonies.

*Nesting habits:* Male Horned Larks may begin singing in January and delineate their territories in early February. They sing, mostly for the benefit of other males, either from the ground or in flight at altitudes of several hundred feet. The flight song ends with a spectacular dive to earth. Taking place mostly at noon and sundown, singing reaches a peak during nest building, egg laying, and incubation. The territory, probably 300 feet square (8,360 m²) or larger, is usually defended by the male. Both adults feed almost entirely within its boundaries.

Nesting reportedly begins when the mean temperature rises above 40°F (4.4°C) for two consecutive days, which sometimes happens in our area in early March. The mating ritual is much like that of the House Sparrow. The male Horned Lark struts before the female, who crouches and flutters her wings. The nest is constructed by the female. Using her beak and feet, she excavates a shallow depression on the sheltered side of a clump of grass. Here she builds a nest of coarse leaves and stems lined with grasses. The rim is level with the ground, and the area near the rim may be paved with pebbles and lumps of dirt. Construction requires from 2 to 4 days. The female lays two to five greenish-gray eggs that are finely speckled with cinnamon brown, often in a dense ring at the large end. Early clutches tend to be smaller than late ones. Performed by the female, incubation takes about 11 days and usually does not begin until the clutch is complete. The male may help care for the young during their 10 days in the nest. Newly hatched Horned Larks have brown skin and long buffy down. Young just out of the nest hop instead of walking like the adults, and 5 days after departure they can fly.

Nests have been found in the Carolinas from early March to mid-July, the species having two or three broods per year in our region. Pairs will continue to renest on the same territory throughout the breeding season unless growth of vegetation makes the habitat unsuitable. Singing ceases after the nesting season, and the birds gather for the winter in flocks sometimes numbering into the hundreds.

*Feeding habits:* Horned Larks consume mostly grass and weed seeds plus some grasshoppers, weevils, spiders, and other animal matter.

*Description:* The Horned Lark's tiny horns are seen only at close range. The species is best recognized by its high-pitched sibilant flight notes, bold black breast band, and unnotched dark tail with white outer feathers. The Prairie Horned Lark (*E. a. praticola*) is the race breeding in the Carolinas. The winter population is composed of this race plus some Northern Horned Larks (*E. a. alpestris*). The line above the eye is yellow in the northern race and white in the prairie race.

# Family Hirundinidae: Swallows

Flying low over waterways, meadows, grain fields, and other open places in pursuit of moths, flies, mosquitoes, and various other insects, swallows emit typically harsh but rather cheerful twitters. A large migrating flock of mixed species may number several hundred birds and can be quite noisy while feeding on the wing or resting on wires over open terrain.

## Tree Swallow
*Iridoprocne bicolor*
5–6¼ in. (12.5–16 cm)

*Range:* Near the coast of the Carolinas, the Tree Swallow is a common spring and abundant fall migrant. It also winters there erratically, often being uncommon at a locality for a few weeks and then suddenly becoming common, especially during cold and windy weather. The species is a common spring migrant from early March through May and an uncommon fall migrant from July to early November over most of our inland counties, becoming scarce toward the mountains. Swallows as a whole seem to be undergoing rapid extensions of breeding range; therefore, it was not particularly surprising when a pair of Tree Swallows were seen feeding young in an old woodpecker cavity beside the New River in northeastern Ashe County, N.C., in June 1979.

*Nesting habits:* Tree Swallows normally nest in isolated pairs, placing grass, straw, and white feathers in a natural cavity, martin gourd, or wooden bird box. They do not linger about the nesting site once the young are well on the wing, but soon gather into flocks and begin moving southward.

*Feeding habits:* See comments on family. In winter Tree Swallows consume many berries from waxmyrtle and bayberry bushes, even though 80% of their annual diet is animal matter.

*Description:* This is the only green-backed swallow that occurs in our region. Brownish young birds may be confused with Bank and Rough-winged Swallows, but the white throat and absence of a breast band separate the Tree Swallow from these two species.

# Bank Swallow
*Riparia riparia*
4¾–5½ in. (12–14 cm)

*Range:* The Bank Swallow is an uncommon to locally fairly common spring and fall transient from late March through May and from early July through September. The main thrust of the migratory movement for this species seems to be across the piedmont in both seasons, and at times during the spring over 100 Bank Swallows can be counted in the large mixed flocks of swallows feeding over large lakes. The species appears to nest locally in the mountains and piedmont of the Carolinas where it is probably overlooked because of its close resemblance to the Rough-winged Swallow, with which it may share a nesting site.

*Nesting habits:* Both adults participate in excavation of the burrow near the top of a nearly vertical embankment. At the end of the burrow, which usually is 2 to 3 feet (0.5–1 m) deep, they build a nest of grass stalks interwoven with finer plant materials and lined with feathers. The four to five pure white eggs hatch in about 14 to 16 days. Both adults incubate eggs and care for the young, which remain in the nest about 18 to 22 days. Shortly before departure they gather at the mouth of the cavity and may take short flights.

*Feeding habits:* See comments on family.

*Description:* The Bank Swallow is brown above and white below with a narrow brown breast band contrasting sharply with the white throat.

---

## Rough-winged Swallow
*Stelgidopteryx ruficollis*
5–5¾ in. (12.5–14.5 cm)

*Range:* The Rough-winged Swallow is a fairly common summer resident throughout the Carolinas, with local abundance varying considerably according to the availability of suitable nesting sites. In the mountains the species does not breed above the middle elevations, but birds forage over the highest peaks. On the Outer Banks the Rough-winged Swallow is only a rare transient. Breeding birds apparently arrive in the Carolinas about mid-March and depart soon after the young are strong on the wing, at some time between early July and early September. Flocks occasionally linger in coastal South Carolina until late January.

*Nesting habits:* Rough-winged Swallows may nest in cracks and crevices in rock cliffs or brick and stone structures such as dams, bridges, and tunnels; take over kingfisher burrows or protruding drainpipes; or excavate their own burrows in road cuts or natural embankments. Normally only one to several pairs will use a single site, but sometimes rather large colonies form at particularly

*Rough-winged Swallow entering nesting burrow*
Samuel A. Grimes

favorable places such as Cliffs of Neuse State Park near Goldsboro, N.C. Excavation most often begins about the first of April. Usually dug near water, the burrow extends from a minimum of 9 inches (22.5 cm) to a maximum of about 6 feet (2 m) into the bank, terminating in a shallow depression that is lined with dry grasses and rootlets. The bulk of the nest varies considerably according to the size of the cavity, and the material rarely includes feathers. Six or seven pure white eggs are

240

laid between early May and early June. Incubation requires about 16 days with the female sometimes assisted by the male. Young remain in the nest up to 3 weeks, and only one brood is raised each year.

*Feeding habits:* See comments on family.

*Description:* Named for the series of small barbs on the outer web of its outermost primary feather, the Rough-winged Swallow is a predominantly brown bird. Its dusky throat and absence of a well-defined breast band separate it from our other brown-backed swallows.

## Barn Swallow
*Hirundo rustica*
6–7½ in. (15–19 cm)

*Range:* Formerly breeding only locally in the mountains and along the coast, the Barn Swallow has extended its range rapidly since the 1940s and now is nesting throughout the Carolinas, being common in most areas but least numerous in southeastern South Carolina. The earliest birds may arrive in mid-March, and a few Barn Swallows may linger along the coast into early winter. Abundant during migrations, Barn Swallows pass northward through the Carolinas mostly from early April to early June, and the return flight is mostly from late July through September.

*Nesting habits:* The bowl-shaped nests of mud pellets mixed with grass and straw are placed atop a rafter or sheltered ledge in a seldom-used building or beneath a bridge or pier. A small projection such as a nail or a mud dauber nest may on occasions offer a suitable starting point for a nest flattened against a wall. Having very weak feet, as do all swallows, the birds of both sexes scoop up and carry the mud pellets with their beaks. The nest usually is lined with white feathers. The four to six white eggs may be spotted with reddish brown all over or mostly in a ring at the large end. Incubation is by the female and requires about 15 days. The male Barn Swallow sleeps beside the nest and may sit upon the eggs when the female is absent, but he apparently does not have a functional brood patch. Both adults care for the young, which remain in the nest 18 days or longer. Active nests have been found in the Carolinas from April to early August, the species being double-brooded in our region. The same nest may be used again, not only for a second brood but also in the succeeding year.

*Feeding habits:* See comments on family.

*Description:* The Barn Swallow has a dark blue back, rusty underparts, and deeply forked tail. Details such as the rusty forehead and white tail spots can be seen at close range. Immature birds have lighter underparts than the adults and may be confused with the Cliff Swallow.

*Barn Swallow feeding young*
William G. Cobey

*Cliff Swallow at nest*
William G. Cobey

# Cliff Swallow
*Petrochelidon pyrrhonota*
5–6 in. (12.5–15 cm)

*Range:* An uncommon transient throughout the Carolinas from early April to late May and from late July to mid-September, the Cliff Swallow breeds locally in the piedmont, showing a preference for nesting sites on tall dams and beneath high bridges crossing large man-made lakes. First reported nesting at Hartwell Dam on the upper Savannah River in the spring of 1965, the species soon was discovered breeding at Kerr Lake on the Roanoke River, at Tuckertown Lake on the Yadkin River, on the Catawba River in South Carolina, and at other sites in piedmont North and South Carolina. In 1977 and 1978 one nest was found at Moore's Landing in coastal South Carolina.

*Nesting habits:* Cliff Swallows return to their colonies about mid-April, and some nests may be completed by the end of the month, while construction of others does not begin until early June. Building requires 5 days or longer. Scooping up balls of mud in their mouths, both adults help build the flask-shaped nest, which often has a neck protruding near the top and curving downward 5 to 6 inches (12–15 cm). Although the walls may be slightly reinforced with straw and horsehairs, these mud structures must be placed in sheltered sites to keep them from being washed away by rainfall. Some pairs renovate nests built the previous year. The nest chamber is scantily lined with feathers and dried grass stems. The four or five eggs are white, perhaps tinged with a creamy or pinkish shade, and almost always spotted with various shades of brown, sometimes in a ring around the egg. Incubation usually lasts about 14 days, and sometimes two broods are raised, the second ones fledging about mid-July. Young are tended by both parents and leave the nest at 16 to 24 days of age. In late July or early August the adults and offspring of a colony may be seen perched on wires along the highway, attracting the attention of even a casual observer. Later they will flock with swallows of their own and other species prior to fall migration. Noted for their gregariousness, Cliff Swallows sometimes nest in mixed colonies with Barn Swallows.

*Feeding habits:* See comments on family.

*Description:* The Cliff Swallow is identified in flight by its buffy rump and unforked tail. At close range the pale forehead, rusty throat, and streaked back can be seen.

---

## Purple Martin
*Progne subis*
7¼–8½ in. (18.5–21.5 cm)

*Range:* A summer resident throughout the Carolinas, the Purple Martin is fairly common to common, particularly in the coastal plain, but its abundance at each locality is controlled by the availability of nesting houses. Among our earliest spring migrants, martins arrive in coastal South Carolina in February or early March, rarely in late January, and reach inland localities by

*Purple Martins*
Bill Faver

mid-March or early April. Fall migration is quite leisurely, beginning in late July, when the local birds gather into large flocks, and continuing into October.

*Nesting habits:* In primitive times Purple Martins nested in old woodpecker holes and other natural cavities in trees and cliffs. Indians erected gourd houses to attract martins to their villages, and early settlers adopted the practice. Nesting boxes for martins should be placed in open terrain from 15 to 25 feet (4.5–7.5 m) above ground. Martins will return to the same site year after year, with the adult males arriving before the females and young males hatched the previous season. If the birds come while their apartment house is down for cleaning and repairs, or to prevent its use by House Sparrows, they will circle the exact spot where it should be and even perch upon it as it is being set in place.

Both sexes build the nest of grass, leaves, and other convenient materials such as twigs, feathers, mud, rags, paper, and string. Nests may be started several weeks before eggs are laid. The four or five slightly glossy white eggs may be laid from mid-April through May. The incubation period varies from 12 to 20 days with 15 apparently the average duration. The female normally assumes all responsibility for incubation, but the male sometimes sits on the eggs. The male assists in feeding the young, often bringing as many food items during a period of observation as does his mate. Young stay in the nest 24 to 28 days, at which time the adults cease feeding them. One or both of the parents remain nearby, waiting to join the offspring once they have flown from the nest. The family party stays together until the young are fully independent, a period of about 3 weeks. Then the group may join other martins to form a huge flock for the southward migration. Purple Martins are normally single-brooded and will not renest if even one nestling survives from the first clutch; however, second clutches may be laid when the first nesting is a total failure, and some third clutches have been reported.

*Feeding habits:* Purple Martins feed mostly on day-flying insects, showing a distinct preference for beetles, dragonflies, wasps, and other fairly large prey. Although they do on occasions take a good number of mosquitoes, their consumption of these predominantly night-flying pests has been greatly exaggerated by some writers.

*Description:* The adult male Purple Martin is completely dark above and below. Females and immature males have dusky throats and white bellies. To distinguish them from swallows, watch for the martins' larger size, broader wings and tail, and iridescent purple upperparts.

# Family Corvidae: Jays and Crows

Bold, noisy, aggressive birds, the corvids figure prominently in folklore, literature, and everyday speech—"sassy as a jaybird" or "as the crow flies." Jays and crows are medium to large in size with long strong legs, large strong feet, and strong straight bills. The nostrils usually are covered with short, stiff, forward-directed bristles. Most corvids will eat anything they can swallow and are thus able to survive changing conditions in a wide variety of habitats.

## Blue Jay
*Cyanocitta cristata*
10–12 in. (25–30 cm)

*Range:* The Blue Jay is an abundant permanent resident throughout the Carolinas, with the population increased in winter by flocks of birds that migrate by daylight from the northern part of the species' range. Blue Jays are at home in any kind of woodlands, but they prefer fairly open pine-oak woods. They are rather quiet about their nests, though at other times they will engage in noisy pursuit of hawks, owls, and snakes, giving alarm cries that are recognized and heeded by almost all woodland birds and mammals.

*Nesting habits:* The nest is a bulky and rather untidy affair made of sticks, twigs, leaves, roots, pine needles, rags, waste-paper, and mud. It may be placed in a small tree, but high horizontal limbs of large oaks and pines seem to be preferred. Often 20 to

*Blue Jay*
Eloise F. Potter

50 feet (6–15 m) or more above ground, the nest is usually not far from the main trunk of the tree. The three to five olive-buff eggs are thickly spotted with brown. First clutches of the season are laid in April and usually are larger in number than second ones. The incubation period is about 17 days, and bob-tailed young leave the nest 17 to 21 days after hatching, though they are still dependent upon their parents for another week or more. First broods often leave the nest the latter part of May, and second broods do so about mid-July. Because the sexes are indistinguishable in the field, no one seems to know exactly the role of the male in nesting activities. Blue Jays do engage in courtship feeding, and males apparently participate in nest construction, feed the incubating female, and help tend the young. Some reports indicate that males relieve the female on the nest, but this appears to be just a matter of covering the eggs or nestlings in the absence of the female rather than true incubation and brooding.

*Feeding habits:* The Blue Jay is omnivorous with vegetable matter apparently predominating in the diet. Although the jay has a bad reputation for robbing nests of other birds, it is only one of many such predators including crows, rat snakes, and house cats. The nest that is not well hidden or well defended will be raided, if not by the jay then by some other animal.

*Description:* This is our only blue bird with a crest and a black neck band. The Blue Jay has an imposing vocal repertoire that includes hawk imitations and raucous cries. One of its most delightful renditions is the rather musical pump-handle call, which is accompanied by an appropriate bobbing motion.

## Black-billed Magpie
(American Magpie)
*Pica pica*
17½–22 in. (45–56 cm)

*Range:* On March 23, 1960, shortly after a great blizzard had raked the Midwest, a Black-billed Magpie visited a feeding station at Chapel Hill, N.C. The bird appeared to be wild, and newspaper publicity brought no word of an escaped cage bird in the region. (hypothetical status)

## Common Raven
*Corvus corax*
22–26½ in. (56–67 cm)

*Range:* The Common Raven is an uncommon, but conspicuous, permanent resident in our higher mountains at elevations above 3,500 feet (1,070 m). After the breeding season, individuals and small flocks, probably young of the year rather than adults, wander into the lowlands, sometimes even to the coast. A number of recent low-elevation sightings, including the discovery of a nest at Pilot Mountain, N.C., suggest that the species may be on the increase in our region.

*Nesting habits:* In February or early March, in a tall conifer or upon some small rock shelf protruding from a high mountain cliff or crag, ravens build a nest of sticks and twigs lined with matted moss or wool. The four to six greenish, brown-splotched eggs usually are laid in March, and incubation takes about 3 weeks. The male feeds the female on the nest, but he normally does not sit on the eggs except when she must leave them in cold or wet weather. Young remain in the nest about a month, or until early May in our area, and the adults continue to feed them even after departure.

*Feeding habits:* Ravens are omnivorous, having a taste for carrion, birds, snakes, and small mammals; but they readily accept anything edible at the garbage dump. In some parts of the country they have learned to rip open plastic garbage bags in search of food.

*Description:* Larger and heavier-billed than a crow, the Common Raven has a shaggy throat and a wedge-shaped tail. Its voice is a hoarse croak.

---

## Common Crow
*Corvus brachyrhynchos*
16–21 in. (40–53 cm)

*Range:* The Common Crow is common and conspicuous throughout the Carolinas at all seasons, but it does not breed at the higher elevations in our

*Common Crows*
M. M. Browne

mountains where it is an infrequent summer visitor. Though seen in a wide variety of fields and open country habitats, crows nest and roost in rather dense woods. Our winter crow roosts are thought to be composed chiefly of flocks that have migrated from the north. When crows flock for the winter, they post lookouts to warn the feeding or roosting birds of impending danger.

*Nesting habits:* Crows mate early in February and begin nest building later that month. During the nesting season the birds are quiet and secretive, remaining in solitary pairs. Usually placed 25 to 70 feet (7.5–21.5 m) above ground and near the trunk on a large horizontal limb of a conifer, the nest is a heavy, compact structure made of sticks and twigs and lined with leaves and grass. Eggs for first clutches are laid from early to mid-March. Numbering four to six, they vary in color from pale blue to olive green and are spotted and blotched with dark brown. Incubation requires about 18 days, and young remain in the nest about a month. Both adults share in nest construction, incubation, and care of the young. In our region a second brood may be raised.

*Feeding habits:* The Common Crow's diet is mostly vegetable matter, notably corn, wheat, oats, and wild berries; but crows also eat many insects as well as crayfish, snakes, lizards, mice, rats, young rabbits, and the eggs and young of other birds. Thus, from an economic standpoint, the species is both beneficial and detrimental. Because of its fondness for corn and young poultry, the crow has been shot, trapped, bombed, and poisoned; but this wary species continues to thrive.

*Description:* This big black bird is best recognized by its voice, the familiar *caw.* The slightly smaller Fish Crow calls in a less strident *ca* or *ca-ha.* Crows fly with a steady rowing wingbeat.

---

# Fish Crow
*Corvus ossifragus*
15–17 in. (38–43 cm)

*Range:* The Fish Crow is another passerine that is in the process of extending its range in the Carolinas. Prior to 1960 the species was regarded as a common permanent resident along the entire Carolina coast and inland along the Savannah River and its tributaries to Greenwood, S.C., where a nest was found on April 1, 1925. In March 1962, four Fish Crows were seen at Raleigh, N.C., and in April 1972 a nest was found in a medium-height pine grove in residential Raleigh. Subsequent reports indicate that the Fish Crow is present locally in the coastal plain and piedmont inland to Clemson, S.C., and Charlotte and Winston-Salem, N.C. Fish Crows first appeared in central North Carolina soon after Common Grackles began breeding locally, and they have been observed in the act of raiding nests in a grackle colony. Fish Crows arrive at Raleigh in early to mid-March and usually depart in November.

*Nesting habits:* Little is known about the nesting habits of the inland Fish Crow population. These birds appear to begin nesting in late March or early April, and they place nests in pine groves, the same habitat preferred by the Common Grackle at inland localities. On the coast nesting begins in late April, and some Fish Crow nests still contain eggs in early June. The nest and four or five eggs are like those of the Common Crow but smaller. Incubation takes 16 to 18 days, and young remain in the nest about 3 weeks. Both parents appear to share fully in building the nest, incubating the eggs, and caring for the offspring. Only one brood is raised, but if the first set of eggs is lost, another will be laid, sometimes in the same nest. Although nests are usually built 30 to 100 feet (9–30 m) high in pines and other tall trees, they may be situated in waxmyrtle bushes only 5 or 6 feet (1.5–2 m) above ground. Fish Crows may nest well removed from others of their kind or in small colonies with several pairs breeding within a radius of a few hundred yards. In autumn Fish Crows flock in preparation for migration, and winter roosts may number several thousand birds.

*Feeding habits:* Fish Crows breeding on the coast habitually raid heron, gull, tern, and shorebird colonies. In addition to the eggs and young of other birds, Fish Crows consume a variety of aquatic life and many wild fruits and berries from such plants as the mulberry, grape, palmetto, holly, and magnolia. Inland, Fish Crows apparently do not feed around the lakes to any appreciable extent. They frequent city dumps, shopping centers, and the nesting sites of Rock Doves and Common Grackles.

*Description:* The Fish Crow is a slightly smaller version of the Common Crow. Its call is a nasal *ca* or *ca-ha* that can be confused with the calls of young Common Crows.

# Family Paridae: Titmice and Chickadees

The Paridae are small, very active, and highly insectivorous birds with nostrils partly covered by short bristles. They have such strong feet and legs that they can perform amazing acrobatics while extracting seeds from cones, plucking berries from the tips of branches, or searching crevices in bark for insects and larvae.

---

## Black-capped Chickadee
*Parus atricapillus*
4¾–5¾ in. (12–14.5 cm)

*Range:* The Black-capped Chickadee reaches the southern limit of its range in the Great Smoky, Great Balsam, and Plott Balsam Mountains of North Carolina. The species appears to have been extirpated from all our other lofty peaks including Mount Mitchell. Black-capped Chickadees breed mostly in the high-altitude spruce-fir forests above 4,000 feet (1,200 m). In winter Black-cappeds tend to withdraw to the lower elevations where they mingle with Carolina Chickadees.

Where Black-capped and Carolina Chickadee breeding populations come together, hybridization may occur. In the Great Smokies and adjacent northern Great Balsams, the Black-capped is regarded as a fairly common permanent resident with no problem of hybridization with Carolina Chickadees. The Plott Balsam population appears to be sound above 5,000 feet (1,500 m), but there is some evidence of interbreeding between the two species below that elevation. The status of the Black-capped population in the southern Great Balsams has not been determined.

Because of hybridization and because Carolina Chickadees breed in some high-elevation hab-

itats where Black-cappeds are not present, one cannot safely assume that any chickadee is a Black-capped simply because it is found in spruce-fir forest above 4,000 feet (1,200 m).

*Nesting habits:* In late April and early May, pairs of Black-capped Chickadees dig their nest cavities from 5 to 60 feet (1.5–18 m) above ground in the trunks of dead trees. At the bottom of the cavity they build a nest of soft plant fibers, hair, wool, feathers, and insect cocoons. Eggs are like those of the Carolina Chickadee but usually slightly larger. Incubation takes 12 to 14 days, and young remain in the nest about 16 days. The male feeds the female during incubation and helps her care for the young. Nesting activities for Black-cappeds begin 2 or 3 weeks later than for Carolinas.

*Feeding habits:* See comments on family.

*Description:* Separating Black-capped and Carolina Chickadees in the field is very difficult and indeed impossible for some individual birds, especially where hybrids occur in certain parts of the range. Compared to the Carolina, the Black-capped is slightly larger, has whiter cheeks and rustier sides, and has broader white edgings to the wing feathers. Black-cappeds tend to be tamer than Carolinas, or at least more curious about human activities. Vocalizations are not entirely reliable field characters because some individuals of both species occasionally deliver incomplete or incorrect songs that can be misleading. If identification is based on song, repetition of the song is essential. The Black-capped sings a clearly whistled *fee-bee,* and its *chick-a-dee-dee-dee* call is slow, deliberate, and about an octave lower in pitch than the hurried call of the Carolina. For more information on the Black-capped Chickadee in North Carolina, see *Chat* 41:79–86.

## Carolina Chickadee
*Parus carolinensis*
4¼–4¾ in. (10.8–12 cm)

*Range:* The Carolina Chickadee is a common permanent resident of woodlands throughout the Caro-

linas. The species is scarce in the mountains at elevations above 4,500 feet (1,380 m), but it may occur as high as 6,000 feet (1,800 m) in habitats not occupied by the slightly larger Black-capped Chickadee.

*Nesting habits:* Carolina Chickadees sometimes take over nest boxes put up for bluebirds or wrens, but they usually prefer to excavate their own nest cavities even where old woodpecker holes are available. Both adults work about 2 weeks at digging the hole in the soft wood of a fence post, decaying stump, or dead stub on a living tree. Height above ground ranges from 2 to 12 feet (0.6– 3.7 m) with an average around 5 or 6 feet (1.5–2 m). At the bottom of the burrow, which may be 6 to 12

*Carolina Chickadee*
William G. Cobey

252

inches (15–30 cm) below the entrance hole, is the nest proper. This is made of plant down and other soft plant fibers, moss, hair, fur, and feathers matted together rather than woven. One side of the nest is built higher than the other to form a blanket that is drawn over the eggs when the bird leaves the nest. April is the usual month for nesting, but egg laying often begins in March and in some seasons does not occur until early May. The four to eight white eggs are speckled with reddish brown, the spots often forming a wreath at the large end of the egg. Incubation requires about 12 to 13 days. The male feeds the incubating female and helps care for the young during their 17 days in the nest. The species is generally considered to be single-brooded, but some pairs apparently rear second broods. After the nesting season Carolina Chickadees flock with titmice, nuthatches, kinglets, and other small birds.

*Feeding habits:* See comments on family. Although highly insectivorous, Carolina Chickadees will be among the first birds to appear at a feeding station to accept a handout of sunflower seeds.

*Description:* This tiny gray bird has a black cap and black bib framing a white cheek patch. Its hurried *chick-a-dee-dee-dee* and whistled *fee-bee, fee-bay* are among the first songs learned by beginning bird students in the Carolinas. Separating the Carolina Chickadee from the Black-capped is a tricky field problem. Outside the known range in the mountains of North Carolina, chickadees found in our region should be assumed to be Carolinas until proved otherwise.

---

## Tufted Titmouse
*Parus bicolor*
6–6½ in. (15–16.5 cm)

*Range:* A common permanent resident throughout the Carolinas, the Tufted Titmouse is a bird of deciduous and mixed woodlands, but it normally does not occur at the highest elevations in the mountains.

*Nesting habits:* Tufted Titmice do not excavate their own cavities, so they readily accept nest boxes and old woodpecker holes. The chosen natural or man-made site may be 4 to 50 feet (1.2–15 m) above ground. Both sexes help build the nest. If the cavity is too deep, the birds will put in a filling of dead leaves, grass, and weed stems. The nest proper is made of green moss and leaves lined with cotton, hair, fur, feathers, and other soft fibers. In coastal South Carolina a piece of cast snakeskin is almost always present. The four to eight white or creamy eggs are profusely spotted with reddish brown. Laying may begin in mid-March in parts of South Carolina or be delayed until early June in the mountains. Requiring 12 to 14 days, incubation is performed entirely by the

*Tufted Titmouse*
Eloise F. Potter

female, who is fed by the male. When she must leave her eggs, she covers them with soft nest materials. Young remain in the nest 15 or 16 days, being fed by both adults and brooded chiefly, if not wholly, by the female. The species is single-brooded, and after the nesting season titmice flock with chickadees, nuthatches, and other small birds.

*Feeding habits:* See comments on family. Titmice frequent bird feeders.

*Description:* This tiny gray bird has rusty sides, a crest, and a shiny black eye. Its calls are much like those of the chickadee, but its whistled *peter-peter-peter* is distinctive.

## Family Sittidae: Nuthatches

Nuthatches are small woodland birds that feed mostly by picking insects from crevices in bark while hitching nimbly headfirst up or, more often, down the trunks of trees. Not having stiffened tails to serve as props while they forage on tree trunks, they must depend entirely on their stout legs, long toes, and sharp claws. Nuthatches also eat seeds and nuts, which they wedge in crevices and pound open with their long heavy bills. This habit of shelling nuts probably is the origin of the family name.

## White-breasted Nuthatch
*Sitta carolinensis*
5–6 in. (12.5–15 cm)

*Range:* The White-breasted Nuthatch is a permanent resident of mature deciduous forests in all sections of the Carolinas. It is fairly common in the mountains except in the spruce-fir forests where it is scarce or absent, uncommon in most of the piedmont, and fairly common in swamps and flood plains throughout the coastal plain. Usually seen as single birds or isolated pairs, White-breasted Nuthatches remain mated all year and nest much earlier than do most other small birds.

*Nesting habits:* White-breasted Nuthatches rarely hollow out their own nest holes. They almost always take over deserted woodpecker holes or other natural cavities from 20 inches to 40 feet (0.5–12 m) above ground. Both adults help line the burrow with bark strips, feathers, fur, caterpillar silk, and other soft fibers. Egg laying begins by early March in coastal South Carolina and by early April in the mountains. The four to six white eggs sometimes have a rosy tinge and always are profusely speckled with reddish brown and lavender. Incubation requires 12 days, and the male brings food to the female. Both parents feed the young in the nest

and during their 2 weeks of dependency following departure. The species is single-brooded.

*Feeding habits:* See comments on family.

*Description:* This small upside-down bird has a blue-gray back and white breast. The male White-breasted Nuthatch has a solid black cap and the female a gray one. The Red-breasted Nuthatch is similar, but its has rusty underparts and a dark line through the eye. The male has a black crown and the female a slate-blue one. The Brown-headed Nuthatch has a brown cap and a light spot on the back of its neck; the sexes are alike.

## Red-breasted Nuthatch
*Sitta canadensis*
4½ in. (11.5 cm)

*Range:* An erratic winter visitor in piedmont and coastal Carolina, the Red-breasted Nuthatch is fairly common to common some years from mid-September to early May and rare or absent others. These winter visitors frequent pine forests, often in association with other small birds. The species is a permanent resident in the spruce-fir and hemlock forests of the North Carolina mountains, being common from April through November. Depending on the local abundance of food, weather conditions, and the influx of migrants from the north, the Red-breasted Nuthatch may be com-

*White-breasted Nuthatch*
Edward Burroughs

*Red-breasted Nuthatch*
Edward Burroughs

mon or absent at high elevations during the winter. Sightings below 3,000 feet (900 m) are rare in the breeding season; but when the spruce-fir seed crop is poor, Red-breasted Nuthatches move down the mountains to feed on the seeds of other conifers. Extralimital breeding was noted in Rockingham County, N.C., in 1975.

*Nesting habits:* Red-breasted Nuthatches mate in March and remain together all year, rarely associating with the flocks of unmated birds. Although a pair may take over an old woodpecker hole, they are more likely to hollow out their own cavity in a rotten stub or dead limb. Height above ground or water may vary from 2 to 120 feet (0.6–37 m), but 10 to 15 feet (3–4.5 m) is average. Both adults share in nest construction, lining the burrow with a pad of soft plant and animal fibers and plastering the surface around the entrance hole with pitch. Applications are made from the beginning of construction and continue as long as eggs or young remain in the nest. The pitch may prevent insects or predators from entering the nest cavity. The four to seven eggs are white with reddish-brown spots. Fresh clutches have been found in North Carolina as early as May 10 and as late as June 14. Incubation, apparently performed chiefly by the female, requires 12 days, and young leave the nest 14 to 21 days after hatching. Both adults care for

the offspring, and the species is single-brooded.

*Feeding habits:* See comments on family.

*Description:* See White-breasted Nuthatch.

---

## Brown-headed Nuthatch
*Sitta pusilla*
4 in. (10 cm)

*Range:* The Brown-headed Nuthatch is a common permanent resident of open pine woods throughout the coastal plain and in most of the piedmont, but in the mountains it is only a rare accidental. Recent records from Swannanoa and Lenoir indicate that the species is extending its breeding range in western North Carolina.

*Nesting habits:* Brown-headed Nuthatches hollow out their own cavities in some partly decayed fence post, tall stump, or dead limb. Several holes may be started before one is selected for use and dug to a depth of about 6 inches (15 cm) below the entrance. Elevations above ground vary from a few inches to about 90 feet (28 m), the usual height being less than 15 feet (4.5 m). The nest chamber is lined with soft plant materials, prominent among them the thin transparent sheaths from pine seeds. The four to six white or creamy eggs are heavily and rather evenly speckled with reddish brown and lavender. Eggs may be

*Brown-headed Nuthatches at nesting cavity*
William G. Cobey

found from early March in coastal South Carolina to mid-May. Incubation requires about 14 days, with the male bringing food to the female. Both parents feed the young, and the family party remains together long after the nesting season is over. The species is single-brooded over most of its range, but two broods may be raised in southeastern South Carolina. Where their ranges overlap, the Brown-headed Nuthatch associates with Red-cockaded Woodpeckers. Other frequent companions are kinglets, titmice, chickadees, Pine Warblers, Downy Woodpeckers, Chipping Sparrows, and Eastern Bluebirds.

*Feeding habits:* Brown-headed Nuthatches feed largely on pine seeds and a wide variety of insects.

*Description:* See White-breasted Nuthatch.

# Family Certhiidae: Creepers

Creepers are an Old World family of small birds with long slender decurved bills and stiffened tail feathers. The tail is used as a prop as the creeper climbs about the trunks and limbs of trees searching crevices in the bark for hidden insects and larvae.

# Brown Creeper
*Certhia familiaris*
5–5¾ in. (12.5–14.5 cm)

*Range:* The Brown Creeper is a fairly common winter resident from mid-October to mid-April in the coastal plain and piedmont sections of the Carolinas. In the mountains of North Carolina it is a permanent resident, breeding mostly in the high-altitude spruce-fir forests and wintering at all elevations, though most commonly at the lower ones. Sometimes the species is rare or absent in winter on certain high peaks such as Mount Mitchell.

*Nesting habits:* Brown Creepers place their nests in knotholes and natural cavities, behind a slab of loose bark on a tall tree stub, or beneath a loose shingle on a building. Lined with feathers, the nest is a loosely formed mass of lichens, moss, grasses, rootlets, spider cocoons, and shredded bark.

*Brown Creeper*
Courtesy Michael A. Godfrey, from *The Winter Birds of the Carolinas and Nearby States*

Nests built behind bark scales may be fastened in place with spider webs and built upward on the sides a little above the nest cup, giving the whole a crescent shape. Although the male brings materials to the nest site, construction apparently is the work of the female. Completion of the nest may require several weeks. Singing may begin at mid-February, but from late March through June is the usual period. In the southern Appalachians nest construction has been noted from late April to mid-June. The five or six eggs may be sparingly or profusely dotted with reddish brown. Incubation takes about 14 days. The male brings food to the female both during nest building and while she is sitting on the eggs. The male also helps feed the young, which leave the nest about 14 days after hatching. Newly fledged birds have been seen in North Carolina from late June to early August. After the breeding season Brown Creepers are often found with chickadees, Golden-crowned Kinglets, and Red-breasted Nuthatches in woodlands of various types.

*Feeding habits:* The Brown Creeper typically feeds by spiraling up the trunk of one tree to search for insects and then flying to the base of the next in preparation for another climb. In winter this species may feed heavily upon pine seeds. Brown Creepers collect insects from cobwebs beneath overhanging roofs or from crevices in the siding of wooden buildings, and they may roost on window ledges and porches. Such a close association with human habitations seems surprising in a woodland species that rarely visits bird feeders.

*Description:* This small brown bird is more easily recognized by its feeding behavior than by its markings. Look for the long slender decurved bill, white eye line, rusty rump, and long stiff tail feathers.

# Family Troglodytidae: Wrens

Wrens are small brown or brownish-gray birds with strong legs, short rounded wings, sharp and usually decurved bills, and tails frequently cocked. They are highly insectivorous birds that live chiefly in hedges, brushy places, woodland tangles, and grassy marshes, foraging mostly on or near the ground. These pugnacious birds greet the intruder with harsh scolding calls. The sexes look alike, and both sing throughout most of the year. Indeed, wrens are among the most gifted and persistent singers in the bird world. The family name means "cave dweller" and derives from the shape of the large and typically domed nest with an entrance on the side. The male builds several nests as part of the mating ritual. The female selects one, usually the best constructed or best hidden, finishes the inside to suit herself, and lays and incubates the eggs. Males often roost in a cock nest, and cowbirds sometimes are fooled into laying there rather than in the real nest. Male wrens rarely incubate, but they may feed the female on the

nest and regularly help care for the young. Wrens usually are multibrooded, and some are polygamous.

---

## House Wren
*Troglodytes aedon*
4¼–5¼ in. (11–13 cm)

*Range:* The House Wren is a common winter resident of brushy areas, thickets, and woodland margins in eastern South Carolina and coastal North Carolina from mid-September to early May; but the species becomes uncommon or rare westward throughout the two states. During the breeding season the House Wren occurs in the North Carolina coastal plain southward at least to Rocky Mount, in the North Carolina piedmont southward to Wake and Mecklenburg Counties, and across western South Carolina from Rock Hill to Clemson. In the North Carolina mountains it nests throughout the lower and middle elevations. The House Wren was discovered breeding in piedmont North Carolina in 1922 and in western South Carolina in

*House Wren*
William G. Cobey

1950. Further range extension can be expected.

*Nesting habits:* The breeding birds arrive in early April and usually depart by mid-October. In many places House Wrens nest only in towns, preferring open residential developments with much shrubbery. They seldom nest in exposed sites and readily accept a gourd or birdhouse, which the male sometimes fills to overflowing with twigs. The five to eight eggs are white and thickly speckled with reddish brown, the tiny spots often concentrated at the rounded end of the egg. The incubation period is 13 days, and young remain in the nest about 2 weeks. Two broods are raised annually, and some males are polygamous. The female may begin finishing a nest for her second clutch before the first brood is fully independent. She may mate the second time with the same male or move into the territory of another male. If she deserts her first family too soon, the young will perish because the male cannot brood nestlings. If the young are old enough to regulate their own body temperature, they may survive, for the male will continue feeding them in the absence of his mate.

*Feeding habits:* See comments on family.

*Description:* The House Wren is a small grayish-brown bird with no conspicuous markings. It has a faint eye line and a moderately long tail. The Winter Wren has heavily barred underparts and a very short tail. Bewick's and Carolina Wrens have prominent white eye stripes. The marsh wrens have white streaking on their backs.

---

## Winter Wren
*Troglodytes troglodytes*
3½–4¼ in. (9–10.8 cm)

*Range:* The Winter Wren is a fairly common permanent resident of the high-altitude spruce-fir community where it breeds and associates with species such as the Golden-crowned Kinglet, Brown Creeper, and Red-breasted Nuthatch. The Winter Wren may withdraw from the highest peaks about mid-November and return in late March or early April. Winter Wrens sing throughout the year, but their concert reaches a peak from late April until mid-July. These birds sometimes perform antiphonally, with the refrain carried by two or more musicians. Outside the mountains the Winter Wren is a fairly common winter resident, occurring from mid-October to mid-April. This woodland species is usually found about stream banks, fallen trees, and dense tangles.

*Nesting habits:* Little is known about the breeding habits of the Winter Wren in the southern Appalachians. The small amount of data available indicates that nests are concealed in upturned roots of fallen trees. The four or five eggs are white, finely dotted with reddish brown. Laying probably takes place about mid-May, and the incubation period is thought to be 14 to 16 days. Young apparently stay in the nest nearly 3 weeks, departing before the end of June. No published records suggest a second brood in the North Carolina population.

*Feeding habits:* See comments on family.

*Description:* This very dark brown wren has a stubby tail, indistinct eye line, and heavy barring on the underparts.

## Bewick's Wren
*Thryomanes bewickii*
5–5½ in. (12.5–14 cm)

*Range:* Formerly a common summer resident in the mountains of North Carolina, where it was one of the several most numerous birds found in the cities

and towns prior to 1900, the Bewick's Wren frequented farmyards and ranged to the highest peaks. By the 1930s, however, the population had declined sharply. Although conclusive data are not available, the almost complete disappearance of the Bewick's Wren from the urban areas of western North Carolina appears to have taken place about the time the House Sparrow and Starling invaded the region. Outside the mountains, breeding has occurred occasionally eastward to Forsyth County, N.C., and to Chester and Aiken Counties, S.C.

Today the Bewick's Wren is uncommon to rare or absent as a breeding bird in the mountains of North and South Carolina. Nesting appears to be confined to rural sites at rather high elevations, habitats still generally free from House Sparrows and Starlings. In the piedmont and coastal plain the species is a rare transient and very rare winter visitor between October and late March. Along the immediate coast it is a rare fall transient from mid-October to early November. In the Savannah River Plant area, which is closed to the public, the Bewick's Wren was a fairly common winter resident during the 1950s; but there is no indication of a comparable winter population elsewhere in South Carolina. Most likely to be found in brushy places and woodpiles or around abandoned buildings, the Bewick's Wren is easily attracted into view by squeaks, scolds, and Screech Owl imitations.

*Nesting habits:* In the mountains Bewick's Wrens may begin nest building before the end of February, carrying twigs and straws into the rafters of an abandoned building, a deserted automobile, a nest box, a natural cavity, or an old tin can. Nest building has been noted in the piedmont in late May. The five to seven eggs are white, irregularly spotted with reddish brown. Dates for egg laying are not available, but two broods are raised in a season. Incubation is by the female and usually takes 14 days. Both adults feed the young in the nest for 14 days and for an additional 2 weeks or more after departure. Once the young are able to fly, they may return to the nest to roost at night. In Clay County, N.C., a brood left the nest on June 9, and fledglings have been seen in the Smoky Mountains as late as July 28. Obviously much remains to be learned about the habits and status of the Bewick's Wren in the Carolinas.

*Feeding habits:* See comments on family.

*Description:* Bewick's Wren has white underparts, a prominent white eye line, and predominantly white outer tail feathers. The tail is long and rounded at the tip. The bird habitually jerks its tail sideways. The Carolina Wren also has a plain brown back, but its buffy underparts readily separate it from the Bewick's Wren.

# Carolina Wren

*Thryothorus ludovicianus*
5–6 in. (12.5–15 cm)

*Range:* South Carolina's official state bird, the Carolina Wren, is a common permanent resident in all sections of the Carolinas; however, in such specialized habitats as salt marshes and high-elevation spruce-fir forests, this species is known only as a postbreeding wanderer. Although Carolina Wrens are found in remote swamps and woodlands, they also frequent farmyards and the residental sections of cities. Their bubbling songs and scolding notes are heard all year long; and a mated pair will remain together from one breeding season to the next, perhaps nesting in the same place for several successive years.

*Nesting habits:* Carolina Wrens build their bulky and often partly domed nests of dead leaves, twigs, rootlets, moss, pine needles, and other convenient materials in natural cavities, woodpiles, birdhouses, mailboxes, flower pots, or almost any other sheltered nook including clothespin bags, caps, and the pockets of coats left hanging on porches or in garages. Eggs number four to six per clutch and are whitish, well spotted with brown and lilac. Incubation, performed wholly by the female, takes 12 to 14 days. Remaining in the nest about 2 weeks, the young are fed by both adults. Two broods are raised ordinarily, but three are common in coastal South Caro-

*Carolina Wren feeding young*
Morris D. Williams

lina where first clutches are laid in late March or early April, with the second and third ones appearing in early June and mid-July. Northward and inland first clutches are laid a little later, and third clutches are not common. This extraordinarily high rate of reproduction is possible because the female lays the next clutch in a nest the male has already prepared for her, and she may begin incubation while he is still feeding the offspring of the previous nesting.

*Feeding habits:* See comments on family.

*Description:* The largest of our wrens, the Carolina has a plain brown back, prominent white eye stripe, and buffy underparts. One of its songs can be rendered as *cheerily, cheerily, cheerily.*

---

## Long-billed Marsh Wren
*Cistothorus palustris*
4–5 in. (10–12.5 cm)

*Range:* The Long-billed Marsh Wren is a common permanent resident of the great coastal marshes. It is found not only in salt marshes but also amid the tall reeds and cattails of freshwater marshes. Some of the breeding birds may withdraw southward in winter, but they are more than replaced by the influx of birds from the north. During migrations Long-billed Marsh Wrens occur inland to our mountains, and an occasional straggler may spend the winter in some marsh far from the coast. Long-billed Marsh Wrens sing energetically, often several at a time, at any hour of day or night. Suddenly a bird will fly upward for several yards, singing on the wing, and then drop silently into the marsh again.

*Nesting habits:* Although they may nest singly, birds of this species tend to be fairly gregarious and often nest in loose colonies. Attached to the stem of a marsh plant growing in shallow water and woven of wet, pliable marsh grass, the nest is a hollow ball about the size of a grapefruit and has an entrance on the side. Four or five dummy nests may be constructed in addition to the one selected by the female. The five to eight eggs are light brown, heavily marked with darker shades of brown. Incubation takes about 13 days. The species is often triple-

brooded, and eggs have been found from late April through early August. The chief cause of nesting failure is high water; thus, the Long-billed Marsh Wren may be comparatively scarce along our coast the year following the passage of a major storm during the nesting season.

*Feeding habits:* In addition to insects common in the diet of all wrens, this species consumes many snails and small crustaceans.

*Description:* The Long-billed Marsh Wren has a prominent white eye stripe and a dark brown back narrowly streaked with white at the shoulders.

## Short-billed Marsh Wren
*Cistothorus platensis*
4 in. (10 cm)

*Range:* The Short-billed Marsh Wren is a fairly common to com-

*Long-billed Marsh Wren*
Heathcote Kimball

*Short-billed Marsh Wren*
John L. Tveten

mon winter resident of the fresh-water and brackish marshes on and near the Carolina coast. Inland the species becomes rare or absent in winter. Fall migrants have been seen inland from early August to early October, and spring migrants occur from late April to mid-May. Long-billed and Short-billed Marsh Wrens often winter in the same habitat, but Short-billeds usually prefer marshes with scattered shrubs.

*Nesting habits:* Although there is no firm evidence that the species breeds in the Carolinas, its globular nests should be sought in northeastern North Carolina amid the sedges, grasses, and other low herbage at a height of not more than 1 or 2 feet (30–60 cm) above ground, mud, or very shallow water. Usually the nest is very well hidden with blades of the growing green grasses woven into the ball and arching over it. The eggs are pure white, and the shells are very thin and fragile. Long-billed Marsh Wrens occasionally lay clutches of white eggs, but their nests tend to be more conspicuous, slightly ovate, attached to taller plants, and over slightly deeper water. The peak of the Short-billed Marsh Wrens' nesting season is from early June to early July.

*Feeding habits:* See comments on family.

*Description:* This very tame little wren has a short bill, a stubby tail, an indistinct eye line, and a brown back with narrow white streaks that extend into the crown.

# Family Mimidae:
# Mockingbirds, Catbirds, and Thrashers

Probably descended from some thrush-like ancestor, all members of this New World family are excellent singers, and most are skillful mimics. The three species found regularly in our region can be separated by voice according to the number of times in succession identical phrases are given. The Mockingbird will sing the same phrase three or more times in a row, the Brown Thrasher but twice, and the Gray Catbird only once. A catbird may give several consecutive mewing sounds, but each will have a different inflection. The voice of this species is more liquid and less strident than that of our other mimics.

## Mockingbird
*Mimus polyglottos*
9–11 in. (22–28 cm)

*Range:* The Mockingbird is our most versatile singer, giving remarkable concerts by day and night throughout most of the year. Some individuals have been reported as being able to imitate the songs of 30 other species. Perched atop some tall snag, chimney, or television antenna, the mocker sometimes becomes so rapturous that it will fly straight up for several feet and drop to its perch again without missing a note. It may move from one perch to another, singing all the way. This magnificent songster is a common to abundant per-

*Mockingbird*
Eloise F. Potter

manent resident in all sections of the Carolinas, but in the mountains it is confined to the lower elevations.

*Nesting habits:* A bird of the roadsides, woodland edges and thickets, hedgerows, and dooryards, the Mockingbird builds its nest 3 to 12 feet (1–3.5 m) above ground in bushes, vines, and trees. The bulky cup of small sticks, twigs, and leaves is lined with grasses and rootlets. Both birds work on the nest, and construction usually requires 3 or 4 days. The three to five greenish-blue eggs are spotted and splashed with reddish brown. The female incubates the eggs for 12 to 14 days. Her mate usually assists in caring for the young, which remain in the nest about 2 weeks. The nesting season begins early in April with eggs for the first brood being laid about the middle of the month, the second clutch in June, and the third in late July or early August. Mockingbirds are quite bold in defense of their nests, attacking humans, cats, snakes, and other birds with a ferocity that does not encourage a second visit. During courtship Mockingbirds face each other and raise their wings repeatedly in a highly stereotyped dance. Wing flashing is seen in single birds at other seasons, possibly a recrudescence of the courtship performance, possibly to startle insects into movement, or just as possibly for some reason not yet considered by ornithologists.

*Feeding habits:* Mockingbirds take nearly equal amounts of animal and vegetable matter; however, insects predominate in spring, and fruits and berries are taken mostly in fall and winter. Mockers have a habit of driving other species from bird feeders during winter. Blue Jays may gang up on the bully mocker, taking turns harassing it until it becomes exhausted or at least decides the goodies in the feeder are not worth the effort of defending them.

*Description:* The gray Mockingbird has white outer feathers on its long tail and large white patches in its wings. See comments on the family for descriptions of Mockingbird, Brown Thrasher, and Gray Catbird vocalizations.

## Gray Catbird
*Dumetella carolinensis*
8–9 in. (20–22 cm)

*Range:* The Gray Catbird is found in all sections of the Carolinas at all seasons, but only along the coast is it truly a permanent resident. In the mountains catbirds are common from mid-April to mid-October, even on some of the highest peaks; but in winter they become rare or absent, lingering only at the lower elevations. In the piedmont catbirds are common in summer and rare or absent in winter. In the coastal plain catbirds are fairly common during

*Gray Catbird*
William G. Cobey

the breeding season, uncommon in winter, and abundant only during migrations. Although they breed but sparingly along most of the immediate coast, catbirds are fairly common here in winter and may be locally abundant in both summer and winter at certain coastal sites such as the Bodie–Pea Island area. Catbirds frequent residential neighborhoods having dense shrubbery as well as all sorts of thickets, especially the damp ones.

*Nesting habits:* The male catbird woos his mate by chasing after her, by strutting before her with wings drooped and tail cocked, and by courtship feeding. The nest is a deep cup of twigs, dead leaves, and grasses, lined with rootlets and secluded in briers, bushes, and trees with thick foliage. Height

above ground ranges from 3 to 15 feet (1–4.5 m), but some nests have been discovered as high as 60 feet (18 m). Both the male and the female work on the nest. If a bird of either sex happens to be on the nest when the other arrives with additional materials, the late-comer will turn its load over to the first bird and begin to search for another suitable item. Construction normally takes 5 or 6 days, but sometimes pairs that have lost a first clutch to a predator will build the new nest very quickly by using almost all the pieces of the first one. The four or five deep greenish-blue eggs are laid about mid-May for the first clutch and in June for the second. Once incubation is well under way, the female rarely leaves her eggs, being fed on the nest by her mate. Incubation requires 12 or 13 days, and young remain in the nest for 10 days. Although males neither incubate nor brood, they do help clean the nest and feed the nestlings. Banding studies indicate that a pair may remain mated to each other through the entire season or that the male may retain a certain territory over a period of years and have a different mate for each of several successive nestings.

*Feeding habits:* Catbirds eat both animal and vegetable matter, with fruits and berries predominating.

*Description:* The Gray Catbird is uniformly dark gray except for its black cap and rusty under-tail coverts. See comments on the family for a description of its voice.

## Brown Thrasher

*Toxostoma rufum*

10½–12 in. (26–30 cm)

*Range:* Found in all sections of the Carolinas at all seasons, the Brown Thrasher is most abundant in the piedmont during the breeding season, and it tends to be scarce or absent at the higher elevations in the mountains. In winter most Brown Thrashers withdraw from the inland counties, although a few hardy birds remain all winter even in the mountains, but only at the lower elevations. In eastern South Carolina and southeastern North Carolina, the Brown Thrasher is common and sometimes locally abundant in winter because of the influx of birds from regions with

*Brown Thrasher*
William G. Cobey

colder climates. The thrasher is a bird of overgrown fields, woodland margins, and residential neighborhoods, favoring drier habitats than those of the Gray Catbird.

*Nesting habits:* The bulky, deeply cupped nest of small sticks and twigs is often well lined with a layer of leaves, grasses, paper, and other soft materials followed by a layer of small twigs and grass stems with an inner lining of well-cleaned fine rootlets. Late-season nests may be less carefully constructed. In the Carolinas nests are placed anywhere from less than 1 foot (0.3 m) above ground to 5 or 6 feet (1.5–2 m) high in briers, vines, and bushy trees. First clutches normally are laid by mid-May, and two or three broods may be raised in a season. Eggs have been found in the Carolinas from early April to early July. The three to six eggs are tinged with green or blue and thickly dotted with reddish brown. The incubation period is said to be from 11 to 14 days, depending upon weather conditions. The nestling period varies from 9 to 12 days, with the average young probably leaving the nest at 11 days of age. Both parents share fully in all nesting chores.

*Feeding habits:* Acorns, wild fruit, and berries are major items in a diet that also includes a large number of beetles and caterpillars.

*Description:* The Brown Thrasher, often mistakenly called "Brown Thrush," is reddish-brown above and coarsely streaked with brown below. The long tail and long decurved bill separate it from the several species of brown thrushes with spotted breasts. The adult Brown Thrasher has a yellow eye. See comments on the family for a description of vocalizations by thrashers, mockers, and catbirds.

---

## Sage Thrasher
*Oreoscoptes montanus*
8–9 in. (20–22 cm)

*Range:* A Sage Thrasher was seen near Nags Head, N.C., on October 5, 1965. A second bird of this Western species was collected near Southern Pines, N.C., on September 19, 1973. It appears that this bird of sagebrush deserts may be considerably more frequent as an accidental on the East Coast than the few published records indicate.

*Feeding habits:* The Sage Thrasher is highly insectivorous, but it also takes some vegetable matter.

*Description:* Much smaller and grayer than the Brown Thrasher, the Sage Thrasher has white in its outer tail feathers and streaking on the back as well as the breast.

# Family Turdidae: Thrushes

Thrushes are migratory woodland birds that are noted for their sweet flute-like songs. They are highly insectivorous, although in season they eat a wide variety of both wild and cultivated fruits and berries, those of flowering dogwood, American holly, and pokeweed being among their favorites in the Carolinas.

---

## American Robin
*Turdus migratorius*
9–11 in. (22–28 cm)

*Range:* The American Robin is the best known and most widely distributed of the North American thrushes. This abundant species winters throughout the Carolinas and breeds in all sections of the two states, but in summer it tends to be scarce or absent along the coast. During the 1970s robins became well established as breeding birds in the vicinity of McClellanville, S.C., the southernmost point on the Carolina coast where nesting is known to occur regularly. Robins nest mostly near residences where lawns, shrubs, and scattered trees are found. After the breeding season robins flock and roost in dense cover such as wooded swamps, where they are often found in company with Starlings and blackbirds. When our dooryard birds move south for the

*American Robin*
Morris D. Williams

winter, they are replaced by flocks of migrants from the north. In spring, northbound flocks visit pastures and large lawns.

*Nesting habits:* The robin usually builds her nest in a crotch if the tree has small limbs or atop a large horizontal limb, but beams of a porch or storage shed will suffice. Sometimes one or more nests may be started and abandoned before one is completed and occupied. Height above ground is variable, 15 to 50 feet (4.5–15 m) being commonplace. The male usually brings nesting materials, but the female is primarily responsible for construction. The nest of grasses, twigs, rootlets, leaves, or perhaps yellowed daffodil foliage is given rigidity with mud, which the bird forms into a cup by pressing her breast against the inner wall while turning her body. The mud is often collected from earthworm castings. The mud cup is lined with dry grasses. Three or four clear blue-green eggs are laid, usually about mid-April for first clutches. Eggs have been found from early April to late July in our region. Incubation requires 12 to 14 days, young remain in the nest about 2 weeks, and two or even three broods may be raised each season. The male does not incubate or brood, but he does help guard the nest. He helps feed the young in the nest and assumes full responsibility after departure. This frees the female to begin making preparations for the laying of the next clutch.

*Feeding habits:* Robins eat worms, insects, fruits, and berries.

*Description:* The American Robin is dark above and rusty below. The head of the male is darker than that of the female. Young robins have heavily spotted breasts until the first molt, which for birds of the first brood usually begins in early July in the Carolinas. During the first winter young birds have red breasts like the adults.

## Wood Thrush
*Hylocichla mustelina*
7½–8½ in. (19–21.5 cm)

*Range:* The Wood Thrush is a common summer resident from coastal Carolina to the lower and middle elevations of the mountains, but in the spruce-fir zone it is replaced by another thrush, the Veery. Wood Thrushes return to their breeding territory in April and depart for their tropical wintering grounds in October; however, there are a few winter records for the Carolinas.

*Nesting habits:* Although the Wood Thrush almost always nests amid mature trees of swamps, woods, and dooryards, it usually places its nest in a shrub or in the main fork of a sapling about 8 to 15 feet (2.5–4.5 m) above ground. The nest is essentially like that of the American Robin, except that the outer wall usually has more leaves and bits of paper or plastic, and the mud cup usually has a lining of rootlets. Eggs normally

*Wood Thrush*
John Trott

number three or four and are greenish-blue, decidedly lighter in color than those of the Gray Catbird. First clutches generally are laid in late April or early May. Incubation requires 13 or 14 days and is performed by the female. The female broods the young during their 12 or 13 days in the nest. Males guard the nest and help care for the young. The species is double-brooded in the Carolinas, and the second nest may be under construction only a couple of days after young leave the first one.

*Feeding habits:* See comments on family.

*Description:* This and the next four species of spotted-breasted thrushes are separated from the Brown Thrasher by their smaller size, shorter tails, and generally olive-brown upperparts. The Wood Thrush is reddish about the head and has rounded breast spots that contrast sharply with the white underparts. The next four species have comparatively indistinct breast spots. The Hermit Thrush has a conspicuous eye ring and a reddish tail, which it constantly raises and lowers. Swainson's Thrush has a buffy eye ring, a buffy cheek, and a buffy wash on the upper breast. The Gray-cheeked Thrush has a gray cheek patch; whitish breast and throat; and an eye ring that, if present at all, is whitish and indistinct. The Veery has completely reddish-brown upperparts. Neither Swainson's nor Gray-cheeked Thrushes have red in the upperparts, and many fall birds of these two species are so similar that they cannot be reliably separated in the field. Consult a field guide for help in identifying this difficult group of birds.

## Hermit Thrush
*Catharus guttatus*
6½–7½ in. (16.5–19 cm)

*Range:* A fairly common winter resident of woodlands throughout the Carolinas from mid-October to early May, the Hermit Thrush is less abundant in the mountains than toward the coast. The bird rarely sings its beautiful liquid song while here. Apparently it sings only briefly just before sunrise and occasionally at dusk, doing so most frequently soon after arrival in fall and shortly before departure in spring. Throughout the daylight hours it gives only a low but distinctive call note.

*Hermit Thrush*
Heathcote Kimball

The Hermit Thrush breeds sparingly in the mountains of southeastern Virginia. A male singing on Roan Mountain, Mitchell County, N.C., in June 1979 might have been nesting, but there was no evidence of a mate or young. Nesting habits of the Hermit Thrush are similar to those of the Veery.

*Feeding habits:* The Hermit Thrush is not at all shy when visiting bird feeders at homes located in or near woodlands. Apple cores and a paste made of peanut butter, corn meal, and melted suet are favorite feeder foods for this species. It usually eats worms, insects, fruits, and berries.

*Description:* This small brown bird with an indistinctly spotted breast and a conspicuous eye ring is easily recognized by its reddish-brown tail, which it raises and lowers several times a minute. See Wood Thrush for a comparative description.

## Swainson's Thrush
(Olive-backed Thrush)
*Catharus ustulatus*
6½–7½ in. (16.5–19 cm)

*Range:* Fairly common spring and fall transients in upland hardwood forests, Swainson's Thrushes move northward in April and May, and they pass through the Carolinas on their return trip to the tropics in September and October. Occasional birds may linger into winter along the coast, but the species cannot be con-

*Swainson's Thrush*
John Trott

sidered a regular winter visitor in our region.

*Feeding habits:* See comments on family.

*Description:* See Wood Thrush for a comparative description.

---

## Gray-cheeked Thrush
*Catharus minimus*
7–8 in. (17.5–20 cm)

*Range:* An uncommon spring and fall migrant, the Gray-cheeked Thrush, like the Swainson's Thrush, is sometimes found along the coast in winter but cannot be considered a regular winter visitor. The Gray-cheeked is seen most often in upland hardwood forests during May and early October.

*Feeding habits:* See comments on family.

*Description:* See Wood Thrush for a comparative description.

---

## Veery
*Catharus fuscescens*
6½–7½ in. (16.5–19 cm)

*Range:* In the mountains of southwestern North Carolina and adjacent Tennessee and Georgia, the Veery reaches the southern limit of breeding in eastern North America. The species can be found not only above 5,000 feet (1,500 m) in the spruce-fir zone but also in deciduous woods from 3,500 to 5,000 feet (1,070–1,500 m) where it overlaps the upper range of breeding for the Wood Thrush.

*Gray-cheeked Thrush*
John Trott

From late May to late July the parking lot at Clingman's Dome in the Great Smoky Mountains National Park is a good place to listen for the Veery's loud descending series of rapid flute-like notes. The evening chorus of the Veery continues until dark. Outside the mountains the species is a fairly common transient that is found mostly in April and May and in September. It is less common near the coast than inland.

*Nesting habits:* Typically, nests are placed on or near the ground in clumps of bushes growing in woods, and those nests closest to the ground often rest upon a bed of leaves. The peak of laying is from late May to early June. The three or four greenish-blue eggs

*Veery*
Heathcote Kimball

are slightly smaller than those of the Wood Thrush. The female incubates the eggs for 10 to 12 days. The male guards the nest and helps care for the young, which remain in the nest at least 10 days. There is no evidence of the species' having a second brood in North Carolina.

*Feeding habits:* See comments on family.

*Description:* See Wood Thrush.

*Eastern Bluebird, male*
William G. Cobey

## Eastern Bluebird
*Sialia sialis*
6–7 in. (15–17.5 cm)

*Range:* Eastern Bluebirds are fairly common permanent residents of our open woodlands, orchards, farmyards, and roadsides.

*Nesting habits:* Bluebirds build a simple nest of grass or pine needles in the bottom of a natural

*Eastern Bluebird, female*
William G. Cobey

cavity in a tree or wooden fence post. They readily accept properly constructed birdhouses and often appropriate rural and suburban mailboxes. Most of the nesting materials are gathered by the female. Four or five pale blue eggs usually are laid, but clutches of white eggs are also found. The female normally does all the incubating, and eggs hatch in 12 or 13 days. The male helps feed the young, which remain in the nest 15 to 18 days. Nesting activity begins early (March or even February in some parts of South Carolina), and three broods may be raised in a season. Eggs have been found from early March to late July in the Carolinas. Birds of the year remain with the parents and may help feed young of subsequent broods. Family bands of Eastern Bluebirds are joined after the nesting season by birds of several other species such as the Pine Warbler, Carolina Chickadee, Tufted Titmouse, Brown-headed Nuthatch, and Chipping Sparrow. Many bluebirds are killed by ice storms, and others perish in oil burners when they attempt to roost in tobacco curing barns; but by far the greatest threat to the species is the shortage of suitable nesting sites. Farmers and suburban homeowners who remove dead trees and branches and erect metal fences must provide nest boxes if they want to keep their bluebird neighbors.

*Feeding habits:* See comments on family.

*Description:* The adult male Eastern Bluebird has a blue back, red breast, and white belly. The female is similar but grayish about the head. Dingy young birds have speckled breasts and prominent white eye rings. The red breast is acquired during a molt that usually occurs prior to the first winter.

---

## Wheatear
*Oenanthe oenanthe*
5½–6 in. (14–15 cm)

*Range:* A bird having the appropriate field marks and behavior of this species was seen on a Charleston, S.C., golf course October 1, 1960. Wheatears are a group of Eastern Hemisphere thrushes that have moved out of the woodlands to frequent open country. Breeding in tundra from northern Alaska to Greenland, the Wheatear winters in the Old World and is a rare accidental southward in the Western Hemisphere to Louisiana, Cuba, and Bermuda. (hypothetical status)

# Family Sylviidae: Gnatcatchers and Kinglets

Nearly 400 species are included in this large family of small, very active birds that have thin bills and weak feet and legs. Most of these species are either Eurasian in distribution, as is the case with the true warblers of the Old World, or circumpolar in the Northern Hemisphere, as with the kinglets; however, the gnatcatchers are a distinctly New World subfamily.

## Blue-gray Gnatcatcher
*Polioptila caerulea*
4–5½ in. (10–14 cm)

*Range:* The Blue-gray Gnatcatcher is a common summer resident of bottomland hardwoods in all sections of the Carolinas, but it usually is not found in the mountains above 2,500 feet (750 m). Gnatcatchers begin arriving in the Carolinas about mid-March, and most of them depart in early October, although a few spend the winter in the lower coastal plain from Wilmington south.

*Nesting habits:* Both adults aid in construction of the nest, which is a lichen-covered cup of grasses, plant down, and feathers saddled on a lateral limb of a tree from 4 to 35 feet (1.2–11 m) above ground, rarely as high as 80 feet (24.5 m). Placed in both deciduous and evergreen trees, nests closely resemble the somewhat smaller ones built by Ruby-throated Hum-

mingbirds. The four to six eggs are white, tinged with green or blue, and speckled with chestnut. Laying takes place from mid-April to early May. Both sexes incubate the eggs, which hatch in about 13 days. Young remain in the nest 10 to 12 days and are fed by both parents. Although the species is single-brooded over most of its range, second broods may be raised in parts of the Carolinas, particularly in southeastern South Carolina. After the breeding season gnatcatchers roam through upland woods with chickadees and titmice.

*Feeding habits:* Gnatcatchers are almost wholly insectivorous, taking cotton leafworms, woodborers, weevils, and flies in addition to gnats.

*Blue-gray Gnatcatcher*
Morris D. Williams

282

*Description:* This tiny blue-gray bird has a prominent white eye ring and white outer tail feathers. Its body may be slightly smaller than that of a kinglet, but the longer bill and tail give it a greater overall length.

---

## Golden-crowned Kinglet
*Regulus satrapa*
4–4¼ in. (10–10.8 cm)

*Range:* The Golden-crowned Kinglet is a common permanent resident in the hemlock and spruce-fir forests of the North Carolina mountains. In a mature grove of white pines near Highlands, the species reaches the presently known southern limit of breeding in the eastern United States. Elsewhere in the Carolinas it is a common winter resident from early October to mid-April, frequenting stands of evergreens and rarely visiting bird feeders.

*Nesting habits:* Built 4 to 60 feet (1.2–18 m) above ground among the slender twigs of spruces or other evergreens, the nest of the Golden-crowned Kinglet is a ball of green mosses mixed with lichens or bits of dead leaves and lined with strips of soft inner bark, fur, rootlets, or feathers. The opening is at the top with the rim contracted above the hollow holding the 5 to 10 creamy eggs that are variably dotted or splotched with brown. The nest is so small that large clutches are deposited in two layers. Late May or early

June appears to be the peak of egg laying in the Appalachian Mountains. The incubation period and length of time offspring remain in the nest apparently are unknown. Young birds have been found out of the nest in North Carolina in late June. A Maine observer reports that newly hatched kinglets are about the size of bumblebees and are fed by both parents, at first by regurgitation and later with whole insects and caterpillars. After the nesting season Golden-crowned Kinglets associate in loose flocks with chickadees, Red-breasted Nuthatches, Brown Creepers, and other small birds.

*Feeding habits:* Golden-crowned Kinglets assiduously pick insects, spiders, and other minute animal life from twigs and leaves of trees.

*Description:* The Golden-crowned Kinglet is a tiny olive-green bird with two white wing bars. It has a dark line through the eye, a white line above it, and a black edge to the golden crown. The female has a yellow crown patch, but the male has a central orange streak dividing the yellow of the crown. Kinglets are very active birds that constantly flick their wings while on the move.

---

## Ruby-crowned Kinglet
*Regulus calendula*
3¾–4½ in. (9.5–11.5 cm)

*Range:* The Ruby-crowned Kinglet is a common winter resident east

*Ruby-crowned Kinglet*
John Trott

of the mountains from late September to early May. In the mountains this species is mostly a spring and fall transient at the higher elevations, preferring the coves and valleys as a winter home. Ruby-crowneds occur in a wide variety of habitats including residential shrubbery, woodland margins, and forests, often showing a preference for conifers.

*Feeding habits:* Constantly flicking its wings and often hovering at the tips of branches, the restless Ruby-crowned feeds almost entirely on animal matter, only occasionally consuming a few weed seeds and berries.

*Description:* The Ruby-crowned Kinglet is a tiny olive-green bird with two white wing bars and a white eye ring that is broken at the top. The male's red crown is seldom seen except when the bird erects these feathers. Ruby-crowneds begin singing in April while still on the wintering grounds, and the song is remarkably loud and rich in tone for so small a creature.

# Family Motacillidae: Wagtails and Pipits

Pipits are sparrow-sized birds with slender, warbler-like bills. While searching the ground for insects, they walk slowly, wagging their tails more or less continually.

## Water Pipit
(American Pipit)
*Anthus spinoletta*
6–7 in. (15–17.5 cm)

*Range:* The Water Pipit is an uncommon transient and rare

*Water Pipit*
Edward Burroughs

winter visitor in our mountains. In the piedmont and upper coastal plain the species is an uncommon to fairly common winter resident. In the low country, however, Water Pipits abound from late October to early May where large open fields have been freshly plowed or burned over. Huge flocks are almost invisible against the dark damp soil as the birds search for food in the furrows and occasionally perch upon a dirt clod or bit of stubble. Water Pipits also visit sandy shores, mudflats, golf courses, and airports. In broad grassy areas they seem to favor the bare spots.

*Feeding habits:* See comments on family.

*Description:* The Water Pipit looks like a thin-billed sparrow with a light eye line, white outer tail feathers, and black legs. The very similar Sprague's Pipit has yellowish legs.

## Sprague's Pipit
*Anthus spragueii*
6–7 in. (15–17.5 cm)

*Range:* Sprague's Pipit is a Western species that probably occurs in the Carolinas far more frequently than the few published records indicate. These pipits have been found as fall migrants on the Carolina coast throughout the month of November. Inland they have occurred at the Savannah River Plant as early as November 1 and as late as January 30; in York County, S.C., on January 25; at Santee National Wildlife Refuge, S.C., on February 21; at Rocky Mount, N.C., from January 5 through March 9; at Raleigh, N.C., on March 18; and at Chapel Hill, N.C., on May 9. In the Carolinas, Sprague's Pipits seem more likely to be found in fields and pastures near Savannah Sparrows than among the Water Pipits.

*Feeding habits:* See comments on family.

*Description:* Sprague's Pipit has yellowish legs but is otherwise similar to the Water Pipit. This is a somewhat solitary species that tends to stay hidden in tall grass or weeds, often flies rather high when flushed before dropping into another clump of vegetation, and does not wag its tail as frequently as does the Water Pipit.

# Family Bombycillidae: Waxwings

Waxwings are named for the colorful waxlike appendages found on some of their wing feathers. The purpose of these droplets, if any, has not been discovered.

## Cedar Waxwing
*Bombycilla cedrorum*
6½–8 in. (16.5–20 cm)

*Range:* Cedar Waxwings breed in woodlands throughout the higher elevations of our mountains, and on rare occasions eastward across the northern half of the North Carolina piedmont to Wake County and Rocky Mount. Although there is no positive evidence of breeding in South Carolina, several June sightings at

Mount Pinnacle, Caesar's Head, and Table Rock State Park indicate that nesting may occur in Pickens and Greenville Counties. From September to mid-May large restless flocks of Cedar Waxwings roam all over the Carolinas.

*Nesting habits:* Billing and courtship feeding are part of the mating ritual. The nesting period begins about mid-May and extends throughout the summer with eggs still in some nests in late August. Waxwings are very erratic in their nesting habits, moving from place to place to take advantage of the local abundance of fruits and berries instead of returning year after year to a chosen site. While soli-

*Cedar Waxwings*
James F. Parnell

tary nesting seems to be the usual case in our region, loose colonies and even several nests in one tree have been reported elsewhere. The birds seem to nest a mile (1.6 km) or so from their supply of ripe fruit. Nests have been found from 4 to 50 feet (1.2–15 m) above ground, but the average appears to be about 20 feet (6 m). Nests may be placed in forks or on horizontal limbs of shrubs, deciduous hardwoods, pines, or firs. Built by both adults, nests are bulky baskets of *Usnea* lichens, twigs, weed stems, grasses, pine needles, plant down, moss, wool, feathers, twine, and almost any other convenient item, with the softer materials being used for the lining. The three to five eggs are ashy gray, sparingly and irregularly dotted with black, blackish brown, or purple. Incubation is primarily, if not entirely, by the female. Hatching takes place in 10 to 16 days, with 12 to 14 probably being average. The female broods the nestlings almost constantly for the first few days, until they have sprouted some feathers. Both parents feed insects to the young during the remainder of their 14 to 18 days in the nest. Two broods may be raised in a season.

*Feeding habits:* Cedar Waxwings eat a variety of wild and cultivated fruits and berries. Privet and pyracantha berries constitute a major source of food in winter. Waxwings also eat some insects and caterpillars, and in spring they eat the buds from fruit trees. While they usually do not visit bird feeders, they do like to drink and bathe where water is available.

*Description:* This crested brownish bird has yellowish underparts, a black mask about the eyes, and a yellow-tipped tail. Adults usually have waxlike red appendages on a few of the wing feathers. Young birds are streaky brown and lack the sealing wax on the wings. The Bohemian Waxwing (*B. garrulus*) of the western United States and Canada has not been recorded in the Carolinas. This larger and grayer species has cinnamon under-tail coverts. Cedar Waxwings have white under-tail coverts.

# Family Laniidae: Shrikes

The most predatory of our passerines, shrikes have strong feet, sharp claws, and a heavy hooked bill with sharp cutting edges. They feed chiefly on mice and insects; but they will take small birds, mostly warblers and sparrows, whenever they can. Having feet designed for grasping rather than walking, shrikes hunt by flying down from exposed perches such as telephone wires to pounce upon their prey, killing vertebrates with a quick blow to the base of the skull. Like many other birds of prey, shrikes will kill more than they can eat when an opportunity presents itself. Shrikes are called "Butcherbirds" because they hang their excess prey on thorns or barbed-wire fences somewhat the way butchers hang slaughtered animals on meat hooks. Although a shrike may eat the prey immediately after it has been impaled, no evidence exists that the bird ever returns to a larder to eat when food becomes scarce.

## Northern Shrike
*Lanius excubitor*
9¼–10¾ in. (23.5–27 cm)

*Range:* The Northern Shrike is a very rare winter visitor in North Carolina. A specimen was taken at Pea Island on December 9, 1909, and the species was reported twice from Ashe County during the 1960s. Northern Shrikes erupt southward erratically and may be overlooked in our region because of their similarity to the Loggerhead Shrike.

*Feeding habits:* See comments on family.

*Description:* The Northern Shrikes that come south are usually the brownish immatures that have a light lower mandible and barred underparts. The black mask of the adult Northern Shrike does not extend across the forehead as it does in the Loggerhead.

## Loggerhead Shrike
*Lanius ludovicianus*
8½–9½ in. (21.5–24 cm)

*Range:* The Loggerhead Shrike is an uncommon to fairly common permanent resident throughout

*Loggerhead Shrike*
Michael Tove

the Carolinas, usually being more numerous in the piedmont than elsewhere. In the mountains the species is confined to the lower elevations during the breeding season and is uncommon to rare at the higher elevations from late July through early April. The resident population is increased in winter by an influx of birds from the north. Shrikes occur in open country where scattered trees, telephone wires, and fences offer suitable perches for hunting small animals.

*Nesting habits:* Loggerhead Shrikes mate in February and may begin laying eggs in early March in southeastern South Carolina, but nesting is often retarded by cold weather. During most seasons, eggs probably are not common until April in the major portion of our region. Built by both adults, the bulky nest of twigs is firmly woven and well padded with weeds, plant fibers, cotton, string, hair, rags, and paper. Normally it is placed 8 to 15 feet (2.4–4.5 m) above ground in the heavily twigged growth of a hedgerow, a young oak, or an apple tree. The four to six creamy eggs are marked with brown and lavender. The species is double-brooded throughout the Carolinas, and third clutches usually are laid in southeastern South Carolina. First clutches normally contain six eggs with one less being laid in each successive set. Incubation requires 13 days or slightly longer, and the male feeds his mate on the nest. Both adults feed the offspring, which remain in the nest about 3 weeks.

*Feeding habits:* Although they normally hunt from a perch, some Loggerhead Shrikes learn to drive birds from feeders into unscreened windows and glass doors, snatching up stunned birds as large as Cardinals. Their food is almost entirely animal matter, ranging from cattle ticks, spiders, and grasshoppers to snakes, lizards, frogs, mice, and small birds. See comments on family for additional information.

*Description:* Sometimes called a "French Mockingbird," the Loggerhead Shrike is a predominantly gray bird with patches of white in the wings and on the outer tail feathers. The black hooked bill and black facial mask separate this species from the familiar Mockingbird. The mask of the Loggerhead Shrike extends across the forehead, but that of the Northern Shrike stops at the bill. The adult Northern Shrike also is a slightly larger bird with a light base to the lower mandible and a lighter shade of gray on the back and crown.

# Family Sturnidae: Starlings

This Old World family is represented in our region by a single introduced species, the ubiquitous Starling.

## Starling
*Sturnus vulgaris*
7½–8½ in. (19–21.5 cm)

*Range:* Sixty Starlings were released in New York City's Central Park in March of 1890. They began to breed at once, and by the early 1920s this European species was nesting in the Carolinas. Today Starlings are found from the Atlantic to the Pacific and from southern Canada to northern Mexico. This is a bird of the cities, farmyards, roadsides, and open groves of trees. In the Carolinas one can escape Starlings only by visiting dense woods and high mountains.

*Nesting habits:* Starlings breed in the Carolinas throughout the year, though more frequently and in greater numbers during spring and summer than in fall and winter. Pairs place their bulky pad of dried vegetable matter in any convenient crevice around buildings and do not hesitate to evict bluebirds, flickers, martins, and other native hole-nesting species from their homes, often destroying their eggs and young in the process. The Starling's four to six eggs are pale bluish and unspotted. Incubation requires about 14

*Starling, breeding plumage*
Elizabeth Conrad

days, and both parents sit upon the eggs. Both adults feed the young, which remain in the nest until fully fledged, a period of 2 to 3 weeks. Each season two or three broods are raised in the same nest. Most passerines swallow or carry away the fecal sacs until the off-spring are able to defecate over the side of the nest. Starlings, however, do not practice nest sanitation, so the site becomes caked with droppings.

In autumn, Starlings form huge flocks, often traveling and roosting with native blackbirds. Starlings frequently roost in noisy hordes on ledges of downtown buildings, where their droppings are unsightly and a hazard to pedestrians. People who must live or work in the vicinity of a major roost are not impressed by the fact that Starlings consume many harmful insects. Ornithologists report that the first great population explosion has ended along the Atlantic seaboard and that the wintering flocks are gradually diminishing.

*Feeding habits:* Insects, caterpillars, and other animal matter compose about half the food taken by the Starling. Vegetable matter includes various fruits and berries, notably mulberries and cherries.

*Description:* The winter Starling is a heavily speckled brownish bird with a short tail and a dark pointed bill. In spring the bill turns bright yellow and the plumage of the head and breast becomes iridescent. Although its own song is squeaky and unimpressive, the Starling possesses the ability to imitate other birds and human whistling.

# Family Vireonidae: Vireos

Vireos are small greenish birds that live in woodlands and feed on insects, often foraging for them in the uppermost branches of tall trees. Fleshy fruits and berries may be taken, particularly in fall and winter. The sturdy vireo bill has an upper mandible that is slightly hooked at the tip.

## White-eyed Vireo
*Vireo griseus*
4½–5½ in. (11.5–14 cm)

*Range:* In the coastal plain and piedmont the White-eyed Vireo is a common summer resident from late March to early October. The species winters sparingly along the coast of South Carolina and occasionally in coastal North Carolina or the inland portions of both states. In the mountains these vireos arrive in early April, breed at the lower elevations, and

*White-eyed Vireo*
Jane P. Holt

wander to the higher elevations in late summer and early autumn. The White-eyed Vireo is a bird of moist thickets and the edges of swamps.

*Nesting habits:* Woven of grasses, bark strips, and other plant fibers, the slightly conical nest is bound together with caterpillar or spider silk and suspended between the forks of a twig, often 2 to 10 feet (0.6–3 m) above ground on a drooping limb of a waxmyrtle, dogwood, sweet gum, or small oak. The exterior of the nest is frequently decorated with moss or lichens. The three or four eggs are white, sprinkled with a few fine black or brown spots about the large end. First clutches usually are laid in late April, and incubation apparently requires about 14 days. Almost nothing is known about the care of the young and their development, but the male parent is thought to share in all the nesting chores. Two broods are raised each season, and a third nesting may be attempted under favorable conditions.

*Feeding habits:* See comments on family.

*Description:* This is our only vireo that has two white wing bars, yellow spectacles, and yellow sides. The white iris of the adult is distinctive, but immature birds have dark eyes and may be mistaken for Bell's Vireos. The song, often imitated by the Yellow-breasted Chat, can be rendered as *chick-per-a-wheeo-chick,* with the first and last syllables accented and the middle ones slurred together.

292

## Bell's Vireo
*Vireo bellii*
4¼–5 in. (10.8–12.5 cm)

*Range:* Bell's Vireo is a Western bird that occurs east of the Appalachian Mountains as a very rare transient and apparently winters at least accidentally in Florida. A fall migrant of this species was seen in open mixed woods at the edge of a golf course in Wake County, N.C., on August 10, 1974. Bell's Vireo has faint wing bars and white spectacles but otherwise is strikingly similar to the immature White-eyed Vireo. (hypothetical status)

## Yellow-throated Vireo
*Vireo flavifrons*
5–6 in. (12.5–15 cm)

*Range:* A fairly common summer resident of mature woodlands in all sections of the Carolinas from early April to early October, the Yellow-throated Vireo breeds in the mountains only at elevations below 3,000 feet (900 m).

*Nesting habits:* Suspended from a fork of a limb 20 to 60 feet (6–18 m) above ground, the cupped nest is woven of plant fibers and is camouflaged on the outside with lichens. The three or four eggs are much like those of the White-eyed Vireo and require 12 to 14 days for incubation. Offspring are thought to remain in the nest about 2 weeks. The species is double-brooded; and the male shares in nest construction, incubation, and care of the young.

*Feeding habits:* See comments on family.

*Description:* The Yellow-throated Vireo has two white wing bars, yellow spectacles, yellow throat and breast, and a blue-gray rump. The heavy hooked bill and yellow spectacles separate it from the Pine Warbler.

## Solitary Vireo
(Blue-headed Vireo)
*Vireo solitarius*
5½–6 in. (14–15 cm)

*Range:* Solitary Vireos are fairly common spring and fall transients in woodlands throughout the Carolinas. Fairly common winter residents in southeastern South Carolina, they winter sparingly northward along the coast and inland, very rarely even in the mountains. Solitary Vireos breed commonly at all elevations throughout the mountains of the Carolinas in both coniferous and deciduous forests. The species also breeds to an undetermined extent in pine woods of the foothills and eastward in North Carolina to Wake and Moore Counties.

*Nesting habits:* Solitary Vireos arrive on their breeding grounds about mid-March, ahead of the main passage of migrants. Nest building begins in late April, and eggs usually are laid in early May for the first clutch and in June for the second. The nest, eggs, and family life are essentially the same as for our other vireos, with the nest usually placed rather low

*Solitary Vireo*
Chris Marsh

and the incubation period probably 11 days or slightly longer.

*Feeding habits:* See comments on family.

*Description:* The Solitary Vireo has a blue-gray head that contrasts noticeably with the greenish back. Other field marks include the white spectacles, white wing bars, and yellowish sides. The blue-gray head and relatively large size separate this species from Bell's Vireo, which also has white spectacles.

## Black-whiskered Vireo
*Vireo altiloquus*
5½ in. (14 cm)

*Range:* The Black-whiskered Vireo breeds in the mangroves and hammocks of southern Florida

and the Florida Keys. On April 1, 1960, about the time this bird normally migrates from South America to Florida, one dead but still warm was found beneath a telephone wire on the causeway to Wrightsville Beach, N.C. On the preceding 2 days there had been a good flow of tropical air on the Atlantic Coast with strong winds from the southwest.

*Feeding habits:* See comments on family.

*Description:* This species has the general appearance of a Red-eyed Vireo, but it has a prominent black line extending from the base of the bill down the side of the throat.

## Red-eyed Vireo
*Vireo olivaceus*
5½–6½ in. (14–16.5 cm)

*Range:* The Red-eyed Vireo is a common summer resident in all sections of the Carolinas from mid-April through mid-October. During the breeding season this species occurs in the mountains up to 5,000 feet (1,500 m) and occasionally a bit higher, but it is found mostly at elevations below 4,500 feet (1,400 m). A few postbreeding wanderers and fall transients occur at the highest altitudes from late June through early October.

*Nesting habits:* This persistent singer nests in both wet and dry deciduous woodlands, and in the latter habitat it is usually the most abundant breeding species. The nest is a deep cup woven of bark, grass, and other plant fibers and lined with pine needles or other soft materials. It may be decorated on the outside with bits of lichen. Caterpillar silk is used to bind the nest together and to suspend it by the rim from a slender fork near the tip of a drooping limb. Nests are placed from 2 to 60 feet (0.6–18 m) above ground in a deciduous shrub or tree. The three of four eggs are white, lightly sprinkled with reddish-brown dots that are concentrated near the large end. First clutches generally are laid in May and second ones in June. Incubation requires 12 to 14 days. The male shares in nest construction, incubation, and care of the young, which stay in the nest about 12 days.

*Feeding habits:* Red-eyed Vireos supplement their highly insectivorous diet with a number of berries, the bright red seeds of the magnolia being one of their favorite foods in autumn.

*Description:* The Red-eyed Vireo is distinguished by the absence of wing bars and the presence of a gray crown, black-bordered white eye line, and red iris. Immature birds have a brown iris. Two other vireos that occur regularly in our region do not have spectacles or wing bars. The Philadelphia has predominantly yellow underparts, and the Warbling has a white eye line that is not bordered with black.

---

## Philadelphia Vireo
*Vireo philadelphicus*
4½–5 in. (11.5–12.5 cm)

*Range:* An uncommon and rarely seen migrant, the Philadelphia Vireo moves northward primarily across the mountains of the Carolinas in late April and early May. During fall migration it may be found in all sections, even on the Outer Banks, from early September through the first week in October. Philadelphia Vireos usually frequent woodland edges and deciduous scrub, but autumn migrants often travel with other species and visit a wide variety of habitats. Look for them in mixed flocks of warblers, woodpeckers, titmice, chickadees, kinglets, and

*Red-eyed Vireo*
Jack Dermid, courtesy North Carolina
Wildlife Resources Commission

nuthatches. The Philadelphia Vireo seems to be a frequent companion of Bay-breasted, Cape May, and Blackburnian Warblers.

*Feeding habits:* See comments on family.

*Description:* Easily mistaken for a warbler, the Philadelphia is our only vireo with plain wings and a yellow breast.

---

## Warbling Vireo
*Vireo gilvus*
5–5½ in. (12.5–14 cm)

*Range:* In most parts of the Carolinas, the Warbling Vireo is a transient, rare in spring and very rare in fall, occurring from late March to early May and from late August to mid-October. In the mountains of northwestern North Carolina, however, it breeds in open groves of deciduous trees adjacent to rivers in the broad valleys and plateaus below 3,000 feet (900 m). Scattered late spring and summer records suggest that the species may breed eastward across the northern edge of the North Carolina piedmont. This would not be particularly surprising, because Warbling Vireos nest eastward into the coastal plain of Virginia.

*Nesting habits:* The nest of the Warbling Vireo is a neatly woven basket of plant fibers lined with grasses, horsehair, and other soft materials and usually suspended 20 to 50 feet (6–15 m) above ground among leafy twigs close to the topmost branch of a tree. Active nests have been found in North Carolina in May and June, and the species apparently is single-brooded. The three to five white eggs have a few scattered spots of reddish brown, dark brown, or blackish brown, with the darker spots predominating. Incubation requires 12 days, and the young do not leave the nest until 16 days after hatching. Newly fledged Warbling Vireos are oddly pale in general appearance, almost white. Both adults share in nest building, incubation, and care of young. The nest is so well hidden that the male often sings with impunity while sitting upon the eggs.

*Feeding habits:* See comments on family. Sometimes Warbling Vireos consume many ladybugs, much to the displeasure of gardeners who like these beneficial little beetles.

*Description:* This drab gray vireo has only one distinguishing feature, a broad white eye line that is not bordered by black.

# Family Parulidae: Wood Warblers

Wood warblers are a New World family of small and highly insectivorous woodland birds with thin straight bills. Most of the warblers that breed in the eastern United States and Canada migrate to Central and South America, or at least to the southeastern United States, for the winter. These migratory flights are made at night, often leading to great mortality in rainy or foggy weather. Some birds crash against television towers, high bridges, and tall buildings. Others become attracted to lighthouses and airport ceilometers, flying in circles about the bright light until they drop from exhaustion or from collisions with each other. Warbler migration, however, provides one of the greatest thrills in bird study.

Budding spring woodlands that were deserted the day before are alive with flitting, singing warblers the morning after the arrival of a big wave of migrants. Upland groves of open, mature hardwoods often teem with warblers in April and May. Another good place to look for warblers in spring is in flood plains having good stands of blue beech, which is also called ironwood. A small defoliating insect attacks these trees at the peak of warbler migration, providing an abundant food supply.

The fall passage is prolonged and quiet, but no less a challenge to the field student. Young birds of the year and postbreeding adults may look quite different from the spring adults, and the few sounds they make are of little help in identifying them. Fall migrant warblers occur in a great variety of habitats, and they are frequently seen near the ground along woodland edges and in mixed flocks with the local Eastern Bluebirds, Pine Warblers, Chipping Sparrows, Carolina Chickadees, and other small birds. Many fall migrants that will not visit a feeding station sometimes come to bathe on the wing in the spray of a lawn sprinkler or on the ground in puddles around it. Such birds can be studied at leisure while they shake and preen on a low perch. Aphid infestations and pokeberries also attract fall migrants.

If you see one bird chasing another during spring or fall migration, look quickly to see who is being chased. Quite often it will be a stranger in the neighborhood, a new species for the season or possibly even a new one for your life list.

---

## Black-and-white Warbler
*Mniotilta varia*
5–5½ in. (12.5–14 cm)

*Range:* The Black-and-white Warbler is most abundant in the Carolinas during the spring and fall migrations, but it can be found somewhere in our region

*Black-and-white Warbler*
John Trott

during every season of the year. A common summer resident in the mountains, it breeds mostly below 5,000 feet (1,500 m) and wanders into the higher elevations after the nesting season. This species also nests in the piedmont and upper coastal plain, becoming uncommon in summer at the eastern edge of its breeding range. The breeding birds arrive between mid-March and early April, and most depart by mid-October, although a few linger throughout the winter in the coastal plain, particularly in southeastern South Carolina.

*Nesting habits:* The Black-and-white Warbler usually breeds in mature hardwood forests, but in parts of the piedmont and coastal plain it nests in swamp hard-

woods. The nest is placed on the ground, often tucked under an exposed root at the base of a tree or under a mat of pine straw beside a fallen log, and it blends so well with its surroundings that it is practically invisible from above. Composed of bark strippings, grasses, and leaves, the nest is lined with hair or rootlets. The four or five white eggs are dotted with reddish brown and lavender gray, sometimes in a wreath pattern. Incubation apparently is primarily, if not entirely, by the female and requires about 12 days. Both adults care for young, and the species is single-brooded. When disturbed by an intruder, the sitting bird may perform a broken-wing act. The period of nestling life is 8 to 12 days; and very shortly after emerging from the nest, the young can climb trunks and branches of trees.

*Feeding habits:* Black-and-white Warblers are insectivorous, and they so closely resemble nuthatches and Brown Creepers in their feeding behavior that the species formerly was called "Black-and-white Creeper."

*Description:* Heavily streaked with black and white, this species has a black crown divided by a white central stripe. The male has a black cheek patch and a black throat patch with white lines separating the cheek from the crown and the throat. Females and immatures lack the dark cheek and throat patches. Black-and-white Warblers can be confused with male Blackpolls, which have a solid black cap.

Prothonotary Warbler, male at nesting cavity
Jack Dermid

## Prothonotary Warbler
*Protonotaria citrea*
5–5½ in. (12.5–14 cm)

*Range:* The Prothonotary Warbler is a common summer resident from early April to late September along the coast and throughout the coastal plain. It also breeds sparingly throughout piedmont South Carolina and inland to Gaston, Iredell, and Forsyth Counties in North Carolina. The species is a rare spring migrant in the mountains from late April to early May. Winter stragglers are very rare. Although probably most abundant in the cypress swamps, the species nests in other types of swamps and in heavily wooded borders of lakes and streams.

*Nesting habits:* Both adults work on the nest of small twigs, leaves, and moss placed in a natural cavity in a tree, stump, or wooden structure. The nest usually is low, only 3 to 15 feet (1–4.5 m) high, and almost invariably over water. The four to seven almost spherical eggs are white and generously splashed with bright reddish brown. Incubation requires about 13 days and seems to be performed by the female alone, with the male feeding her on the nest to some extent. Both adults tend the young, which leave the nest at 10 to 11 days of age. The species is double-brooded in our region, eggs usually being laid in early May for first broods and in late June for second ones.

*Feeding habits:* See comments on family.

*Description:* The Prothonotary Warbler is predominantly yellow with a shiny black eye and blue-gray wings and tail. Males are more golden yellow than the females. Named for the papal chief notary, who wears a bright yellow robe, the Prothonotary Warbler probably should be called the "Golden Swamp Warbler." Then, at least, bird-watchers would not have to wonder whether to accent the second syllable, as is heard quite frequently, or the third, as logically should be preferred.

---

## Swainson's Warbler
*Limnothlypis swainsonii*
5½–6½ in. (14–16.5 cm)

*Range:* Dr. John Bachman of Charleston, S.C., discovered this elusive warbler on the Edisto River in 1833, and Audubon named it for the English artist-naturalist William Swainson. Present from early April to late September, the Swainson's Warbler breeds uncommonly in suitable habitat throughout South Carolina and in both the coastal plain and the southern mountains of North Carolina. Apparently the species is absent from piedmont North Carolina except as a rare transient and a very local nester. In the eastern counties, Swainson's Warbler usually nests

where there are impenetrable swampy thickets with extensive stands of cane. In the mountains, it nests below 3,000 feet (900 m) in the steep, rugged, densely vegetated river gorges draining the Blue Ridge plateau. Here it is usually found in thickets of rhododendron, laurel, and dog hobble. In both situations the habitat effectively discourages all but the most dedicated ornithologists.

*Nesting habits:* Nests are bulky masses of leaves lined with fine rootlets. Built by the female, they are placed 1 to 10 feet (0.3–3 m) above ground in palmettos, cane, bushes, or tangled vines. The general appearance is that of a cluster of dead leaves lodged in a crotch by high water. The three, sometimes four, eggs are globular and creamy white, occasionally lightly spotted with reddish brown or tinged with blue or green. Eggs have been found in the Carolinas from early May to early July. Incubation is by the female and requires 14 or 15 days. The female is a very close sitter, at least once having accepted insects from the fingers of an intruder; and if forced from the nest, she will feign a broken wing. Both parents share in the feeding of the young, which remain in the nest 12 days or longer and beg food from their parents an additional 2 or 3 weeks. Males may continue singing into August, but there is no firm evidence of a second brood.

*Feeding habits:* See comments on family.

*Swainson's Warbler feeding young*
James F. Parnell

*Description:* This very plain brown warbler has a solid rusty cap and a white eye line. Swainson's resembles the brownish Worm-eating Warbler, which has a dark crown that is divided and bordered by conspicuous buffy streaks. The song of the Swainson's Warbler is easily confused with that of the Louisiana Waterthrush, but Swainson's typically has fewer syllables, often three low slurred notes followed by an ending like the last two notes of the Hooded Warbler's song.

---

# Worm-eating Warbler
*Helmitheros vermivorus*
5–5¾ in. (12.5–14.5 cm)

*Range:* The Worm-eating Warbler migrates throughout the Carolinas, being an uncommon tran-

sient from mid-April to mid-May and from mid-August to early October. In late September it may be locally numerous in brushy mountain lowlands. The species is uncommon to fairly common as a breeding bird in the mountains, preferring hilly deciduous forests from 1,800 to 3,000 feet (550–900 m) in elevation. It is uncommon to rare or absent in the piedmont and coastal plain during the breeding season. This is a terrestrial bird, feeding for the most part on the ground and nesting there.

*Nesting habits:* Well hidden under a drift of dead leaves, the nest of decayed or partly skeletonized leaves usually is lined with hair, fine grass, or the reddish-brown flower stems of hair moss. The three to six slightly glossy white

*Worm-eating Warbler*
John L. Tveten

eggs are variably spotted with brown, the markings usually being somewhat concentrated at the large end. The female incubates the eggs about 13 days, with the male sometimes feeding her on the nest. Young leave the nest about 10 days after hatching and remain with the parents for some time after departure. Apparently, only one brood is raised.

*Feeding habits:* The species' name appears to be a misnomer because the Worm-eating Warbler consumes a wide variety of animal matter including bees, spiders, insects, and insect larvae. It forages by walking on the ground and along limbs.

*Description:* See Swainson's Warbler for a comparative description.

# Golden-winged Warbler
*Vermivora chrysoptera*
5 in. (12.5 cm)

*Range:* In the mountains of southwestern North Carolina, the Golden-winged Warbler is a locally fairly common summer resident at the middle elevations around 2,000 to 4,000 feet (600–1200 m) where old fields and forest clearings are growing up in bushes and young trees. The right-of-way for high-voltage transmission lines is a good place to look for it. Males sometimes sing from perches on the huge towers. The species is a rare transient in the piedmont, very rare in the coastal plain, and apparently absent on the immediate coast except as a very rare fall migrant. Golden-winged Warblers arrive on the breeding grounds about mid-April and depart by late September.

*Golden-winged Warbler, male at nest*
John Trott

Migrants seem to pass through the Carolinas from late April through early May and from late August through September, usually being found in bottomland hardwood forests, especially in spring.

*Nesting habits:* The coarse, bulky nest of bark strippings, grass, and other plant fibers may be placed on bare ground, on a mat of dead leaves, or very near the ground in clumps of weeds, ferns, or briers. The birds tend to tilt the nest opening so the plant materials on the ragged upper rim can partly conceal the cup below. The four or five eggs are white, variably spotted or wreathed with gray and reddish brown. Laying apparently begins in the Carolinas in late May; incubation is by the female and requires 10 to 11 days; and young stay in the nest about 10 days. The species appears to be single-brooded.

*Feeding habits:* Despite their habit of nesting on the ground, Golden-winged Warblers frequently feed very high in tall trees, foraging at the tips of branches even before the buds open in spring.

*Description:* The male is a predominantly gray bird with a black bib, black eye patch, yellow crown, and large yellow wing patch. Females and immatures have the same general pattern, but they are less boldly marked.

---

## Blue-winged Warbler
*Vermivora pinus*
5 in. (12.5 cm)

*Range:* The Blue-winged Warbler occurs sparingly during the breed-

Blue-winged Warbler, male
John Trott

ing season in the extreme south-western tip of North Carolina at elevations between 1,500 and 2,000 feet (450–600 m). Elsewhere in the Carolinas the species is known only as a transient, uncommon in the mountains and along the fall belt and rare in most parts of the piedmont and coastal plain. The migrants pass mostly from late April through early May and from mid-August through September, occurring mainly in bottomland hardwoods. Apparently territorial male Blue-winged Warblers have been found at several places in western Graham and Cherokee Counties, N.C., in June and July and at one site in Pickens County, S.C., in June. There is however, no documented nesting record for the Carolinas.

*Nesting habits:* The Blue-winged Warbler has essentially the same nesting habits as the Golden-winged Warbler, but the nest is often very deep and narrow, like an inverted cone.

*Feeding habits:* See comments on family.

*Description:* The Blue-winged Warbler resembles a Prothonotary, but it has a black line through the eye and two white bars on the blue-gray wing. Its buzzy song is quite different from the ringing tones of the Prothonotary.

*Hybrids:* Where their ranges overlap, Golden-winged and Blue-winged Warblers hybridize. The well-marked offspring of such matings once were thought to be separate species, the Brewster's

Warbler and the Lawrence's Warbler. Both hybrid forms have been found in the Carolinas, mostly as spring migrants. Consult a field guide for information on identification of hybrid warblers.

---

## Bachman's Warbler
*Vermivora bachmanii*
4¼–4½ in. (10.8–11.5 cm)

*Range:* The rarest of American wood warblers and an endangered species, the Bachman's Warbler apparently frequents canebrakes

and thickets both within and along the borders of mature hardwood swamp forests. Bachman's Warblers begin arriving in Charleston County, S.C., in early March and have not been seen there later than July 19. Recent sightings have been reported from the vicinity of Mayrant's Reserve in the Francis Marion National Forest. In 1891 two specimens were taken at Raleigh, N.C., one on April 27 and the other on May 22. Their occurrence apparently was accidental.

*Bachman's Warbler, male*
John H. Dick

*Nesting habits:* Bachman's Warbler was discovered in I'On Swamp, Charleston County, S.C., in 1833; and its nests have been found here, sometimes near those of the Swainson's Warbler, in scrub palmetto, clumps of cane, low bushes, and vines. Placed only 2 or 3 feet (0.6–0.9 m) above ground, the nest may be made of cane leaves, grasses, weed stalks, skeletonized leaves, and Spanish moss. The three to five white eggs usually are laid in late March or early April. Almost nothing is known about the family life of the Bachman's Warbler. The species is thought to be single-brooded.

*Feeding habits:* Although the Bachman's Warbler nests very near the ground, it generally feeds 20 feet (6 m) or more above the surface, often in the very tops of tall cypresses where its small size and deliberate movements might cause it to be mistaken for a vireo. Instead of flitting from tree to tree the way most warblers do, this elusive species will sing or forage in one tree and then suddenly take flight toward another tree well out of sight. Birds occurring at the edges of the swamp forest tend to forage closer to the ground than do those found in heavy timber.

*Description:* Bachman's Warblers strongly resemble the Hooded, but they lack the Hooded's prominent white tail spots. The black bib of the adult male Hooded extends upward in a point that touches the base of the bill at the chin. The adult male Bachman's has a yellow chin, and a highly variable portion of the throat also may be yellow. Although not shown in popular field guides, the small patch of yellow at the bend of the Bachman's wing is a useful field mark.

*John Bachman:* The Reverend John Bachman (1790–1874) was pastor of Saint John's Lutheran Church in Charleston, S.C., for 60 years. A truly remarkable naturalist, Bachman not only discovered two avian species new to science (Swainson's Warbler and Bachman's Warbler) but also befriended John James Audubon while he labored to complete *The Birds of America.* Bachman wrote the entire text for the pioneer book on American mammals, *The Viviparous Quadrupeds of North America.*

## Tennessee Warbler
*Vermivora peregrina*
4½–5 in. (11.5–12.5 cm)

*Range:* During spring migration the Tennessee Warbler is uncommon in the mountains and appears to be confined to the lower and middle elevations. It becomes very rare eastward toward the fall belt, being almost completely absent from the coastal plain in this season. The peak of spring migration is in late April and early May. In fall the Tennessee Warbler is more abundant, being common in the mountains and occurring from the highest peaks to the barrier beaches from very late August through October, particularly between mid-September and mid-October.

*Feeding habits:* See comments on family. Look for Tennessee Warblers in deciduous woods, usually in the treetops. Many fall migrant warblers, including this species, have been noticed visiting trees heavily infested with aphids.

*Description:* Spring males resemble a Red-eyed Vireo with a dark eye and a bill that is thin even for a warbler. This is our only warbler that has completely white underparts in spring. Fall birds can be confused with the Philadelphia Vireo. Consult a field guide for tips on identifying spring females and fall birds.

## Orange-crowned Warbler
*Vermivora celata*
5 in. (12.5 cm)

*Range:* Usually found in the Carolinas from early October through early May, the Orange-crowned Warbler is a fairly common winter resident in southeastern South Carolina, becoming uncommon northward along the coast and rare to very rare inland, where it is known only as a transient.

*Feeding habits:* The Orange-crowned Warbler often forages on or near the ground.

*Description:* This dull greenish bird is best recognized by the absence of tail spots, wing bars, and prominent head markings. The orange crown is rarely seen, the dark stripe through the eye may be indistinct, and the streak-

*Tennessee Warbler, fall plumage*
John Trott

ings on the underparts are faint. Immature Tennessee Warblers have white under-tail coverts, but those of the Orange-crowned are yellow.

---

## Nashville Warbler
*Vermivora ruficapilla*
4½–5 in. (11.5–12.5 cm)

*Range:* The Nashville Warbler is a rare spring and fall migrant that is more likely to be seen in the central and western counties than in the coastal plain. Migrants pass through the Carolinas from late April to mid-May and from mid-August to mid-October. While still far from common, this species appears to be more plentiful east of the Appalachians now than it was in the 1940s and 1950s.

*Feeding habits:* In spring the Nashville Warbler usually is a treetop bird, but in fall it often forages near the ground in thickets and woodland edges.

*Description:* The mostly greenish Nashville is our only warbler that has a gray head, prominent white eye ring, unstreaked yellow throat and breast, no wing bars, and no tail spots.

*Nashville Warbler, male*
Michael Tove

*Northern Parula*
John Trott

## Northern Parula
(Parula Warbler)
*Parula americana*
4½ in. (11.5 cm)

*Range:* A fairly common to common summer resident of swamps and damp woodlands throughout the Carolinas, the Northern Parula is most numerous near the coast, scarce in the western piedmont, and generally absent from the mountains above 5,200 feet (1,600 m). Spring migrant parulas begin arriving in southeastern South Carolina— where a few individuals may have spent the winter—in early March, but they do not reach most of our region until late March or early April. The species is rarely seen in the Carolinas after October. From mid-April to early May, when the majority of spring migrants pass through the Carolinas, parulas frequently sing from large shade trees well removed from water.

*Nesting habits:* Nest building begins soon after Northern Parulas return to their breeding grounds. The nest is usually suspended about 25 feet (7.5 m) high from a lateral branch of a tree standing in or near water. Where Spanish moss is available, the nests invariably are concealed in its streamers, the nest proper being woven of fine grasses and strands of moss. Elsewhere the birds weave together strands of the hanging gray lichen, *Usnea.* The entrance to the nest is always on the side of the cluster. The three to five eggs are white, speckled around the large end with reddish brown and lilac. Laying for first clutches usually takes place in late April or early May. Incubation apparently is the duty of the female, and it probably requires 12 to 14 days. Both parents care for the young, but the duration of the nestling period has not been determined. Two broods are often raised near the coast; one probably is the usual number per season in the mountains. Singing decreases rapidly in July, and the ascending buzzy trill is rarely heard in late summer and autumn.

*Feeding habits:* See comments on family.

*Description:* The Northern Parula is our only blue-backed warbler with a yellow throat. The adult male has an irregular rusty band separating the yellow throat from the yellow upper breast; this mark is absent in females and imma-

tures. Both adults have a greenish patch on the back.

*Hybrids:* Parulas occasionally interbreed with Yellow-throated Warblers, producing the hybrid Sutton's Warbler. This form is found in South Carolina from time to time, but there is no published record from North Carolina. Sutton's Warbler resembles the Yellow-throated but has unstreaked sides and a greenish patch on the back.

## Yellow Warbler
*Dendroica petechia*
4½–5¼ in. (11.5–13 cm)

*Range:* The Yellow Warbler breeds from the mountains of North and South Carolina eastward to Dare and Wake Counties, N.C., and to Chester and Anderson Counties, S.C. The species is a fairly common summer resident in northwestern South Carolina, in the lower elevations—up to about 3,000 feet (900 m)—of the North Carolina mountains, and in the western piedmont of North Carolina. It becomes uncommon to rare or locally absent toward the eastern edge of its range. Outside its breeding range, the Yellow Warbler is a transient from early April through May and from July through October. The nesting birds arrive in early or mid-April in wet thickets and streamside shrubbery, especially black willows. In the mountains they also nest in farmyards. Migrants passing northward through the breed-

*Yellow Warbler, male*
Heathcote Kimball

ing territory frequent both the lowlands and upland groves, arriving 2 or 3 weeks after the summer residents. Yellow Warblers seldom are seen around their nesting places after July, and during this same month they reappear in coastal South Carolina where they do not breed. A few stragglers are found in early winter, usually on the coast but on very rare occasions inland to the mountains.

*Nesting habits:* The male may help the female build the nest, which usually is situated about 7 to 12 feet (2–3.5 m) above ground in a crotch of a small tree, shrub, or climbing rose bush. The compact symmetrical cup of cotton, plant down, or other soft plant fibers is often lined with hair. If the nest is parasitized by a cowbird, the Yellow Warbler almost always builds another atop the one containing the alien egg. Sometimes a nest may have five or six stories. In May or June the Yellow Warbler lays four or five white eggs that are generously speckled and splashed with shades of brown and lilac. The incubation period is about 11 days. The male does not sit upon the eggs or brood young, but he stands guard and feeds the female on the nest. The young remain in the nest about 9 to 12 days, being fed by both parents. The birds begin moving southward as soon as the offspring are fully independent.

*Feeding habits:* See comments on family.

*Magnolia Warbler, male*
John Trott

*Description:* This is our only warbler with a yellow breast and yellow tail spots. The male has conspicuous reddish streaks on the breast; the female has faint streaks.

---

## Magnolia Warbler
*Dendroica magnolia*
4½–5 in. (11.5–12.5 cm)

*Range:* The Magnolia Warbler is a fairly common spring and common fall transient in the mountains and piedmont, becoming uncommon to very rare eastward. The species is more likely to be seen along the coast in fall than in spring. The spring passage takes place from late April through mid-May, and the fall passage occurs mostly from late August through October. During the late 1800s the Magnolia Warbler was reported as breeding in Buncombe County, N.C.; and there are several recent June and July records of the species from Mount Mitchell in Yancey County, N.C., and from the Mitchell County, N.C., side of Roan Mountain. However, the most southerly modern nesting record is from Giles County, Virginia. Although the species nests in spruce, fir, and hemlock trees, spring migrants are found in hardwoods, and fall migrants visit all kinds of wooded habitats.

*Feeding habits:* See comments on family.

*Description:* The Magnolia is our only warbler that has a rectangular white patch on each side of the tail about midway of its length. These spots are noticeable only when the tail is fanned. The spring male looks much like a yellow-throated and yellow-breasted Myrtle Warbler with a broad white wing patch instead of two white wing bars. Magnolias have yellow on the rump but not on the crown.

*Cape May Warbler, spring male*
Heathcote Kimball

## Cape May Warbler
*Dendroica tigrina*
5–5½ in. (12.5–14 cm)

*Range:* The Cape May Warbler is known in the Carolinas as a spring and fall transient. In late April and early May the species is fairly common in the mountains and most of the piedmont, becoming uncommon to very rare in the eastern piedmont and coastal plain. In fall migration the species occurs throughout the Carolinas from late August to early November, with the peak of fall passage probably being from late September through mid-October. Like most transient warblers, this species is usually seen in hardwoods in spring and in various types of woods and thickets in fall.

*Feeding habits:* Although Cape May Warblers are highly insectivorous, they are fond of ripening grapes and do considerable damage to this crop during fall migration.

*Description:* The adult male Cape May Warbler is unmistakable

*Cape May Warbler, fall male*
Heathcote Kimball

with his heavily streaked yellow underparts, rusty cheek patch, large white wing patch, and yellow rump. Females and immatures are very difficult to identify, and use of a field guide is recommended.

## Black-throated Blue Warbler
*Dendroica caerulescens*
5 in. (12.5 cm)

*Range:* The Black-throated Blue Warbler is a common summer resident in the mountains of North and South Carolina from mid-April through mid-October. As a

*Black-throated Blue Warbler, male*
John Trott

spring and fall transient the species is found throughout the Carolinas, more commonly in the western counties than toward the coast, from mid-April to mid-May and from early September through October.

*Nesting habits:* Generally nesting near a brook or spring in hardwood forests above 2,800 feet (850 m) in elevation, this warbler places its nest from 10 inches to 3 feet (25–90 cm) above ground in the fork of a shrub (rhododendron, mountain laurel) or in rank weeds (often rattleweed) and ferns growing between rocks and fallen trees in heavily timbered ravines. Accompanied by the male, the female gathers all the nesting materials and does all the con-

struction. The nest exterior is composed chiefly of rhododendron and grapevine bark strippings bound together with spider webs and interwoven with other kinds of bark, rotten wood, and moss. The interior of the cup is neatly lined with moss, fern rootlets, hair, or fine grass. The four eggs are laid in late May or early June. They are whitish and marked with brown and lilac either all over or in a wreath at the large end. The female incubates the eggs for about 12 days and broods the young, which stay in the nest about 10 days. The male helps feed the offspring and clean the nest. It is not unusual to hear Black-throated Blue Warblers singing after the nesting season in August and September.

314

*Feeding habits:* See comments on
family.

*Description:* Both the handsome
male with his blue back, black
throat and sides, and white belly,
and the dingy female can be distinguished by the small white
patch near the base of the primaries. Young males look almost
exactly like the adult males.

Cairns's Warbler (*D. c. cairnsi*)
is the race of the Black-throated
Blue Warbler that breeds in our
mountains. It is named for John S.
Cairns, a resident of Weaverville,
N.C., who did a great deal of
important ornithological work in
the North Carolina mountains
during the 1890s.

Yellow-rumped Warbler, male in spring
plumage
Edward Burroughs

# Yellow-rumped Warbler
(Myrtle Warbler, Audubon's
Warbler)
*Dendroica coronata*
5–6 in. (12.5–15 cm)

*Range:* The Yellow-rumped
(Myrtle) Warbler is a common
winter resident of the Carolinas
from late September or early
October to mid-May. In midwinter Myrtle Warblers may become
locally scarce or absent in our
mountain counties, but they are
abundant throughout the winter
along the coast.

*Feeding habits:* In winter Myrtle
Warblers eat the fruits of various
plants, especially those of the
waxmyrtle and bayberry. They
also eat many small insects,
which they may pick from the
bark and leaves of trees and
shrubs or pursue on the wing like
tiny flycatchers. Myrtle Warblers
frequently visit bird feeders and
bird baths, thus usually becoming
the first warbler species met by
the beginning bird student.

*Description:* The Yellow-rumped
Warbler is our only bird that has a
yellow cap, yellow rump, and yellow patches on each side of the

Yellow-rumped Warbler, female or winter
male
William S. Justice

breast. In many brownish fall Myrtles the yellow patches are dull and difficult to see.

Among the vast numbers of Yellow-rumped Warblers wintering in the Carolinas, a very rare individual may be of the yellow-throated Western subspecies group, the Audubon's Warbler (*D. c. auduboni*). One such bird was collected at Rocky Mount, N.C., on February 28, 1970. Myrtles with creamy throats can be confused with the Audubon's Warbler.

## Black-throated Gray Warbler
*Dendroica nigrescens*
4½–5 in. (11.5–12.5 cm)

*Range:* This species breeds in the western United States and occurs accidentally on the East Coast. One Black-throated Gray Warbler was seen on Bull's Island, S.C., on December 13, 1941; another was found at Orton Plantation near Wilmington, N.C., on December 30, 1965. In both cases the birds were seen at close range by experienced observers. This black-throated species has a diagnostic tiny yellow spot in front of its eye. (hypothetical status)

## Townsend's Warbler
*Dendroica townsendi*
4½–5 in. (11.5–12.5 cm)

*Range:* A male Townsend's Warbler and a possible female were reported from Nantahala in the North Carolina mountains on April 24, 1975. This Western species is an extremely rare accidental in the eastern United States. It resembles a Black-throated Green Warbler with a black cheek patch and a yellow breast. (hypothetical status)

## Black-throated Green Warbler
*Dendroica virens*
4½–5¼ in. (11.5–13 cm)

*Range:* During spring migration the Black-throated Green Warbler is fairly common in our western counties from mid-April to mid-May, becoming uncommon to very rare eastward across the Carolinas. Fall migrants pass throughout the Carolinas, mostly from mid-September to early November. Although this species breeds very locally in our central counties, it nests principally in the hemlock ravines and spruce-fir forests of our mountains and in the cypress swamps and river bottoms of the lower coastal plain. The birds arrive on the breeding grounds in late March or early April.

*Nesting habits:* Nests are placed 3 to 75 feet (1–23 m) or higher on horizontal limbs of large trees, in crotches of tall saplings, or in tangles of vines. The nest is a neat cup of bark strips, grass, leaves, rootlets, and conifer needles. Egg laying occurs on the coast between mid-April and mid-May and in the mountains between mid-May and mid-June. The three or four eggs are white, speckled and wreathed with brown and lilac. The incubation period is thought to be about 12 days, and the young probably stay in the nest about 10 days. The female appears to be chiefly responsible for nest construction, incubation, and brooding; but both adults feed the young and clean the nest.

*Feeding habits:* See comments on family.

*Description:* This is our only warbler with wing bars and a large yellow cheek patch that encircles the eye. Several Western species are confusingly similar, but only one of these has been reported in our region. Reference to field guides is recommended.

# Cerulean Warbler
*Dendroica cerulea*
4–5 in. (10–12.5 cm)

*Range:* During spring and fall migration the Cerulean Warbler is uncommon in the mountains, becoming rare to very rare or absent toward the coast. The spring passage occurs from early April to early May, and the fall passage from July until mid-September. The Cerulean Warbler population seems to be increasing in the eastern United States. Although the species definitely breeds in North Carolina, its range and nesting habits are not well known. Apparently it breeds in the Great Smoky Mountains

National Park, where singing males have been heard in June at elevations from 1,200 to 5,358 feet (365–1640 m); along N.C. Route 28 between Fontana Village and Tuskeegee in Graham County; on the slopes of the Green River valley in southwestern Polk County; along U.S. Route 21 in northeastern Wilkes County; and along the Roanoke River from the Occoneechee Neck section of Northampton County downstream into Bertie and Martin Counties. The species formerly nested at Morganton, Statesville, and Greensboro.

*Nesting habits:* Cerulean Warblers tend to be gregarious during the breeding season, favoring the canopy of mature hardwood forests with an open understory then as well as during migration. As many as 20 males may be heard singing at a particularly favorable locality, but the nests apparently are rather widely dispersed throughout the general vicinity. The shallow compact cup of bark fiber, weed stalks, lichens, moss, and grass is bound on the outside with spider silk and resembles a Blue-gray Gnatcatcher nest. Placed high in a deciduous tree, well away from the main trunk and amid a cluster of twigs, the nest usually is impossible to see from the clearing below even when an adult is making regular trips to it to feed the begging nestlings. The three to five eggs are white, variably dotted or blotched with brown. Incubation apparently is performed by the female, and the incubation period is estimated to be 12 to 13 days. The male may assist in the feeding of the offspring. In North Carolina adults have been seen feeding young out of the nest as early as May 28 and others still in the nest as late as June 16.

*Feeding habits:* See comments on family.

*Description:* The Cerulean is our only warbler with a blue back and a white throat. The female is paler than the male and lacks the narrow dark band that separates his white throat from the white breast with streaked sides.

## Blackburnian Warbler
*Dendroica fusca*
4¼–5½ in. (10.8–14 cm)

*Range:* The Blackburnian Warbler is a fairly common spring and fall transient in the North Carolina mountains and in northwestern South Carolina, becoming uncommon to very rare toward the coast. The peaks of migration are from late April through mid-May and from late August to mid-October. Although Blackburnian Warblers have been found in the mountains of South Carolina in June, no evidence of breeding has been obtained. Blackburnian Warblers are fairly common summer residents in the mountains of North Carolina, mostly at elevations above 3,000 feet (900 m). They

arrive on the breeding grounds in our spruce-fir, hemlock, and northern hardwood forests about mid-April and depart by mid-October.

*Nesting habits:* The nest usually is placed from 5 to 80 feet (1.5–24.5 m) above ground in a coniferous tree, often a hemlock. At times it is near the tip of a drooping branch, but probably it is most often saddled on a horizontal limb 6 to 10 feet (1.8–3 m) from the main trunk. The nest is rather bulky, usually a densely woven mass of small twigs, plant down, lichens, and rootlets lined with horsehair, fine grasses, and feathers. Egg laying begins in late May in our region, but some females may still be building nests at mid-June. The four or five white eggs are dotted and splashed with brown and gray, often in a wreath around the large end. The incubation period is unknown, and little is known about the family life of this species except that both parents feed the young.

*Feeding habits:* See comments on family.

*Description:* The male Blackburnian is our only warbler with an orange cap and a bright orange throat patch. The adult female can be confused with the Yellow-throated Warbler; look for her tiny yellow crown patch and the white streaks on her back.

318

## Yellow-throated Warbler
*Dendroica dominica*
4¾–5¾ in. (12–14.5 cm)

*Yellow-throated Warbler*
Jack Potter

*Range:* The Yellow-throated Warbler is a common breeding species throughout the coastal plain and a fairly common one elsewhere in the Carolinas; but in the mountains it is confined to the lower elevations, favoring pines below 2,500 feet (750 m). The birds arrive on the breeding grounds from early March to early April and depart by late September or early October. The species is an uncommon but regular winter resident in southeastern South Carolina and a rare winter straggler northward along the coast.

*Nesting habits:* Nest construction is entirely or almost entirely by the female. In the coastal plain swamps and bottomlands, Yellow-throated Warblers prefer to build their nests, composed of bits of bark, rotten wood, fine grasses, weeds, and feathers, in a clump of Spanish moss with the entrance hole on one side of the garland. Elsewhere the birds build in pine woods, placing the nest near the tip of a horizontal branch in a cluster of needles and burs. Nests are usually 15 to 60 feet (4.5–18 m) above ground, but they have been found from 3 to 100 feet (1–30 m) or higher. The four greenish-white eggs are spotted near the large end with brown and lavender gray. Very little is known about the family life of the Yellow-throated Warbler. The incubation period is thought to be about 12 days. In coastal South Carolina the species is double-brooded, first broods often being fully fledged by late April. No one has determined how far northward and inland the Yellow-throated Warbler is able to raise two broods per season; but apparently the species is single-brooded in the mountains, where young leave the nest about mid-June.

*Feeding habits:* See comments on family.

*Description:* The Yellow-throated Warbler is a gray-backed bird with a white eye line, black sideburns, yellow throat, white belly, heavily streaked sides, two white wing bars, and white tail spots. The hybrid Sutton's Warbler (see Northern Parula) is similar to the Yellow-throated except for the unstreaked sides and a greenish patch on the back. This very rare form has been found in South Carolina several times, but there is no published record from North Carolina.

## Chestnut-sided Warbler
*Dendroica pensylvanica*
5 in. (12.5 cm)

*Range:* The Chestnut-sided Warbler is a fairly common spring transient in the mountains and western piedmont between late April and mid-May, becoming uncommon to very rare toward the coast. As a fall migrant from mid-August to late October, the species is fairly common in the eastern counties, but it remains rare along the coast. Chestnut-sideds are common summer residents in our mountains, breeding at elevations of 2,000 to 6,300 feet (600–1,900 m) where man and nature have created suitable openings in the forest. This species thrives in the brushy habitat that springs up following forest fires and lumbering operations. No doubt the Chestnut-sided is more plentiful now than before the arrival of white settlers when it was largely confined to the mountain balds.

*Nesting habits:* Built by the female, the nest of weeds, grasses, and leaves is lined with fine grasses, rootlets, and hair. It is placed in a fork or crotch about 3 feet (1 m) above ground in bushes, vines, or small saplings. The three or four eggs are white, variously speckled and splotched with brown and gray. The peak of laying in our region appears to be from late May through early June. Incubation requires about 12 days and is performed by the female; but both adults feed the young, which remain in the nest about 10

*Chestnut-sided Warbler, pair feeding young*
John Trott

320

to 12 days. The species appears to be single-brooded.

*Feeding habits:* See comments on family.

*Description:* Both sexes have a greenish-yellow crown, a narrow black patch about the eye, and white underparts marked only by a chestnut streak down each side. Consult a field guide for tips on identifying the immature, which has a plain yellowish-green back, two yellow wing bars, and solid white underparts.

## Bay-breasted Warbler
*Dendroica castanea*
5–6 in. (12.5–15 cm)

*Range:* Known only as a transient in the Carolinas, the Bay-breasted Warbler in spring is uncommon in the western counties and very rare toward the coast. The species is more likely to occur in the eastern counties in fall than in spring. Spring migrants pass through our region from late April to mid-May, and the considerably more plentiful fall migrants can be expected from early September through October.

*Feeding habits:* See comments on family.

*Description:* The spring male has a streaky back and two white wing bars that, along with the chestnut crown, throat, and sides, clearly distinguish him from all our other warblers. Spring females and fall birds are easily confused with other species. Identification

of some individuals may be impossible even with the aid of a field guide.

## Blackpoll Warbler
*Dendroica striata*
5–5¾ in. (12.5–14.5 cm)

*Range:* In both spring and fall the Blackpoll Warbler is among the latest of the migrating warblers. The majority of the northbound birds pass through the Carolinas between late April and early June. Fall migrants may be found from late August to mid-November, but the peak period is in the latter part of October. In spring the Blackpoll is a common migrant in the central portion of our region, being only fairly common in the mountains and near the coast. In fall it is rare in the mountains and uncommon to fairly common elsewhere.

*Feeding habits:* See comments on family.

*Description:* In spring the male Blackpoll has a distinctive solid

*Blackpoll Warbler, male*
Heathcote Kimball

black cap, white cheek patch, and yellow feet and legs; otherwise he resembles the Black-and-white Warbler. Spring females and fall birds are finely streaked and difficult to identify, but their yellowish feet and legs help separate them from similar species. A field guide should be consulted.

---

## Pine Warbler

*Dendroica pinus*

5–5¾ in. (12.5–14.5 cm)

*Range:* The Pine Warbler is a common permanent resident of pine forests throughout South Carolina and in all but the upper piedmont and mountain counties of North Carolina. In the mountains the species is found only at the low elevations. Here and in the upper piedmont of North Carolina, it is a fairly common transient, an uncommon summer resident, and a rare winter straggler. An influx of migrants causes the Pine Warbler to become locally very common in the eastern counties in fall and winter.

*Nesting habits:* The breeding season for the Pine Warbler extends from March into June, and during this time the birds may raise as many as three broods. Nests are usually 30 to 50 feet (9–15 m) above ground, but they range from 10 to 135 feet (3–41 m) high. Invariably located in pine trees, they may be saddled on a large horizontal limb, concealed in needles at the tip of a branch, or hidden in a cluster of cones. The nest is a compact cup of bark strips, weed stems, twigs, and grasses, lined with pine needles, hair, or feathers. Nests lined with Eastern Bluebird or Cardinal contour feathers are particularly colorful. The outside may be decorated with cobwebs. The four or five grayish-white eggs are speckled with brown and lilac, often with a wreath at the large end. The incubation period is thought to be about 12 days, and the male may assist the female in this duty. Both adults feed the young, but the duration of the nestling period has not been determined. During the nesting season Pine Warblers tend to stay high in the trees, but in August they flock with Eastern Bluebirds, Chipping Sparrows, Brown-headed Nuthatches, Carolina Chickadees, and Tufted Titmice. Throughout the autumn these mixed flocks spend much time feeding and bathing on and near the ground, often attracting rarely seen fall migrants as temporary companions.

*Feeding habits:* This species spends more time foraging in and beneath pines than do our other warblers.

*Description:* The coloration of Pine Warblers is highly variable, ranging from spring males with brilliant yellow breasts to fall females with only a hint of yellow. Learn the Pine Warbler's trill, which is slower and more musical than that of the Chipping Sparrow, and watch for this combination of field marks: two prominent white wing bars, white tail spots, white belly, unstreaked back, and indistinct eye stripe. The bill of the Pine Warbler is heavier than average for warblers.

## Kirtland's Warbler
*Dendroica kirtlandii*
5¼–6 in. (13–15 cm)

*Range:* Believed to have a total population of less than a thousand individuals, the Kirtland's Warbler nests among the jack pines in one small section of central Michigan and winters in the Bahama Islands. Careful management of its specialized breeding habitat and systematic removal of Brown-headed Cowbirds and their eggs have been undertaken to protect this rare and endangered species.

Kirtland's Warblers are very rare transients in the Carolinas, having been recorded in late April and early May as well as from early September through October. Pre-1935 spring and fall records suggest a straight-line migratory route between the Bahamas and Michigan with the birds striking the South Carolina coast in Charleston and Beaufort Counties. Post-1935 fall migration data, however, indicate that south-bound birds tend to wander eastward across Lake Erie, northern Ohio, and Pennsylvania before turning south along the eastern Piedmont and inner coastal plain. Three fall records from Rocky Mount, N.C., three from Eastover, S.C., and one from Aiken, S.C.,

support this hypothetical route. In addition, a Kirtland's Warbler was seen on the south shore of Kerr Lake on September 1, 1974, about a mile (1.6 km) above the Virginia state line and about 55 miles (90 km) northwest of Rocky Mount. In our region, fall migrant Kirtland's Warblers appear to frequent thickets and woodland edges on high ground just beyond the wet margins of lakes and swamps. The Kerr Lake bird was with a flock of Pine Warblers.

*Feeding habits:* See comments on family.

*Description:* Kirtland's Warbler is gray above and predominantly yellow below with black streaks on the back and sides, two white wing bars, white tail spots, white belly, and white eye ring. This very tame species wags its tail in the manner of the Prairie and Palm Warblers. Of the gray-backed warblers that occur in our region, this is the only one that habitually wags its tail.

## Prairie Warbler
*Dendroica discolor*
4¼–5 in. (10.8–12.5 cm)

*Range:* From early April to mid-October, the Prairie Warbler is a very common summer resident along the North Carolina coast. The species becomes less numerous inland toward the mountains, where it is locally uncommon or fairly common in brushy places on open hillsides at the lower altitudes. It also becomes scarce as a

*Prairie Warbler*
Chris Marsh

*Prairie Warbler, male*
Michael Tove

breeding bird in southern South
Carolina. A few Prairie Warblers
may be found in winter along the
coast northward to Wilmington,
N.C., but the species apparently
does not occur regularly throughout the season in our region.

*Nesting habits:* The nest is usually 2 to 10 feet (0.6–3 m) above
ground in a sapling growing in an
overgrown field, thicket, or
second-growth clearing. The well-
made cup of weeds, plant down,
grasses, and leaves is lined with
hair, fine grasses, or pine needles.
First clutches may be laid in
April, but early May probably is
the rule over most of the our
region. The four or five white eggs
are speckled and wreathed with
spots of brown and lavender. Incubation requires 12 to 13 days, and
young remain in the nest 8 to 10
days. The female apparently does
all the nest building, incubating,
and brooding; but both adults feed
the young. It is not clear whether
late egg dates represent second
broods or result only from renesting after loss of the first clutch.

*Feeding habits:* See comments on
family.

*Description:* Olive-green above
and predominantly yellow below,
the Prairie Warbler has two white
wing bars, dark streaking on the
sides, white tail spots, and white
under-tail coverts. The adult male
may have rusty streaks on his
back, and his song rapidly ascends
the chromatic scale. Prairie Warblers habitually wag their tails

and closely resemble another tail-
wagger, the Palm Warbler, which
has a yellowish rump and yellow
under-tail coverts. Palm Warblers
have rusty caps in spring.

---

## Palm Warbler
*Dendroica palmarum*
4½–5½ in. (11.5–14 cm)

*Range:* Over most of our region
the Palm Warbler is a fairly common transient found in spring
from early April to mid-May and
in fall from mid-September
through November. It is very
common along the Carolina coast
in fall. As a winter resident, it is
common in southeastern South
Carolina, but irregular elsewhere
in the two states. This tail-
wagging warbler frequents hedgerows, edges of fields, yards,
gardens, roadsides, and the sandy
barrier islands.

*Feeding habits:* Palm Warblers
feed on or near the ground. Fall
migrants apparently eat a variety
of berries as well as insects.

*Palm Warbler*
William G. Cobey

*Description:* See Prairie Warbler for a comparative description.

___

## Ovenbird
*Seiurus aurocapillus*
5½–6½ in. (14–16.5 cm)

*Range:* The Ovenbird is a common summer resident from early April through October in the mountains of North and South Carolina up to about 5,000 feet (1,500 m) and across piedmont North Carolina. The species also breeds to some extent in the South Carolina piedmont and the inland portion of the North Carolina coastal plain. Ovenbirds occur as transients throughout the Carolinas, more abundantly inland than along the coast. Winter stragglers are found occasionally, particularly in southeastern South Carolina. The Ovenbird favors rather dry hilly forests with a moderate understory; the canopy may be either pines or hardwoods.

*Nesting habits:* Built entirely by the female, the ground-level nest is made of grass, leaves, pine needles, and other plant materials. It has a domed roof and a side entrance. Beneath the dome is a lining of hair and fine rootlets or grasses upon which the bird deposits four or five white eggs, spotted mostly at the large end with brown and gray or lilac. The ovenlike nests are usually placed in slight depressions near paths or other openings in the forest and are often sheltered by shrubs, fallen branches, or leaf litter. The female incubates the eggs about 12 days, and she occasionally may be fed on the nest by the male. Both adults feed the young, which stay in the nest 8 to 10 days. The

*Ovenbird at nest*
Heathcote Kimball

family party remains together until the offspring are about 5 weeks old. Although single-brooded, Ovenbirds will lay again if the first nesting attempt should fail.

*Feeding habits:* While foraging on the ground for insects and small mollusks, Ovenbirds and water-thrushes walk with a teetering motion in the manner of the Spotted Sandpiper. *Seiurus* means "tail waving."

*Description:* The Ovenbird has a plain olive back and a heavily streaked white breast. Its head pattern separates it from the waterthrushes, which also feed on the ground and wag their tails. Look for the Ovenbird's prominent white eye ring and black stripe above the eye. Adults have rusty crowns.

---

## Northern Waterthrush
*Seiurus noveboracensis*
5–6 in. (12.5–15 cm)

*Range:* A fairly common spring and fall transient across the central part of the Carolinas, the Northern Waterthrush is uncommon toward the mountains and the coast. The main passages occur from mid-April through May and from mid-August through early October.

*Feeding habits:* Waterthrushes are likely to be found feeding on the margins of sluggish water in swamps, wet thickets, woodland streams, and even along the edges

of marshes. They often forage on floating debris.

*Description:* Olive-brown above and heavily streaked below, the two waterthrushes are separated by their head patterns. The Northern has a creamy stripe above the eye, its throat is finely streaked between the heavy jaw stripes, and its comparatively short bill is almost conical. The Louisiana has a prominent white stripe above the eye, its throat is white between the heavy jaw stripes, and its long bill is rather heavy for a warbler. Ovenbirds have a complete eye ring and a dark stripe above the eye. All three species walk with a teetering motion in the manner of the Spotted Sandpiper.

---

## Louisiana Waterthrush
*Seiurus motacilla*
6 in. (15 cm)

*Range:* in the Carolinas, the Louisiana Waterthrush is a fairly common summer resident from mountains below 3,500 feet (1,070 m) to the fall belt. It nests at least sparingly in the northern portion of the North Carolina coastal plain and occurs throughout the coastal plain as an uncommon to rare migrant. The breeding birds arrive in the Carolinas by late March and begin moving southward about mid-July, nearly all having left the Carolinas by early September. Louisiana Water-thrushes inhabit the borders of

Louisiana Waterthrush
Morris D. Williams

woodland streams, especially rocky, fast-flowing ones.

*Nesting habits:* The nest is placed in a sheltered nook in the steep bank of a stream, often in the outer curve of a bend, perhaps under some exposed roots or over-hanging ferns. On a substantial platform of wet leaves stuck together by the mud on them, the waterthrush builds a neat cup of twigs, mosses, and weed stems, lined with dry grasses and hair. The four or five eggs are white or pinkish-white, speckled all over with brown and gray. Incubation requires 12 to 14 days. Apparently the female does all the incubating and brooding, but the male partic-ipates in nest construction and assists in feeding the young,

which probably remain in the nest about 10 days.

*Feeding habits:* Although the Louisiana Waterthrush eats mostly insects and spiders, it sometimes eats snails, other small mollusks, and tiny fish. It often forages on floating debris.

*Description:* See Northern Waterthrush for a comparative description.

## Kentucky Warbler
*Oporornis formosus*
5½ in. (14 cm)

*Range:* The Kentucky Warbler is a fairly common summer resident in the mountains below 3,500 feet (1,070 m) and eastward to the fall belt. It breeds locally and perhaps

328

Kentucky Warbler, nesting female
John Trott

sparingly throughout the coastal plain. The birds arrive in the bottomland hardwoods of the breeding grounds from early to late April and depart mostly from August to mid-September, but a few stragglers may be found in October.

*Nesting habits:* Usually built on or very near the ground at the base of a bush, the nest is a bulky mass of dead leaves, lined with grass, bark strips, rootlets, and pine straw. Laid in May or June, the four or five white eggs are sprinkled with reddish brown and lilac gray. Incubation requires 12 or 13 days. Apparently the female is solely responsible for nest construction, incubation, and brooding; but the male helps feed the offspring, particularly after they

leave the nest. The period of dependency may last nearly a month, 10 days in the nest and up to 17 days after departure. The brief sojourn on the breeding grounds and the male's minor role in the care of the young indicate that the species is single-brooded.

*Feeding habits:* See comments on family.

*Description:* Olive-green above and completely yellow below, the Kentucky Warbler has yellow spectacles and black sideburns.

## Connecticut Warbler
*Oporornis agilis*
5¼–6 in. (13–15 cm)

*Range:* The Connecticut Warbler is a rare transient found mostly, but not exclusively, in the mountains and western piedmont. In the eastern counties this species is seen much more often in fall than in spring, with most of the birds occurring along the coast. Spring migrants usually pass through the Carolinas from about May 10 to the end of the month. Fall migrants occur mostly from early September through October. Migrating Connecticut Warblers frequent wet thickets.

*Feeding habits:* This species forages on the ground, walking in the manner of the Ovenbird.

*Description:* Two gray-hooded warblers occur in the Carolinas, the Connecticut and the Mourning. Both have olive backs and yellow underparts extending from the base of the hood to the tip of the under-tail coverts. The Connecticut is the larger and duller-colored of the two, and it has a complete eye ring, white in the adult and buffy in the immature. The Mourning Warbler has no eye ring in spring, and males have an irregular dark smudge on the throat portion of the gray hood. Fall Mourning Warblers, however, have an eye ring that is broken by a dark line running through the eye.

## Mourning Warbler
*Oporornis philadelphia*
5–5¾ in. (12.5–14.5 cm)

*Range:* The Mourning Warbler is a regular, but still very rare, spring

and fall migrant in the mountain and piedmont sections of the Carolinas, occurring from very late April to late May and from late August to early October.

*Feeding habits:* This slow-moving and secretive bird usually forages close to the ground in woodland clearings and thickets.

*Description:* See Connecticut Warbler for a comparative description.

## Common Yellowthroat
*Geothlypis trichas*
4½–5½ in. (11.5–14 cm)

*Range:* From late March or early April to mid-October, the Common Yellowthroat is found throughout the Carolinas, being a very common species toward the coast but only fairly common in the mountains above 5,000 feet (1,500 m). Yellowthroats winter from the eastern piedmont throughout the coastal plain of the Carolinas, becoming more numerous along the coast. They like habitats such as brushy fields, hedgerows, wet thickets, and marshes.

*Nesting habits:* The nest usually is well hidden in low bushes, cane, cattails, or clumps of grass, often only a few inches above ground or water. Made of coarse grass, leaves, and strips of bark, the rather bulky structure is lined with fine grasses. The male apparently does not regularly assist the

Common Yellowthroat, male feeding young
Morris D. Williams

female with construction. The three to five eggs are white, variably spotted with black and brown. In coastal Carolina, first clutches are laid in late April or early May, and second ones in June. Incubation requires about 12 days and is performed by the female. The male sometimes brings food to the nest for the female to eat while she is incubating or for her to feed to the newly hatched nestlings. On the fourth day he begins delivering food directly to the young, which remain in the nest 9 or 10 days.

*Feeding habits:* See comments on family.

*Description:* Olive above and predominantly yellow below, the male Common Yellowthroat has a broad black mask and sings *witchity-witchity-witchity.* The female is brownish and wrenlike. Look for the white belly that in all plumages separates the yellow throat and breast from the yellow under-tail coverts.

---

## Yellow-breasted Chat
*Icteria virens*
6¾–7½ in. (17–19 cm)

*Range:* The Yellow-breasted Chat is a fairly common to common summer resident in deciduous thickets at the low and middle elevations in the mountains and throughout the piedmont section of the Carolinas, but it is uncommon on and near the coast. The birds begin arriving on the breeding grounds in mid-April, and most of them have departed by the end of September, although a

*Yellow-breasted Chat*
Morris D. Williams

few stragglers can be found in winter, mostly along the coast.

*Nesting habits:* Placed 1 to 5 feet (0.3–1.5 m) above ground in briers (often blackberry) or a sapling, the bulky nest is made of weed stems, grass, and leaves. It is lined with fine grasses and rootlets. Both adults apparently participate in nest construction. The three to five white eggs are variably marked with brown spots. The incubation period has not been determined definitely, but 11 days is thought to be normal for the species. Although the female does all the incubating and brooding, the male at least assists in the feeding of the offspring, which remain in the nest 8 days or perhaps slightly longer. From time to time during the breeding season, the chat may be seen singing lustily while making a clownish, floppy-winged flight, either rising into the air and returning to the same perch or moving from one perch to another. Flight songs have been reported in other warbler species including the Common Yellowthroat, Louisiana Waterthrush, Ovenbird, Blue-winged Warbler, and Prothonotary Warbler.

*Feeding habits:* Although the Yellow-breasted Chat is predominantly insectivorous, it consumes many wild fruits and berries in season.

*Description:* More easily heard than seen, the chat is a ventriloquist that makes its presence known with a noisy repertoire of squawks, chuckles, whistles, and imitations of other species, notably the White-eyed Vireo. Chats usually stay well hidden in dense tangles of saplings, bushes, and briers. This large, heavy-billed warbler has a plain olive back, white spectacles, bright yellow throat and breast, and white belly and under-tail coverts. The white under-tail coverts and large size clearly separate the chat from the Common Yellowthroat, which has the same general color pattern except for its yellow under-tail coverts.

## Hooded Warbler
*Wilsonia citrina*
5½ in. (14 cm)

*Range:* The Hooded Warbler is a common summer resident of moist deciduous woodlands throughout the Carolinas, arriving on the coast in late March and at inland localities in early to mid-April. Fall migration begins in early August, and most of the birds have moved southward by early October.

*Nesting habits:* Usually the nest is built 2 to 4 feet (0.6–1.2 m) above ground in a low bush or in the top of a clump of cane. Tangles of briers are favorite sites. Normally the compact nest is made of cane leaves, bark strips, weed stems, and pine needles and lined with fine grasses, hair, rootlets, or the black inner fiber of Spanish moss. Early May appears to be the peak of egg laying. The three to five creamy eggs are variably marked with brown and lilac. The incubation period is 12 days. Apparently the female builds the nest and does all the incubating and brooding; but the male assists

*Hooded Warbler, nesting female*
Hollis J. Rogers

*Hooded Warbler, male*
John L. Tveten

in feeding the young. When they leave the nest at 8 days of age, the offspring are unable to fly; but they have well-developed legs and are remarkably self-sufficient. Although most pairs probably raise only one brood per season, second and third sets of eggs have been reported.

*Feeding habits:* See comments on family.

*Description:* The yellow forehead and cheeks of the male Hooded Warbler are surrounded by a black cap, neck band, and bib that are joined together to form the hood. Plain olive back, plain yellow underparts, and white tail spots are like those of the female, which has a dark cap and yellow throat. Female Hoodeds are easily con-

fused with Wilson's and Bachman's Warblers. Listen for the male Hooded's loudly whistled *weet-a-wee tee-o* rendered with a rising inflection on the next to the last syllable.

---

## Wilson's Warbler

*Wilsonia pusilla*
4½–5 in. (11.5–12.5 cm)

*Range:* Wilson's Warbler is an uncommon to rare spring and fall transient that is more likely to be found in the piedmont and mountains than in the coastal plain. The spring passage occurs mostly from late April through mid-May. The fall movement extends from mid-August through September with stragglers sometimes found

Wilson's Warbler, male
Norme D. Frost

later. This species likes thickets, especially willows.

*Feeding habits:* See comments on family.

*Description:* Plain light olive above and plain bright yellow below, the male Wilson's Warbler has a small black cap that sharply contrasts with the bright yellow forehead. Females and immatures are similar with an olive crown. In all plumages the Wilson's Warbler lacks white in the tail.

## Canada Warbler
*Wilsonia canadensis*
5–5¾ in. (12.5–14.5 cm)

*Range:* Although the Canada Warbler is a fairly common to common summer resident in the North Carolina mountains from 3,400 feet (1,040 m) to the tops of the highest peaks, the species is an uncommon migrant in the piedmont counties, becoming rare to absent toward the coast. Spring migrants are found mostly in May. After mid-August the breed-ing birds begin wandering into the lower elevations of the mountains; but fall migration does not begin until late August, and it continues into early October. Canada Warblers frequent dense growths of rhododendrons and other shrubs, especially those near small mountain streams.

*Nesting habits:* The bulky nest of dry weeds is lined with fine plant fibers and hair. It is placed on or near the ground, often on a moss-covered log or stump. Beneath the projecting bank of a stream is another favored site. The four or five white or slightly buffy eggs are speckled with brown or gray, primarily around the large end. Egg laying apparently takes place in late May or early June, but the incubation period (probably about 12 days) and number of days the young stay in the nest are unknown. The female is thought to do all the incubating and brood-ing, with the male helping feed the young and clean the nest.

*Feeding habits:* See comments on family.

*Description:* Plain gray above and bright yellow below, the male Canada Warbler has yellow spectacles and a black necklace dangling across the upper breast. The necklace may be faint or even lacking in females and immatures, but the yellow spectacles (very pale around the eyes) and some-what greenish unspotted tail make identification of poorly marked birds possible.

*American Redstart, adult male*
John Trott

*American Redstart, female*
John Trott

## American Redstart
*Setophaga ruticilla*
5–5½ in. (12.5–14 cm)

*Range:* The American Redstart is found throughout the Carolinas as a spring and fall migrant, and it breeds extensively in the inland portions of the two states. Redstarts nest in the mountains up to about 2,500 feet (750 m), throughout the North Carolina piedmont, and at least sparingly in the North Carolina coastal plain. In South Carolina evidence of breeding outside the mountains and foothills comes from Richland, Sumter, and Georgetown Counties. Spring migrants begin arriving in early April and are most numerous in the piedmont. Fall migration occurs from mid-August through October, with the species often very common during this season. Stragglers are found occasionally into winter.

*Nesting habits:* The breeding birds frequent wooded streams, especially extensive bottomland forests, placing nests 5 to 20 feet (1.5–6 m) above ground in a fork of a bush or small tree, often a birch. Built by the female, the nest is a deep, compact cup of shredded plant fibers bound together with spider webs and lined with grass, fine plant fibers, and hair. The four white eggs are speckled with gray and brown, chiefly around the large end, and usually are laid about mid-May. The species normally is single-brooded. Incubation requires about 12 days and is performed by the female. She also does all the brooding, but the male helps feed the young and clean the nest. Off-

spring remain in the nest about 9 days. In piedmont North Carolina many breeding males have little or no black in the plumage, thus resembling females and perhaps causing bird students to overlook some mated pairs.

*Feeding habits:* See comments on family. Redstarts feed by flycatching more often than do most of our other warblers.

*Description:* The fully.adult male American Redstart is our only predominantly black warbler. The sides, bases of the flight feathers, and bases of the outer tail feathers are touched with orange. The female is gray above and white below with white spectacles and yellow spots on the sides, wings, and tail. First-year males resemble females; but the yellow spots may be tinged with orange, and the throat and upper breast may be irregularly dotted with gray and black. Young males wear the female-like plumage through the first nesting season.

# Family Ploceidae: Weaver Finches

This Old World family is represented in our region by a single introduced species.

## House Sparrow
(English Sparrow)
*Passer domesticus*
6¼ in. (16 cm)

*Range:* The House Sparrow is an abundant permanent resident throughout the Carolinas, being scarce or absent only in those habitats well removed from human settlements. This European species, which is quite different from our native sparrows, was introduced in Brooklyn, New York, in the 1850s. By the 1870s it had reached Raleigh and Charleston.

Today House Sparrows can be found in the United States from coast to coast, in southern Canada, and in Mexico. Although these birds consume various harmful insects, they are considered pests because they build unsightly nests; are frequent hosts for mites and lice; and often drive Eastern Bluebirds, Cliff Swallows, and other less aggressive native species from their nesting chambers.

*Nesting habits:* House Sparrows have been found breeding in the Carolinas during every month of the year, but the nesting season generally lasts from March through September. Bulky nests of grass and weed stems lined with

*House Sparrow, adult male*
Elizabeth Conrad

feathers may be hung in trees or placed in crevices of buildings. Both sexes build. House Sparrows are multibrooded, but reports of more than two successful broods per year are not adequately documented. The courting male House Sparrow struts before the female with his wings drooped and his tail cocked. She responds by crouching, fluttering her wings, and begging food like a baby bird. The four to seven eggs are dull white, variably speckled and spotted with purple and gray. Incubation lasts 12 or 13 days and is performed by the female. Young remain in the nest about 15 days and are cared for by both adults.

*Feeding habits:* The spread of the House Sparrow has been facilitated by its varied diet. It consumes grains, fruits, and vegetables as well as insects and garbage.

*Description:* House Sparrows are brown birds with dingy white underparts. The male has a gray crown, black bill, and black bib. The female has a wide pale eye line and a light, often yellowish, bill. Having no distinctive markings, the female House Sparrow is frequently confused with our native sparrows.

# Family Icteridae: Blackbirds and Allies

Icterids have strong feet and legs and a pointed, conical bill; but otherwise these species show little obvious similarity in appearance or behavior.

## Bobolink
*Dolichonyx oryzivorus*
6½–7½ in. (16.5–19 cm)

*Range:* Found throughout the Carolinas during migrations and fairly common to common except in the mountains, flocks of Bobolinks occur from mid-April to late May and from mid-August to mid-October. In spring the males usually arrive a week or more before the females. In fall the species is considerably more numer-

ous along the coast than inland. Look for flocks of Bobolinks in hay meadows, grain fields, and marshes. Bobolinks once nested at North Wilkesboro, N.C., and numerous summer records from the mountains of North Carolina and adjacent Tennessee indicate a small and erratic breeding population in the region.

*Nesting habits:* Male Bobolinks usually reach the breeding grounds a few days ahead of the females and choose a site in a hay, clover, or grain field. Like Redwinged Blackbirds, Bobolinks are colonial and males sometimes take more than one mate. Arriving females are attracted to the colony by the males' songs and plumage displays that include erection of the buffy patch on the nape.

In a shallow depression in the ground amid dense vegetation, the female builds a scanty cup of coarse grass and weed stems and lines it with finer grasses. In late May or early June the female lays four to seven slightly glossy pale gray or buff eggs that are irregularly dotted and blotched with various shades of brown. She incubates the eggs for about 13 days, and young remain in the nest about the same length of time. Both parents tend the offspring, which hide in the field for several days after they leave the nest and before they learn to fly. Bobolinks are single-brooded. Nests are very hard to find because the female runs through the concealing vegetation for a distance when leaving her nest or returning to it.

*Feeding habits:* Sometimes called "Ricebirds," Bobolinks used to inflict heavy damage upon the rice crop in the Carolinas during fall migration; but today rice is not a major agricultural crop, and Bobolinks are no longer driven away with guns and torches. On the northern breeding grounds the species feeds mostly on insects and weed seeds, and fall migrants in the Carolinas often eat wild rice and various grass and weed seeds.

*Description:* In spring male Bob-olinks are black on the face and underparts, yellowish-buff on the nape, and distinctively marked with large white patches on the wings and lower back. Females and fall males are buffy with a boldly striped crown. In all plumages Bobolinks have short and sharply pointed tail feathers that resemble those of a woodpecker.

---

## Eastern Meadowlark
*Sturnella magna*
8½–11 in. (21.5–28 cm)

*Range:* The Eastern Meadowlark is a common permanent resident throughout the Carolinas, frequenting meadows, pastures, large lawns, fields, roadsides, and grasslands but avoiding woodlands.

*Nesting habits:* Nests are usually placed in a depression in a wide expanse of grass and concealed by an overhanging tuft of grass. The nest of coarse grasses is lined with finer materials. Egg laying occurs from late April through July. The three to five eggs are white with reddish-brown and purple spots. Incubation requires about 2 weeks and is performed by the female. Normally the male helps care for the young during their 11 or 12 days in the nest and assumes almost full responsibility for the first brood while the female begins building her second nest. Some males, however, may be polygamous.

*Feeding habits:* Meadowlarks feed mostly on insects.

*Eastern Meadowlark at nest*
William G. Cobey

*Description:* Meadowlarks are predominantly brown above and yellow below with white outer tail feathers and a bold black V across the breast.

## Western Meadowlark
*Sturnella neglecta*
8½–11 in. (21.5–28 cm)

*Range:* During the winter the local meadowlark population is increased by many migrants from the north. These sometimes include a few Western Meadowlarks, which can be separated reliably from Eastern Meadowlarks only by song or by examining the bird in hand. The Western Meadowlark is an accidental found in the Carolinas very rarely between late November and early March.

*Feeding habits:* See Eastern Meadowlark.

*Description:* Consult field guides and recordings of meadowlark songs.

## Yellow-headed Blackbird
*Xanthocephalus xanthocephalus*
9–11 in. (22.5–28 cm)

*Range:* The Yellow-headed Blackbird is a rare accidental in the Carolinas between early August and early May. It is most likely to be found among the vast hordes of Common Grackles, Brown-headed Cowbirds, and Red-winged Blackbirds that winter in the eastern counties.

*Feeding habits:* Yellow-headed

*Yellow-headed Blackbird, male*
James F. Parnell

Blackbirds eat insects, including many agricultural pests; grains, with a preference for oats; and weed seeds.

*Description:* The adult male Yellow-headed Blackbird is completely black except for a white patch in the wing and bright yellow plumage on the head, neck, and upper breast. First-winter males and brownish females lack the distinct white in the wing. The female's yellow plumage is less conspicuous than that of the male; larger size and lack of streaking separate the female Yellow-headed from Red-winged Blackbirds with yellow or orange throat patches.

## Red-winged Blackbird
*Agelaius phoeniceus*
7¼–10 in. (18.5–25 cm)

*Range:* The Red-winged Blackbird is a common to abundant permanent resident of fields, marshes, lake margins, and other open hab-

*Red-winged Blackbird, male*
Bill Duyck

*Red-winged Blackbird, female*
Jack Dermid

itats throughout the Carolinas. An influx of fall migrants from the north causes the species to become locally extremely abundant during winter in the vicinity of roosting places. Roosting blackbirds may become a nuisance. Once Red-winged Blackbirds have dispersed to their nesting grounds, they become good neighbors, breeding in small colonies in marshy places and consuming great quantities of grass and weed seeds and harmful insects.

*Nesting habits:* Built entirely by the female and woven of marsh grasses, the deeply cupped nest is securely attached to the stems or supporting branches of reeds, cattails, or bushes growing in or near water. The nesting season extends from April into June, but the peak of laying is in early May. The three to five pale bluish eggs are dotted and scrawled with black markings. Incubation, performed by the female, requires about 11 days. Males help feed the nestlings, but females appear to be primarily responsible for care of the young during their 10 or 11 days in the nest. Polygamy is not unusual among Red-winged Blackbirds, but pairs frequently are loyal to each other through a nesting season. The species appears to be mostly single-brooded in our region, but replacement clutches are laid if eggs are destroyed. After the nesting season Red-winged Blackbirds separate into flocks, and the sexes do not associate with each other again until the next spring.

*Feeding habits:* Red-winged Blackbirds eat insects, grains, and weed seeds.

*Description:* The shiny black male with his yellow-bordered red patches at the bend of the wing can be confused with no other bird that occurs in our region. Females and young males are brownish and heavily streaked above and below; some individuals may show yellow or orange patches on the throat or a touch of red on the wing. First-winter males are similar to adult males but have a somewhat mottled appearance.

*Mixed-species blackbird roosts:* Every winter many localities in the Carolinas become roosting sites for vast numbers of blackbirds. Mixed-species roosts may be composed of American Robins, Starlings, Red-winged Blackbirds, Rusty Blackbirds, Common Grackles, and Brown-headed Cowbirds. The density of birds in these roosts has resulted in considerable debate regarding population dynamics of the species involved. Some ornithologists believe that monocultural farming processes and increased acreage under cultivation have contributed to a population explosion among some species. Others maintain that the spreading human population has consistently reduced available roosting habitat. In any case, when the birds roost in or near suburban residential areas and shopping centers, local citizens are upset by the noise and droppings.

Numerous control programs have been instituted, ranging from attempts to frighten the birds by making loud noises to killing them with guns or chemicals. Other than achieving very local short-term success, these efforts have been ineffective. Problem roosts should be reported to the state representatives of the United States Fish and Wildlife Service, which has employees trained in the use of the control methods currently considered most effective.

## Orchard Oriole
*Icterus spurius*
6–7½ in. (15–19 cm)

*Range:* During the breeding season the Orchard Oriole is a common resident of the coastal plain and a fairly common one in the piedmont and in some mountain valleys. At the higher altitudes it is known only as a transient. Orchard Orioles begin arriving in the Carolinas in early April, and most individuals depart in July and August; however, winter stragglers are found from time to time. True to its name, the Orchard Oriole frequents orchards, groves of shade trees, open woodlands, and the edges of fields.

*Nesting habits:* Both members of the pair participate in construction of the nest, which is a bag woven of green grasses that yellow as they dry out. It is suspended by the rim from a fork near the tip of a drooping branch from 7 to 70 feet (2–20 m) above ground or water. Evergreens and large deciduous trees such as oaks seem to be preferred nesting sites, but bushes and banners of Spanish moss are also used. Although the male gathers materials, the female apparently does all the weaving. Orchard Orioles often nest in close association with Eastern Kingbirds. The three to five bluish eggs are marked with spots and scrawls of brown and lilac. Laying usually takes place in May or June, incubation is by the female and lasts about 12 to 14 days, and young fledge in 11 to 14 days. The male feeds his incubating mate, helps protect the nest, and helps care for the offspring. The species is normally single-brooded.

*Feeding habits:* Orchard Orioles are highly insectivorous, but they also eat mulberries, pokeberries, and nectar.

*Description:* The fully adult male Orchard Oriole is a black bird with orange-red underparts, rump, and wing patch. The female is greenish-yellow with two white wing bars. The first-year male is similar to the female but has a black throat patch.

*Orchard Oriole, adult male*
Heathcote Kimball

*Orchard Oriole, female*
Heathcote Kimball

346

## Northern Oriole
(Baltimore Oriole, Bullock's
Oriole)
*Icterus galbula*
7–8 in. (17.5–20 cm)

*Range:* The Baltimore Oriole
(*I. g. galbula*), the Eastern form of
the Northern Oriole, is a fairly
common summer resident in
mature deciduous trees bordering
wide streams and fields in the
mountain valleys north of Asheville, N.C. The species also breeds
to an undetermined extent locally
and sporadically eastward across
the Carolinas. As a migrant
throughout the Carolinas, it is
generally uncommon, but it
becomes common along the coast
in fall. From mid-September to
late April, Baltimore Orioles are
fairly common winter residents in

*Northern Oriole, adult male*
Eloise F. Potter

the eastern and central counties
where they show a preference for
towns with much broad-leaved
evergreen shrubbery and many
bird feeders.

*Nesting habits:* The nest is a 6-
inch-deep (15-cm-deep) bag woven
of plant fibers, often including
string or yarn. Usually it is

*Northern Oriole, female or young male*
Elizabeth Conrad

attached 25 to 30 feet (7.5–9 m) above ground to the terminal twigs of a drooping branch of a deciduous tree. Although the male may assist her by bringing materials, the female is the nest builder. The four to six eggs are larger than those of the Orchard Oriole but essentially the same in appearance. Laying takes place mostly in May and June; incubation is by the female and requires about 12 to 14 days; and young remain in the nest about 2 weeks. The male stays with his family until the young are strong on the wing, although he usually plays only a minor role in their care and feeding. Baltimore Oriole nests often last through the winter and are quite conspicuous in leafless trees.

*Feeding habits:* Baltimore Orioles eat many insects and caterpillars, but they also take grapes and other fruits and berries. In winter they visit holes drilled by Yellow-bellied Sapsuckers. At bird feeders they are partial to oranges, pound cake, and a paste made of melted suet, peanut butter, and yellow corn meal.

*Description:* The black-and-orange male Baltimore Oriole is a spectacular bird. The female has a mottled back, two white wing bars, and golden-yellow underparts. Young males are similar to the female.

Bullock's Oriole (*I. g. bullockii*), the Western form of the Northern Oriole, has been recorded twice in North Carolina. A small flock appeared at a bird feeder in Morehead City in early December of 1959 and remained in the vicinity until the following March. One Bullock's Oriole visited a feeder at Southern Pines in the winter of 1974–1975. The male Bullock's is similar to the male Baltimore, but the Western form has less black on the head and more white in the wings.

## Rusty Blackbird
*Euphagus carolinus*
8½–9½ in. (21.5–24 cm)

*Range:* The Rusty Blackbird is a common winter resident throughout South Carolina from mid-October through April. In North Carolina the species is mostly a spring and fall transient, but it winters erratically throughout the state and sometimes is locally abundant, particularly in the eastern counties. The species frequents freshwater swamps, wet woodlands, fields, and pigpens adjacent to streams and ponds. It often associates with grackles, cowbirds, and Red-winged Blackbirds.

*Feeding habits:* Food items for the Rusty Blackbird are insects, weed seeds, and waste grain.

*Description:* Rusty and Brewer's Blackbirds are very difficult to separate in the field. Use of a field guide is recommended.

# Brewer's Blackbird
*Euphagus cyanocephalus*
8¾–10¼ in. (22–24 cm)

*Range:* Brewer's Blackbird is an irregular but sometimes locally common winter resident in the Carolinas from late November through mid-April. This Western species appears to be more numerous around Asheville, N.C., than elsewhere in our region, but it is probably overlooked by those unfamiliar with it. Brewer's Blackbirds visit cattle feed lots and generally avoid fields and marshes where hordes of other blackbirds congregate.

*Feeding habits:* Principal foods for Brewer's Blackbirds are insects and seeds.

*Description:* See Rusty Blackbird.

# Boat-tailed Grackle
*Quiscalus major*
Male 15–17½ in. (38–45 cm)
Female 11½–13½ in. (29–34 cm)

*Range:* The Boat-tailed Grackle is a common permanent resident of coastal Carolina where it seldom wanders far from salt and brackish waters.

*Nesting habits:* On the ground or on perches such as bushes or telephone poles, courting males posture grandly, ruffling their feathers, spreading their wings and tails, bowing, jumping about, and vocalizing excitedly. In the midst of this great activity, the birds may point their beaks skyward and remain immobile for a few seconds or even minutes. Suddenly the pose is broken, and active pursuit of mates is resumed. Boat-tailed Grackles nest in colonies, and males are decidedly polygamous. Nesting sites may be bushes or tall grasses in marshes or shade trees in towns near salt water. Nests are bulky affairs woven of heavy grasses, deeply cupped, securely fastened to the supporting stems, and reinforced with mud. Eggs are laid mostly in April and May, but sometimes nesting extends into June. The species is single-brooded, laying second clutches only when first ones are lost. The three to five eggs are bluish-white, scrawled and splashed with dark brown, black, and purple markings. Incubation requires about 2 weeks, and young remain in the nest about 3 weeks. The males do not assist in any manner in the building of the nest, incubation of eggs, or care of offspring. Indeed, males are seldom seen near the nests once the eggs have been laid.

*Feeding habits:* Boat-tailed Grackles feed chiefly on small aquatic animals, but they also take various other items including seeds and fruits.

*Description:* Iridescent black males with their long keel-shaped tails can be confused in our region only with the smaller Common Grackle. Female Boat-taileds are much smaller than males and have brown plumage that sometimes appears almost golden on the breast. In flocks composed of both sexes, the contrast in size and color separates Boat-taileds from Commons.

---

## Common Grackle
(Purple Grackle, Bronzed Grackle)
*Quiscalus quiscula*
10½–13 in. (26.5–33 cm)

*Range:* The Common Grackle is an abundant species found in all sections of the Carolinas in all seasons, but it is not particularly numerous in the mountains and does not breed at the higher elevations. One race of this species, the Florida Grackle (*Q. q. quiscula*), breeds throughout South Carolina and northward along the North Carolina coast. Another race, the Purple Grackle (*Q. q. stonei*), extended its breeding range southward into the Carolinas during the present century, most rapidly since 1950. Still a third race, the Bronzed Grackle (*Q. q. versicolor*), is known only as a transient and winter resident, mostly in the western counties.

Common Grackles occur in a wide variety of habitats and are gregarious at all seasons. Winter roosting concentrations of blackbirds may contain a million or more Common Grackles. Watch and listen in late winter and early spring for displaying males facing each other and giving the ruff-out squeak. This marks the onset of courtship activities.

*Nesting habits:* Although the Florida race usually builds its nests in bushes near fresh water, the Purple race usually nests in small colonies in pines or other conifers. The male helps gather nesting materials, but construction is apparently the work of the female. Made of twigs and grasses, the bulky structures are sometimes reinforced with mud and are frequently lined with grasses and feathers. The four to six eggs usually are laid in April or early May. They are greenish-white, heavily blotched and scrawled with dark brown and gray markings. Incubation requires about 12 to 14 days, and young apparently remain in the nest about 12 to 15 days. Although males help defend nests from predators and help care for the young both in the nest and after departure, they apparently do not incubate eggs.

*Feeding habits:* Feeding mostly in open fields and grassy places, Common Grackles eat a great deal of vegetable matter, including sprouting corn, corn in the ear, and waste grain. They also consume insects, caterpillars, crayfish, mollusks, and minnows.

*Description:* Larger than a robin but considerably smaller than a crow, the iridescent black Common Grackle has a keel-shaped tail. Females and young of the year have shorter tails than adult males, and the fold down the center is less pronounced; but the wedged shape of the tail still is adequate to separate grackles from Rusty and Brewer's Blackbirds.

*Boat-tailed Grackle, male*
William G. Cobey

*Common Grackle*
Edward Burroughs

## Brown-headed Cowbird
*Molothrus ater*
7–8 in. (17.5–20 cm)

*Range:* First reported breeding in the Carolinas in the mid-1930s, Brown-headed Cowbirds now can be found in all sections of the region throughout the year. They are most abundant in the coastal plain and piedmont in winter, and adults are generally scarce in July and August.

*Brown-headed Cowbird, male*
Edward Burroughs

*Nesting habits:* Cowbirds build no nests of their own, but rather lay their eggs in the nests of other birds. Females lay very early in the morning. An egg of the host species is removed the day before laying, later the same day, or perhaps the next day. Normally the female deposits only one egg per nest, but more than one female may lay in a given nest. Cowbird eggs are highly variable in size, ground color, and markings; however, they are almost always larger than those of the parasitized species. The incubation period varies from 11 to 14 days, with the cowbird eggs usually hatching before those of the host species. Even if the cowbird hatches later, this large and aggressive nestling usually survives. Brown-headed Cowbird young do not deliberately eject the eggs and young of the hosts. Fledgling cowbirds normally leave the nest at 10 days of age and soon flock with others of their own species. Females apparently remain in the vicinity of the nest and lead the young away once they are independent of the foster parents.

The most frequently reported hosts in the Carolinas are the Rufous-sided Towhee, Red-eyed Vireo, and Wood Thrush. Various warblers and finches often make successful hosts. Gray Catbirds and American Robins eject cowbird eggs, and many other species abandon parasitized nests. If the alien egg is accepted, many foster parents manage to fledge one or more of their own young along with the cowbird. There is no evidence that cowbirds have created serious problems for hosts in the Carolinas. Fortunately, females tend to lay in the nests of abundant and multibrooded species. In a given season one female may lay a total of 10 to 12 eggs deposited in several clutches separated by intervals of a few days to a few weeks. The fledging of young cowbirds in June, July, and August indicates that the eggs are laid by summer-resident birds rather than by northbound migrants.

*Feeding habits:* Cowbirds eat insects, waste grain, and weed seeds. Their name derives from their habit of feeding in pastures and barnyards about the feet of the livestock. In winter they often occur in mixed flocks with grackles and blackbirds.

*Description:* Brown-headed Cowbirds have stout conical bills that are much shorter than those of grackles and blackbirds. When they feed on the ground, their tails tilt upward. Males are greenish-black with a brown head, and females are uniformly gray. Immatures are similar to females, but the breast is faintly streaked.

# Family Thraupidae: Tanagers

Tanagers are colorful and predominantly tropical birds with long stout bills.

## Western Tanager
*Piranga ludoviciana*
6½–7½ in. (16.5–19 cm)

*Range:* The Western Tanager is a very rare accidental in the Carolinas, occurring mostly as a winter visitor at feeding stations from December through March. The species normally winters south of the United States.

*Feeding habits:* Insects provide most of the food, but a significant amount of fruit is taken.

*Description:* The male is mostly yellow with black tail and wings, one wing bar yellow and the other white, and a variable amount of red on the head. The female is similar, but she has a greenish back and no red about the head.

*Western Tanager, male*
Richard A. Rowlett

## Scarlet Tanager
*Piranga olivacea*
6½–7½ in. (16.5–19 cm)

*Range:* The Scarlet Tanager is a common summer resident in the southern Appalachian Mountains, breeding mostly at elevations between 1,500 and 5,000 feet (450–1,500 m). The species also breeds throughout the piedmont of North Carolina and northwestern South Carolina. Although a few nest in the inner coastal plain of North Carolina, Scarlet Tanagers generally are rare migrants below the fall belt. Partial to deciduous forests, the Scarlet Tanager arrives on its breeding grounds by late April or early May, and most individuals have left for the tropics by mid-October.

*Nesting habits:* The nest, probably built by the female, is a shallow cup of grasses placed on a horizontal tree limb, often that of an oak, well out from the main trunk and usually about 20 to 40 feet (6–12 m) above ground. The three to five eggs are greenish-blue, speckled with reddish brown. Performed by the female, incubation requires 13 or 14 days. Young remain in the nest about 2 weeks. Males may help feed their offspring until they are fully fledged, or they may leave the care of the young almost entirely to the female. The species is single-brooded.

*Scarlet Tanager, male in breeding plumage*
Charles E. Newell

*Feeding habits:* Although Scarlet Tanagers occasionally eat fruit, they are mostly insectivorous with a strong taste for caterpillars.

*Description:* Breeding male Scarlet Tanagers are our only birds with bright red bodies and jet black wings and tails. In fall males molt and temporarily resemble females. Females are greenish-yellow with black wings and tails; their bills are smaller and darker than those of female Summer Tanagers.

---

## Summer Tanager
*Piranga rubra*
7–8 in. (17.5–20 cm)

*Range:* The Summer Tanager is a common summer resident throughout the Carolinas, but in the mountains it breeds only at the lower elevations, mostly below 2,000 feet (600 m). The birds are present in wooded residential districts and open woodlands from mid-April to mid-October.

*Nesting habits:* The male is not known to participate in nest construction. Nests are shallow cups of grass placed well out from the main trunk on a horizontal limb of a pine or deciduous tree, often an oak, and usually 10 to 40 feet (3–12 m) above a roadway or clearing in the woods. The three or four greenish-blue eggs are dotted with brown and lavender. Eggs usually are laid in late May or June, and the species is single-brooded. Incubation lasts about 12 days and is performed by the

*Summer Tanager, male at nest*
William G. Cobey

*Summer Tanager, female at nest*
William G. Cobey

female. The male feeds his mate during incubation, helps defend the nest, and helps feed the young and clean the nest. Under normal conditions offspring probably remain in the nest about 12 days.

*Feeding habits:* Summer Tanagers eat a variety of fruits and berries, but insects apparently constitute the bulk of their diet in most seasons. They eat many wasps and bees, and they often hover beneath the eaves of houses while foraging for spiders and insects. They also hunt from a perch like a flycatcher.

*Description:* The adult male Summer Tanager is our only all-red bird without a crest. Unlike the male Scarlet Tanager, he retains his bright plumage throughout the year. Although the females normally are dull greenish-yellow birds, partly and completely red ones are found from time to time. Compared to the female Scarlet Tanager, the female Summer has less darkness in the wings, more orange-yellow in the underparts, and a larger, lighter-colored bill. Young resemble the female.

# Family Fringillidae: New World Seedeaters

All members of this family are equipped with stout conical bills used for crushing the seeds that constitute their chief source of food in winter. Finches also eat buds and berries in season, and in spring and summer insects and their larvae are the major source of food. Nestling finches are fed almost exclusively on animal matter. After the nesting season most fringillids gather into flocks that may roam widely in search of food. Some winters large numbers of northern finches such as Evening Grosbeaks, Purple Finches, and Pine Siskins appear at feeders in the Carolinas, causing much excitement among bird-watchers.

Although there are many variations, the general pattern of family life among fringillids is for the female to build the nest with little or no help from her mate. She incubates the eggs and broods the young, but the male brings food to her and helps guard the nest. After the eggs hatch, both parents feed the offspring and clean the nest. Males frequently take full charge of the recently fledged brood while the female prepares a nest for the second or third clutch of eggs.

## Cardinal
*Cardinalis cardinalis*
7½–9¼ in. (19–23.5 cm)

*Range:* The Cardinal is the state bird of North Carolina, and the species is a very common permanent resident throughout the Carolinas. Found in every con-

*Cardinal, male*
John Trott

*Cardinal, female*
Jack Dermid

ceivable type of wooded habitat, but favoring woodland margins and residential shrubbery, the "Redbird" is among the first visitors at a new bird feeder.

*Nesting habits:* In late March or early April the male Cardinal begins offering his mate tidbits, this tender exchange often taking place right on the feeding tray for all to behold. Soon thereafter the female is busy building her nest, which is usually placed 3 to 15 feet (0.9–4.5 m) above ground in a bush, tree, or tangle of vines. Composed of weed stems, twigs, strips of bark, and other pliable plant fibers, the nest may have leaves or pieces of paper interwoven and a lining of fine grasses. The three or four eggs are whitish and well spotted with lavender and brown. Laying for first clutches usually begins about mid-April. Incubation requires 12 or 13 days and normally is the task of the female, although the male may sit upon the eggs briefly from time to time. Young usually remain in the nest about 10 days and are fed by both parents. Two or three broods may be raised in a season.

*Feeding habits:* See comments on family.

*Description:* Although the Cardinal is not our only red bird, it is our only red one with a prominent crest. The male is bright red, the female brownish. Because young Cardinals have touches of orange on the upper breast, eyebrows, and crest, they are sometimes mistaken for Pyrruloxias. Listen for the Cardinal's whistled *pretty–pretty–pretty* and *three cheers.*

---

## Rose-breasted Grosbeak
*Pheucticus ludovicianus*
7–8½ in. (17.5–21.5 cm)

*Range:* The Rose-breasted Grosbeak breeds commonly in the North Carolina mountains at altitudes of 3,200 to 5,000 feet (975–1,500 m), but the species is known in the piedmont only as a fairly common spring and fall transient from mid-April to late May and from mid-September to mid-October. In the coastal plain it is an uncommon to rare migrant. Winter stragglers are found occasionally. Rose-breasted Grosbeaks favor mature deciduous forests during migration and on the breeding grounds.

*Nesting habits:* The nest is a shallow cup of twigs, grass, and other plant fibers placed 3 to 20 feet (1–6 m) above ground in a bush or tree. Laid in May, the three to five greenish-blue eggs are heavily spotted with reddish brown. Incubation takes 12 to 14 days, and young remain in the nest 9 to 12 days. The male shares fully with the female in all aspects of family life including nest building, incubation, and care of young—a notable exception to the usual behavior of fringillids.

*Feeding habits:* See comments on family.

*Rose-breasted Grosbeak, adult male*
James F. Parnell

*Description:* Black above and white below, the male has a prominent triangular patch of rose on the upper breast. The brown-streaked female resembles a female Purple Finch with broad white wing bars and a broadly striped crown. In flight the male flashes rosy wing linings and the female golden ones.

## Black-headed Grosbeak
*Pheucticus melanocephalus*
7–8½ in. (17.5–21.5 cm)

*Range:* An accidental from the West, the Black-headed Grosbeak is a very rare fall transient and winter visitor seen mostly at bird feeders in the Carolinas. The species normally winters south of the United States.

*Black-headed Grosbeak, male*
Edward Burroughs

*Feeding habits:* See comments on family.

360

*Description:* The male resembles a male Rose-breasted Grosbeak but has golden underparts and a streaked back. The female is similar to the female Rose-breasted but more finely streaked. Both sexes have lemon-yellow wing linings.

## Blue Grosbeak
*Guiraca caerulea*
6¼–7½ in. (16–19 cm)

*Range:* A fairly common to common summer resident of the coastal plain and piedmont, the Blue Grosbeak also breeds locally and sparingly in the mountains at altitudes up to about 4,000 feet (1,220 m). The species inhabits brushy open country such as hedgerows, thickets, and aban-doned fields. Blue Grosbeaks normally arrive about mid-April and depart by mid-October, but a few individuals sometimes linger into winter.

*Nesting habits:* Usually placed from 3 to 8 feet (1–2.5 m) above ground in a fork of a bush or small tree, the rather bulky nest of weed stems, leaves, and grass may contain pieces of cast snakeskin, cotton, rags, or paper. It may be lined with rootlets or horsehair. The three or four unmarked eggs are very pale blue. Laying takes place from late May to mid-July, and two broods may be raised in a season. The female apparently incubates the eggs about 12 days. Both adults feed the young during their 13 days in the nest, but the male tends the first brood after depar-

*Blue Grosbeak, male feeding young*
James F. Parnell

ture while the female builds her second nest.

*Feeding habits:* Blue Grosbeaks often perch on roadside wires, watching for the insects that make up the bulk of their diet. Grain and weed seeds are the chief sources of vegetable matter.

*Description:* Both the blue male and the brown female are recognized by the very heavy bill and two wide brown wing bars. Blue Grosbeaks are easily confused with the Indigo Bunting, which is a smaller bird with a relatively small bill and no conspicuous wing bars. Blue Grosbeaks habitually flick their tails sideways. Male Blue Grosbeaks appear almost black at a distance, but male Indigo Buntings glint metallic blue in sunlight.

*Indigo Bunting, male*
Edward Burroughs

## Indigo Bunting
*Passerina cyanea*
5–5¾ in. (12.5–14.5 cm)

*Range:* From mid-April to mid-October the Indigo Bunting is a common summer resident of brushy fields, woodland edges, and other clearings in most parts of the Carolinas; but in the mountains the species is not known to breed above 5,200 feet (1,585 m), and in eastern South Carolina its distribution is localized. Winter stragglers are found occasionally.

*Nesting habits:* The female builds a nest of weed stems, grasses, and leaves 1½ to 15 feet (0.4–4.5 m) above ground in a crotch of a

sapling, bush, or stout weed. The three or four pale bluish-white eggs are laid from mid-May to mid-July, and two broods are raised in a season. Incubation is performed by the female and requires 12 or 13 days. The female also appears to be entirely responsible for the feeding and care of the young until they leave the nest at about 10 days of age. The male remains near the nesting site, singing persistently from an elevated perch and defending the nest from intruders. After the young have fledged, the male helps provide for them and may even assume complete responsibility for the brood while the female begins renesting.

*Feeding habits:* See comments on family.

*Description:* In breeding plumage, the male Indigo Bunting is an iridescent blue bird without wing bars. The female is almost uniformly brown with the underparts faintly streaked and slightly lighter than the upperparts. Some females are tinged with blue. Young birds resemble the female, but they have faint whitish wing bars and streaks on the back and breast. After the breeding season, males molt and temporarily resemble females. Molting males are blotched with brown and blue.

## Painted Bunting
*Passerina ciris*
4¼–5½ in. (10.8–14 cm)

*Range:* The Painted Bunting is a common summer resident of coastal Carolina from Carteret County, N.C., southward. In South Carolina some breeding occurs inland to the fall belt, mostly along the flood plains of major rivers. A pair seen feeding young at Washington, N.C., in early June of 1970 plus April and early May sightings at Clinton, S.C., Stanly County, N.C., and Tarboro, N.C., suggest that the species may be extending its range northward and inland. Painted Buntings are most numerous in the dense shrub thickets of the barrier islands and adjacent mainland. Males usually arrive on the breeding grounds by mid-April, followed in about a week by the females. Most Painted Buntings migrate southward before the end of October, but a few individuals are found in winter, some of them having appeared regularly at feed-

*Painted Bunting, male*
John Trott

ing stations from midwinter until the beginning of the nesting season.

*Nesting habits:* The male announces his presence by singing from conspicuous perches and defends his territory in fierce battles that may end fatally for the weaker bird. Usually placed less than 20 feet (6 m) above ground in a bush, tree, or clump of Spanish moss, the nest is a cup of grass, leaves, and weed stems lined with hair or fine grass. First clutches are laid about mid-May, and three broods may be raised in the Charleston area. Northward the number of broods is reduced to two, or possibly only one. The three or four eggs are white, spotted and splashed with brown. Incubation takes about 11 days, and young remain in the nest about the same length of time. The female is solely responsible for nest construction, incubation, and care of young in the nest. Continuing to feed her fledged brood unassisted, the female begins building a fresh nest at a new site. When the nest is finished, sometimes in as little as 2 days, the male suddenly begins to court her. On the eve of egg laying, he takes full charge of the first brood, which the female then abandons.

*Feeding habits:* See comments on family.

*Description:* Purple head, green back, and red rump and underparts make the fully adult male

Painted Bunting unmistakable. The bright greenish-yellow female has a narrow eye ring.

---

## Dickcissel
*Spiza americana*
5½–7 in. (14–17.5 cm)

*Range:* Primarily a bird of the prairies, the Dickcissel was common in the Atlantic States during most of the nineteenth century; but its numbers declined in the eastern part of its range until it became virtually absent during the first quarter of the twentieth century. Today the species occurs only locally and erratically east of the Appalachians. Small breeding colonies are found from time to time in weedy fields, wheat fields, and other open habitats of the Carolina piedmont; and individuals occasionally appear at bird feeders in winter, more often along the coast than inland. Although some spring and fall migrants traverse the Carolinas, there is no definitely known time for their passage. The breeding season extends from mid-May through July.

*Nesting habits:* The female builds her well-concealed nest on or very near the ground. It is a bulky affair of coarse weed and grass stems interwoven with leaves and whatever plant fibers may be convenient, the interior being lined with fine grasses, rootlets, or hair. The three to five pale blue eggs are unmarked. Incubation requires 12 to 13 days, and young leave the nest when about 8 days old. A second brood may be raised. The male takes no part in caring for the eggs or young. Some males depart soon after incubation has begun, but others remain in the vicinity, singing and giving alarm at the approach of an intruder.

*Feeding habits:* See comments on family.

*Description:* Dickcissels bear a superficial resemblance to House Sparrows. The male has a yellow breast marked by a black V that makes him look like a stubby-billed miniature meadowlark. The female has a bluish bill and a touch of yellow on the breast. Both sexes have a reddish-brown patch at the bend of the wing.

## Evening Grosbeak
*Hesperiphona vespertina*
7–8½ in. (17.5–21.5 cm)

*Range:* First recorded in North Carolina in 1922 and in South Carolina in 1951, Evening Grosbeaks are erratic winter residents throughout the Carolinas, scarce some seasons and abundant others with the extent of the invasion depending upon the availability of natural food supplies in eastern Canada. In our region grosbeaks tend to be most numerous in pine forests and in urban areas having many bird feeders well stocked with sunflower seeds. Although a few birds arrive sooner and depart later, the major flocks arrive in November and leave in late April. As yet no winter roost has been

*Evening Grosbeak, male*
Robert F. Soots Jr.

*Evening Grosbeak, female*
Robert F. Soots Jr.

discovered in the Carolinas, but elsewhere pines and other evergreens appear to be preferred winter roosting sites. The same conditions that cause many Evening Grosbeaks to move south for the winter often cause unusual numbers of Pine Siskins, Purple Finches, and crossbills to visit the Carolinas. Bird-watchers refer to these seasons as "big northern finch winters."

*Feeding habits:* See comments on family. Evening Grosbeaks provide much excitement for the backyard birder who is financially able to feed his voracious guests. Many observers have noted that grosbeaks tend to leave the feeders before midafternoon.

*Description:* The male Evening Grosbeak is more colorful than the female, which usually is the case with our winter finches. He is our only winter finch with a yellow forehead and large white wing patches.

## Purple Finch
*Carpodacus purpureus*
5½–6½ in. (14–16.5 cm)

*Range:* Although a few individuals may arrive in August and linger throughout May, Purple Finches are common winter residents in the Carolinas only from about mid-October to late April. Like Evening Grosbeaks, Purple Finches travel in flocks and frequent bird feeders where sunflower seeds are in generous supply. The Purple Finch is a fine singer, and these birds may be

*Purple Finch, adult male*
Elizabeth Conrad

*Purple Finch, female or immature*
Eloise F. Potter

heard singing in the Carolinas from the first warm days in February until they migrate northward.

*Feeding habits:* In fall Purple Finches eat many wild seeds and berries, and in spring they feast upon the buds and flowers of maples, sweet gums, tulip trees, cherries, and various other deciduous trees.

*Description:* The adult male Purple Finch looks like a streaky sparrow that has been dipped in raspberry juice. Females and immatures are brown with coarsely streaked breasts. In all plumages the Purple Finch has a heavy jaw stripe and a white belly. Most individuals have a lyre-shaped tail. House Finches are similar, but they are finely streaked even on the belly, have a straight slightly notched tail, and lack the jaw stripe. First-winter males may have just a touch of red on the forehead, chin, and rump; but older males may have nearly as much red as the Purple Finch. Female House Finches are so finely streaked that they appear almost gray beside a brown-plumaged Purple Finch. Although the two species are about the same length, the House Finch is slimmer and thus appears smaller than the Purple Finch.

# House Finch
*Carpodacus mexicanus*
5½–6 in. (14–15 cm)

*Range:* House Finches being sold illegally in New York were released by a store owner on Long Island in 1940, and this Western species now breeds southward at least to Greenville, S.C., and winters into Georgia. The House Finch first appeared in North Carolina at a bird feeder in Wake County during the winter of 1962–1963; the first positive record for South Carolina came in December 1966. The species is rapidly increasing as a winter resident of towns and cities throughout the Carolinas, and it is fairly common at some localities in piedmont North Carolina. Since 1974 evidence of breeding has been reported from Winston-Salem, Charlotte, Greensboro, and Raleigh, N.C., and from Greenville, S.C., in June 1979. Continued expansion of nesting range is expected.

*Nesting habits:* House Finches will nest almost anywhere: on the ground, in cavities in trees and buildings, or in abandoned nests of other birds, particularly orioles. The female builds the nest almost without help from her mate. In California, House Finch eggs are found from late February to early August, with the peak of laying apparently in late April and early May. As many as three broods may be raised in a season, a fact that helps account for the species' rapid range extension along the Atlantic seaboard. Eggs usually number four or five and are bluish-white, delicately spotted and streaked with olive, brown, or

*House Finch, male*
Edward Burroughs

*House Finch, female*
Elizabeth Conrad

black. The incubation period varies from 12 to 16 days, and young remain in the nest about 14 to 16 days. The female incubates eggs and broods the young. The male feeds his mate upon the nest, and both parents feed the nestlings. The chicks attempt to defecate over the rim, but the nest soon becomes fouled around the edges; the interior, however, remains clean. The House Finch tends to return to the same nest both for the second brood of the season and in subsequent years.

*Feeding habits:* Food consists chiefly of weed seeds; nevertheless, where House Finches are numerous, damage to fruit crops may cause significant economic loss.

*Description:* This species resembles the Purple Finch but has a finely streaked belly and lacks the heavy stripe at the jaw. Young males with just a touch of red on the forehead can be mistaken for redpolls. See Purple Finch for a comparative description.

## Pine Grosbeak
*Pinicola enucleator*
9–9¾ in. (22.5–25.5 cm)

*Range:* The Pine Grosbeak is a very rare winter visitor in the Carolinas. This northern finch was first recorded in North Carolina in 1951 and in South Carolina in 1962. It has been found in our region as early as mid-September and as late as May 30. Sightings

Pine Grosbeak, male
Charles E. Newell

usually occur during winters when the influx of Evening Grosbeaks and other northern finches ranges from moderate to very heavy. Pine Grosbeaks apparently travel in small flocks, five being the largest number seen at once in the Carolinas, and do not visit bird feeders regularly.

*Feeding habits:* As their name implies, Pine Grosbeaks eat the seeds and buds of pines and other conifers, but in winter they also take the fruits and seeds of deciduous trees.

*Description:* These surprisingly tame finches are about the size of a Cardinal. Superficially resembling male Purple Finches, male Pine Grosbeaks have black bills and prominent white wing bars. Female Pine Grosbeaks are olive-gray with white wing bars and black bills. First-year males resemble females, but they have touches of red on the upperparts, especially the head and rump.

## Common Redpoll
*Carduelis flammea*
5¾ in. (14.5 cm)

*Range:* Common Redpolls first appeared in the Carolinas soon after the turn of the century, and they remain rare and erratic winter visitors. Found between late October and early April, redpolls are most likely to be seen during major winter finch invasions.

*Feeding habits:* Although Common Redpolls occasionally visit bird feeders during their sojourn with us, they apparently prefer the natural food supply of forb and grass seeds found in weedy fields. Their feeding behavior is much like that of the American Goldfinch.

*Description:* Redpolls are small, heavily streaked birds with stout yellowish bills. Adult Common Redpolls have the foreparts and rump more or less washed with red. The bright red cap and black chin are diagnostic. Immature male House Finches have the bright red forehead but lack the black chin.

## Pine Siskin
*Carduelis pinus*
4½–5¼ in. (11.5–13 cm)

*Range:* Like the Evening Grosbeak, the Pine Siskin may be extremely abundant one winter and almost impossible to find the next. Siskins occur throughout the Carolinas from late October to early May. In the mountains they

*Pine Siskin*
David Whitehurst

teristic the Pine Siskin shares with other small birds that begin laying as early as March. The three to six very pale blue or greenish-blue eggs are delicately spotted with light brown and thinly scrawled with black. The incubation period is 13 days, and young remain in the nest about 15 days. Only the female has a brood patch, but the male brings her food and helps care for the young. Apparently the species is double-brooded in some regions, if not throughout its range.

*Feeding habits:* See comments on family. In winter Pine Siskins travel in flocks, often in company with American Goldfinches, and sometimes descend upon feeders in droves. Siskins show a definite preference for seeds of pines and sweet gums. The birds reportedly continue feeding in flocks even during the nesting season.

*Description:* The tiny Pine Siskin is a finely streaked bird with bright yellow patches in the wings and on each side at the base of the tail. The bill is rather long and slender for a finch, and the tail is deeply notched.

can be found in small numbers at elevations above 4,800 feet (1,470 m) throughout the summer and early fall. That the species breeds southward to the Great Smoky Mountains National Park seems almost beyond doubt, but as yet no positive evidence of nesting has been obtained from our region.

*Nesting habits:* The typical Pine Siskin nest is placed in a conifer at medium height or lower and well out from the main trunk. Concealed by dense foliage on a horizontal limb, the shallow cup of twigs and other plant materials is well lined with soft fibers such as fur and moss. The male is attentive to the female during nest building, but apparently he just superintends the work. The nest is rather large in relationship to the size of the builder, a charac-

## American Goldfinch
*Carduelis tristis*
4½–6 in. (11.5–15 cm)

*Range:* Most abundant in winter, the American Goldfinch can be found in all sections of the Carolinas throughout the year, but it becomes scarce or locally absent toward the coast in summer. Win-

American Goldfinch, male acquiring
breeding plumage
William S. Justice

American Goldfinch, winter male
Edward Burroughs

ter flocks visit weedy fields, thickets, residential areas, and various types of woodlands.

*Nesting habits:* The nest is built by the female. Usually placed less than 15 feet (4.5 m) above ground in an upright fork of a bush or low tree growing along a stream or the edge of a thicket, the compact nest is woven of grasses, strips of bark, and other plant fibers and lined with down from cattails or thistles. Goldfinches are late breeders, nests rarely being built before thistles mature in the latter part of June. Thistles provide both food and nesting materials. Some eggs are still being incubated in mid-September. The four to six eggs are unmarked bluish-white, and incubation requires 12 to 14 days. The female goldfinch sits upon the eggs almost constantly, and she is fed by her mate. Both adults feed the young, which leave the nest at 11 to 15 days of age. Only one brood is raised, and the birds begin flocking soon after the breeding season.

*Feeding habits:* See comments on family. Goldfinches and some other small finches are partial to thistle seeds.

*Description:* The breeding male American Goldfinch is unmistakable with his canary-yellow body, black-and-white wings and tail, and jaunty black cap pulled down on his forehead. Breeding females and winter birds of both sexes are dull greenish- or brownish-yellow, but they have the distinctive black-and-white pattern in the wings and tail.

## Red Crossbill
*Loxia curvirostra*
5½–6½ in. (14–16.5 cm)

*Range:* The Red Crossbill probably is the most unpredictable and mysterious bird found in our region. Some winters, flocks of crossbills visit much of North Carolina and northern South Carolina from early November to late spring; but other winters, the species appears to be absent outside the mountains. The real mystery is when and where the birds breed. Although no nest with eggs or young has been found in North Carolina, various reports of adults building nests and feeding fledglings with bills still uncrossed (as early as March 29 and as late as mid-June) indicate that Red Crossbills breed in the Appalachians southward at least to the Great Smoky Mountains National Park and Highlands, N.C. The mystery is compounded by the fact that on May 6, 1964, an immature Red Crossbill about 5 weeks old was collected along with an adult male and an adult female in breeding condition in Wake County, N.C. Allowing 14 to 18 days for incubation places the date of egg laying about the middle of March. At Southern Pines, N.C., a female was seen feeding a recently fledged bird on September 1, 1974. Adults with fledglings were seen at Raleigh and Southern Pines in the spring of 1976. Late May to mid-June sightings eastward to Roanoke Rapids, Clayton, and Fayetteville, N.C., and south to Charleston County, S.C., suggest the possibility of widespread nesting in the Carolinas outside the mountains. Bird-watchers should study carefully the activities of Red Crossbills lingering anywhere in our region after the first of March, because such birds may be breeding locally.

*Nesting habits:* Red Crossbills usually place their bulky nests from 10 to 40 feet (3–12 m) above ground in conifers. The male superintends construction but apparently does not participate in it. The three to five eggs are tinged with green or blue and are variably dotted, splotched, and scrawled with brown and black. The female does all the incubating and brooding, but the male feeds her upon the nest and helps her care for the young, which remain in the nest at least 17 days.

*Feeding habits:* Crossbills feed mostly on conifer and sweet gum seeds. Although they can and do eat sunflower seeds, they may visit a bird bath and ignore a nearby feeder full of seeds.

*Description:* Crossbills can be identified satisfactorily even if the crossed mandibles cannot be seen. Adult males are dull red above and below with solid black wings and tail. Females are yellowish-brown with dark wings and tail; the back is streaked but not the underparts. Immature males are similar to females but mottled with red. Very young birds have uncrossed bills. Red Crossbills are about the size of a Purple Finch.

## White-winged Crossbill
*Loxia leucoptera*
6¼ in. (16 cm)

*Range:* White-winged Crossbills appear erratically in the North Carolina piedmont and mountains from late December to early February during major flights of wintering northern finches. Sometimes flocks of 50 to 250 birds are found in spruce-fir forests in the mountains, but most sightings are of single birds or flocks numbering less than 20 individuals.

*Feeding habits:* White-winged Crossbills are partial to the seeds of conifers.

*Description:* Similar to the Red Crossbill, the White-winged in all plumages has two broad white wing bars. The adult male is rosy red. Females are yellowish-brown and finely streaked above and below. Immature males are similar to the female but mottled with red. Our only other red bird with broad white wing bars is the Pine Grosbeak, which is about the size of a Cardinal and has uncrossed mandibles.

## Green-tailed Towhee
*Pipilo chlorurus*
7–7¾ in. (17.5–19.5 cm)

*Range:* An accidental from the western United States, the Green-tailed Towhee was recorded once in South Carolina when a specimen was taken near Charleston on January 18, 1921.

*Feeding habits:* See Rufous-sided Towhee.

*Description:* Smaller than a Rufous-sided Towhee, this species looks much like a Swamp Sparrow with greenish wings and tail.

## Rufous-sided Towhee
*Pipilo erythrophthalmus*
7½–8¾ in. (19–22 cm)

*Range:* The Rufous-sided Towhee is a common permanent resident throughout the Carolinas, but the species tends to withdraw from the higher mountains during the winter. Towhees are birds of thickets, overgrown fields, woodland margins, and residential shrubbery.

*Nesting habits:* On or very near the ground, the female builds the cup of bark strips, grasses, dead leaves, twigs, rootlets, and other plant fibers. The two to five white eggs are generously marked with reddish-brown spots that tend to be heaviest at the large end, where they may form an almost solid cap. Incubation lasts 12 to 13 days and is performed by the female, but occasionally the male may bring her a bite of food. Although brooding is left entirely to the female, the male regularly helps feed the young, which develop very rapidly and remain in the nest only 7 days. Normally two broods are raised, and third ones are not uncommon under favorable conditions. First clutches may be laid in April, but early May is the usual time.

*Rufous-sided Towhee, male*
James F. Parnell

*Rufous-sided Towhee, female*
John Trott

*Feeding habits:* While feeding, towhees often make a great deal of noise by scratching with both feet to expose seeds and insects hidden beneath leaf litter.

*Description:* The black-backed male and brown-backed female Rufous-sided Towhees are easy to recognize, but the streaky-brown fledglings do not favor either parent. The careful observer may notice that some adult males have red eyes while others have white or yellowish eyes. Some birds have more white in their tail feathers than others, and the voices are distinctly different. These variations occur among three different races that breed in the Carolinas and a fourth that is a very rare winter visitor. Often called "Joree" or "Chewink" in imitation of its calls, the Rufous-sided Towhee sings *drink-your-tea*, ending with a highly variable trill.

## Lark Bunting

*Calamospiza melanocorys*
5¼–7½ in. (13.5–19 cm)

*Range:* The Lark Bunting is a very rare transient and winter visitor along the Carolina coast from early September to mid-April. The species has been found inland from late April to early May. Although a Lark Bunting was in Cumberland County, N.C., once in July, the species is not known to breed in our region.

*Feeding habits:* See comments on family.

*Description:* The male is black with a broad white patch on the leading edge of each wing. The female is streaky brown with a white slur in the wing.

## Savannah Sparrow
(Ipswich Sparrow)

*Passerculus sandwichensis*
4½–6½ in. (11.5–16.5 cm)

*Range:* The Savannah Sparrow is a winter resident of fields and short-grass habitats throughout North and South Carolina, arriving about mid-September and remaining until mid-May. The species is abundant toward the coast and uncommon in the mountains.

*Feeding habits:* See comments on family.

*Description:* This small short-tailed sparrow is streaked below, and some individuals look like miniature Song Sparrows. Yellow in the eye stripe, when present, and the notched tail readily separate this species from similar ones.

At least six different races of the Savannah Sparrow occur in the Carolinas. These vary considerably in size and general coloration, but only one is readily distinguishable in the field, that being the Ipswich Sparrow (*P. s. princeps*). Formerly considered a separate species, this large and pale form of the Savannah Sparrow frequents the sand dunes nearest the ocean from early November through March. The northern end of Pea Island appears

*Savannah Sparrow*
James F. Parnell

to be the best place in the Carolinas to look for the rare and elusive Ipswich Sparrow, although it probably visits all our undeveloped beaches.

## Grasshopper Sparrow
*Ammodramus savannarum*
5 in. (12.5 cm)

*Range:* The Grasshopper Sparrow is a fairly common summer resident in the mountains and piedmont and an uncommon winter resident over most of the coastal plain, becoming fairly common along the South Carolina coast. A few birds winter occasionally in the western counties. Grasshopper Sparrows frequent grassy and weed-grown places such as fields, pastures, neglected meadows, and airports.

*Nesting habits:* Built in a slight depression in the ground, the flimsy but well-hidden nest of dried grasses usually is arched over on the back and sheltered by a bush, clump of grass, or clod of dirt. Eggs have been found in the

*Grasshopper Sparrow*
Morris D. Williams

Carolinas from late May through mid-September, and two broods are raised each season. The three to five white eggs are variably speckled with reddish brown. Incubation apparently requires about 12 days; young remain in the nest 9 days. Although several nests may be found in a suitable meadow, the species is not truly colonial because each male proclaims with a grasshopper-like song his own rather large territory, usually 1 to 3 acres (about 1 hectare).

*Feeding habits:* Insects, particularly grasshoppers, are a favorite food. Strips of weeds in fences along roads and airport runways seem to be preferred feeding places.

*Description:* This small short-tailed sparrow has a buffy unstreaked breast. The head is relatively large for the size of the bird. Listen for the song, which is like that of the grasshopper.

## Henslow's Sparrow
*Ammodramus henslowii*
5 in. (12.5 cm)

*Range:* Henslow's Sparrow is a fairly common, but secretive, winter resident of coastal South Carolina from mid-October to mid-April. It winters in small numbers north to southeastern North Carolina. As a rare spring and fall transient the species occurs inland to the mountains. Records indicate that during the 1930s and 1940s the species bred at least locally or erratically from Stumpy Point in Dare County, N.C., westward to Chapel Hill and Statesville and southward to Charlotte, N.C., and Greenville County, S.C. There is no indication that it currently nests in the Carolinas. This sparrow is most likely to be found in low-lying old fields, lush meadows, and the margins of watercourses, where it runs about in dense vegetation and behaves more like a mouse than a bird. It often associates with Bobolinks, Eastern Meadowlarks, Savannah Sparrows, and Grasshopper Sparrows.

*Nesting habits:* During the breeding season, Henslow's Sparrows tend to form loose colonies. The nest and eggs resemble those of the Grasshopper Sparrow. Egg laying begins about mid-May in states to the north of us; so any Henslow's Sparrows present in the Carolinas from early May through August should be suspected of nesting locally.

*Feeding habits:* Although the Henslow's Sparrow is highly insectivorous, it consumes an appreciable number of grass and weed seeds.

*Description:* This short-tailed and big-billed sparrow has streaked underparts, striped crown, greenish head, and rusty wings. Young Henslow's resemble Grasshopper Sparrows.

## Le Conte's Sparrow
*Ammospiza leconteii*
4½–5½ in. (11.5–14 cm)

*Range:* This elusive, marsh-loving sparrow is an erratic winter resident in the southern half of South Carolina from late October to late April. Some seasons it is fairly common in salt marshes and broom-sedge fields around Charleston, but at other times it is almost impossible to find. In North Carolina, Le Conte's Sparrow is known as a very rare transient, occurring in fall from late October into early January and in spring only in the latter part of April; but a few undetected individuals might spend the entire winter in the coastal region.

*Feeding habits:* See comments on family.

*Description:* Le Conte's is a buffy-breasted sparrow with streaked sides, a rusty nape, and a white crown stripe. The white crown stripe separates this species from the Sharp-tailed Sparrow, which is similar in size and shape. Some Sharp-taileds show a great deal of buffiness and are easily confused with Le Conte's Sparrows.

## Sharp-tailed Sparrow
*Ammospiza caudacuta*
5–6½ in. (12.5–16.5 cm)

*Range:* Sharp-tailed Sparrows are common to abundant winter residents of the coastal salt marshes from late September to late May. Many individuals undoubtedly pass over the inland portions of the Carolinas during spring and fall migrations, but these birds are rarely seen unless they collide with a television tower or some other obstacle. Sharp-tailed Sparrows breed southward to Chincoteague Island in Virginia, but no acceptable evidence of nesting has been obtained from the Carolinas.

*Nesting habits:* This potential breeder nests in the higher, drier portions of the salt marsh. The nest and eggs resemble those of the Seaside Sparrow, but the Sharp-tailed's grassy cup tends to be more bulky.

*Feeding habits:* Sharp-tailed Sparrows seek food, mostly animal matter, in the densely vegetated salt marshes at low tide. They gather on islands and shorelines at high tide. At first glance a promising marsh may seem deserted, but a few squeaks from the birdwatcher will entice the inquisitive little sparrow to hop upon a stem of marsh grass.

*Description:* If no two individuals seem alike, do not be surprised. Several different races of the Sharp-tailed Sparrow occur in the Carolinas, and they vary considerably in size and coloration. This short-tailed sparrow has a dark cap above a buffy-orange triangular face pattern that frames a gray ear patch.

## Seaside Sparrow
*Ammospiza maritima*
5¼–6¼ in. (13.5–16 cm)

*Range:* The Seaside Sparrow is a common permanent resident of salt marshes throughout coastal Carolina.

*Nesting habits:* Built only of dried grasses, the nest is placed very close to the ground and attached to upright stems of marsh plants growing in the wetter portions of the salt marsh, often in rushes and cordgrasses. Laying takes place in late April or early May, and second broods may be raised. The three or four white eggs are heavily spotted with reddish brown. Incubation takes about 12 days, and young apparently stay in the nest about 10 days.

*Feeding habits:* Small marine animals predominate in the diet of the Seaside Sparrow.

*Description:* This dark, short-tailed, and long-billed sparrow has a yellow spot between the eye and the base of the bill.

## Vesper Sparrow
*Pooecetes gramineus*
5½–6½ in. (14–16.5 cm)

*Range:* The Vesper Sparrow is a fairly common spring and fall transient throughout the Carolinas, with migrants noticeable mostly from mid-October to mid-November and in March and April. The species is fairly common in southeastern South Carolina in winter, but to the north and inland it becomes uncommon, scarce, or locally absent at midwinter. In the North Carolina mountains the species breeds southward to Buncombe and Haywood Counties, and scattered June through August sightings suggest

*Seaside Sparrow*
James F. Parnell

*Vesper Sparrow*
James F. Parnell

the probability of nesting southward to the Great Smoky Mountains National Park. Apparently it has nested accidentally on occasions at Greensboro, Rocky Mount, and Wilmington, N.C. The Vesper Sparrow nests on grassy mountain balds and in pastures, cultivated fields (hay, wheat, and corn), and abandoned fields, taking frequent recourse to adjacent woodlands. At other seasons, however, it forages in plowed fields, stubble fields, and short-grass habitats.

*Nesting habits:* The nest of grasses is built beneath fallen dead weeds or at the base of a bush or weed, usually where vegetation is sparse and low at the time of construction, although it may become dense before the eggs hatch. The four creamy or greenish eggs are variably blotched, dotted, and scrawled with rusty brown. First clutches are laid in April, and the species is double-brooded. Incuba-

tion requires about 12 days and is chiefly the work of the female. Both adults feed the young and clean the nest. The young may stay in the nest anywhere from 7 to 14 days, and they remain at least partly dependent on the adults until about 30 to 35 days old. As soon as the male can care for the first brood, the female begins a second nest.

*Feeding habits:* See comments on family.

*Description:* At first glance a Vesper Sparrow may look like a Song Sparrow that has lost its central breast spot. Watch for the Vesper's narrow eye ring, rusty patch at the bend of the wing, and white outer feathers on a slightly notched tail.

## Lark Sparrow
*Chondestes grammacus*
5¾–6¾ in. (14.5–17 cm)

*Range:* The Lark Sparrow is an uncommon but regular fall migrant along the coast. Elsewhere in the Carolinas it is a very rare migrant. The species winters sparingly along the coast, arriving in early August and usually departing by mid-April. Fall migrants frequent the edges of brushy thickets and have been known to bathe under the spray from lawn sprinklers. Although some records suggest the possibility of accidental nesting in piedmont North Carolina, there is at present no known breeding site in our region.

*Feeding habits:* See family.

*Description:* This is one of our most distinctively marked sparrows. The head pattern features a crown broadly striped with white, a chestnut ear patch, and a bold black jaw stripe. The breast is white with a central black spot. The long tail is rounded and edged with white; it resembles the tail of the Rufous-sided Towhee. Young birds may have lightly streaked breasts without the central spot, but the tail and face are enough like those of the adult to make identification fairly easy.

## Bachman's Sparrow
(Pine Woods Sparrow)
*Aimophila aestivalis*
5½–6¼ in. (14–16 cm)

*Range:* In the coastal plain Bachman's Sparrows breed in open pine woods with undergrowths of bushes and grass, but in the piedmont they nest in abandoned fields with scattered saplings and tall grasses. During the breeding season Bachman's Sparrows are fairly common where longleaf pine occurs; elsewhere they are uncommon to rare. In winter the birds tend to withdraw from the northern and western counties, but some remain all year at least as far north as southeastern North Carolina.

*Nesting habits:* The grass nest is usually domed or arched over and almost always impossible to find. Built on the ground at the base of a bush or clump of grass, it often has a hidden passageway extending outward from it. The female builds the nest and incubates the four or five eggs, which, unlike those of most sparrows, are pure white. The nesting season is highly variable, but first clutches usually are laid by late April or early May. The incubation period apparently is about 12 to 14 days, and most observers agree that the male helps feed the young. Two or three broods may be raised in a season. This sparrow, except for singing males, is so secretive that very little is known about its breeding habits.

*Feeding habits:* More insectivorous than many sparrows, this species eats some grass, sedge, and pine seeds.

*Description:* At a glance, which usually is all you get, Bachman's looks like a dingy Field Sparrow. The bill, however, is not pink; the upper mandible is dark and the lower one is light, perhaps a bit yellowish. Reference to field guides is recommended.

## Dark-eyed Junco
(Slate-colored Junco, Oregon Junco)
*Junco hyemalis*
5¾–6½ in. (14.5–16.5 cm)

*Range:* The Dark-eyed (Slate-colored) Junco breeds at elevations above 3,000 feet (900 m) in our mountains and is an abundant winter resident throughout

*Dark-eyed Junco*
John Trott

the Carolinas from early October to mid-April, occasionally to early May. Slate-colored Juncos (*J. h. carolinensis*) breeding in the southern Appalachians are permanent residents of various woodland habitats and are found even in winter to the tops of the highest peaks, although many individuals wander to the lower elevations after the nesting season. Winter-resident birds are a different race (*J. h. hyemalis*).

*Nesting habits:* The female builds the nest of moss, rootlets, and plant stems, usually placing it on an embankment either in a crevice or beneath overhanging ferns or grass. First clutches are laid in late April or early May, and second or perhaps third clutches may be found well into August. The three to five grayish eggs are variably speckled with reddish brown. Incubation lasts 12 to 13 days and apparently is the work of the female. She also does the brooding, but both parents feed the young, which leave the nest at about 12 days of age.

*Feeding habits:* Nestlings are fed exclusively on animal matter, but grass and weed seeds predominate in the diet of the adults. Juncos flock for the winter, feeding on roadsides, lawns, and fields, usually adjacent to coniferous woods. Sometimes large numbers of "Snowbirds" visit feeders, particularly after a substantial snowfall.

*Description:* This small slate-gray bird has a white belly and white outer tail feathers.

The influx of winter birds from the north and west sometimes includes a few Oregon Juncos (*J. h. oreganus*). Once considered a separate species, this well-marked race of the Dark-eyed Junco has been recorded several times in piedmont and coastal North Carolina, but it has yet to be reported from South Carolina. The Oregon Junco has a black or gray hood that contrasts sharply with its brown back and pinkish-tan sides. The pink sides extend forward approximately to the bend of the folded wing, giving the Oregon a distinctive miniature-towhee appearance. Some Slate-colored Juncos may be brownish, but they never show a sharp line between the dark hood and the light sides. Reference to a field guide is recommended.

## Tree Sparrow
*Spizella arborea*
6–6½ in. (15–16.5 cm)

*Range:* A rare winter resident of the mountains and northwestern piedmont counties of North Carolina, the Tree Sparrow occurs irregularly eastward to the coast and southward to Hilton Head Island, S.C., from late October to early May. Apparently the species avoids the higher mountains.

*Feeding habits:* Tree Sparrows are usually found in small flocks, often along with other sparrows, feeding on weed seeds in old fields or perched in the sun on nearby trees and bushes.

*Description:* The Tree Sparrow resembles a Field Sparrow with a dark central breast spot. Look for its two-toned bill, dark jaw stripe, and dark legs.

*Tree Sparrow*
Richard A. Rowlett

## Chipping Sparrow
*Spizella passerina*
5–5¾ in. (12.5–14.5 cm)

*Range:* Although at least a few can be found in all sections of the Carolinas throughout the year, Chipping Sparrows are most numerous in the western counties during the breeding season. In winter they occur over much of the piedmont but are much more numerous toward the coast, where they are uncommon in summer. Chippies frequent open pine woods, woodland edges, roadsides, residential lawns, and brushy fields.

*Nesting habits:* The female builds a nest of fine weed stems, rootlets, dry grasses, and leaves, lining it with hair or fine grasses. Nests may be placed on the ground, in vines or bushes, or on horizontal limbs of trees as high as 30 or 40 feet (9–12 m) above ground. The three to five pale greenish-blue

*Chipping Sparrow*
Edward Burroughs

eggs are wreathed at the large end with dots of black and purple. Fed by her mate, the female incubates the eggs for 11 to 14 days, depending on air temperature. She eats the shells after the chicks emerge, and both adults begin feeding the nestlings less than half an hour after hatching. The female does almost all the brooding, but she may be relieved by the male in cool weather. Young can leave the nest when 10 days old and are capable of sustained flight in another 4 days. First clutches usually are laid in May, and two or even three broods may be raised in a season. When nesting is over, Chipping Sparrows form flocks, often in company with Eastern Bluebirds, Pine Warblers, and Field Sparrows.

*Feeding habits:* See comments on family.

*Description:* This small clear-breasted sparrow has a black bill, rusty crown, white stripe over the eye, and black stripe through it. The gray rump is apparent even in young birds with streaky crowns.

## Clay-colored Sparrow
*Spizella pallida*
5–5¾ in. (12.5–14.5 cm)

*Range:* A rare transient, the Clay-colored Sparrow is seen along the Carolina coast in fall from mid-September to mid-November, but most often in October. This Western species occurs on very rare occasions in

*Clay-colored Sparrow, immature*
Richard A. Rowlett

the piedmont in fall and spring. In North Carolina it has been recorded during October in Orange and Franklin Counties. As a spring transient it has been seen between April 20 and May 9 as far east as Raleigh, N.C., and as far west as Clemson, S.C. The Clay-colored Sparrow has been found at Charleston, S.C., in December and early January, but it is not considered a regular winter resident there.

*Feeding habits:* See comments on family.

*Description:* Similar to the immature Chipping Sparrow, the Clay-colored has a striped crown, brown cheek patch, dark chin stripe, and buffy rump. Young Chipping Sparrows have a gray rump, and the streaky crown lacks a clearly defined central stripe. Reference to a field guide is recommended.

# Field Sparrow
*Spizella pusilla*
5½–6 in. (14–15 cm)

*Range:* Field Sparrows are common permanent residents of roadsides, fields, and abandoned pastures in most parts of the Carolinas; but in the higher mountains they tend to be scarce in summer and absent in winter.

*Nesting habits:* Built by the female, the frail cup of grasses and weed stems may be lined with fine grasses, rootlets, or hair. The nest may be placed directly on the ground in a tuft of grass or a foot (0.3 m) or so above ground in a bush. Sometimes nests are found 10 feet (3 m) high in the topmost tuft of a young pine. The two to five pale bluish-white eggs are variably spotted with reddish brown. Laying begins in late April in coastal South Carolina and continues well into July. The incubation period averages about 12 days, and two or three broods may be raised. The female usually does all the incubating and brooding, but the male may relieve her occasionally. Both adults feed the young and clean the nest. Offspring are ready for departure when 7 or 8 days old, and the female begins work on her new nest as soon as the male can care for them alone.

*Feeding habits:* See comments on family. Family parties gather into flocks in autumn, and hundreds of Field Sparrows may be found feeding together in weed-grown fields.

*Field Sparrow*
Elizabeth Conrad

*Description:* This is our only sparrow with a rusty cap, white eye ring, pink bill, pink legs, and clear breast. The eye ring combined with the absence of prominent facial marks gives the Field Sparrow a blank expression on its face.

## Harris' Sparrow
*Zonotrichia querula*
7½ in. (19 cm)

*Range:* Harris' Sparrow is an accidental winter visitor to the Carolinas. Single birds have been seen, usually in mixed flocks of White-crowned and White-throated Sparrows, in piedmont North Carolina, in Buncombe and Polk Counties in the North Carolina mountains, in northwestern

South Carolina, and at Huntington Beach State Park on the South Carolina coast. Harris' Sparrows normally winter west of the Mississippi River.

*Feeding habits:* See comments on family.

*Description:* Slightly larger than a White-throated Sparrow, the adult Harris' has a pink bill and a distinctive black crown, face, and bib; its sides are streaked. Immature birds have the pink bill and streaked sides plus a blotchy band across the breast; the buffy cheek and absence of the yellow spot before the eye separate young Harris' from fall White-throated Sparrows.

## White-crowned Sparrow
*Zonotrichia leucophrys*
6½–7½ in. (16.5–19 cm)

*Range:* The White-crowned Sparrow is a locally fairly common winter resident found from early October to mid-May in the northern coastal plain of North Carolina, throughout the piedmont of North and South Carolina, and in the mountain valleys. The species occurs along the coast as a regular fall migrant and rare winter resident, but it is seldom reported from the inner coastal plain south of Neuse River. Flocks of White-crowned Sparrows winter in hedgerows and brushy areas adjacent to large open fields. White-crowneds appear to have become more numerous in the Carolinas during recent years.

*Feeding habits:* See comments on family.

*Description:* White-crowned Sparrows have a light bill (pink or yellowish), an erect posture, and a

*White-crowned Sparrow, immature*
Robert H. Lewis

crew-cut look about the crown that readily separate them from the slightly smaller White-throated Sparrow. Head stripes are white in the adult and buffy in the immature, but birds in both plumages have an unmistakable military bearing.

## White-throated Sparrow
*Zonotrichia albicollis*
6½–7 in. (16.5–17.5 cm)

*Range:* The White-throated Sparrow is an abundant winter resident throughout the Carolinas from early October to mid-May. Stragglers have been found in June and July, but there is no evidence of breeding in our region. This species occurs in almost every type of habitat and is common in urban areas as well as in fields, thickets, forests, and swamplands.

*Feeding habits:* Most of the time the White-throated Sparrow feeds on the ground, scratching with both feet for seeds and insects.

*White-crowned Sparrow*
Richard A. Rowlett

White-throated Sparrow
Edward Burroughs

However, in the fall it consumes many wild berries, and in spring it ascends to the treetops to feast upon tender buds.

*Description:* In all plumages this sparrow has a striped crown, a white throat patch, and a yellow spot between the eye and the bill; but in dingy fall birds the yellow spot may be very difficult to see. Listen for the song, two clear whistles followed by three quavering ones. New Englanders render this as "Old Sam Peabody, Peabody, Peabody."

## Fox Sparrow
*Passerella iliaca*
6¾–7½ in. (17–19 cm)

*Range:* The Fox Sparrow is a fairly common winter resident throughout the Carolinas, usually being more abundant in severely cold winters than in mild ones. In

years of major flights, the birds may arrive in late October, and a few sometimes linger into early May. At other times none appear until December, and all have departed before the end of March. Fox Sparrows frequent coniferous woods and woodland thickets, rarely visiting urban bird feeders except when snow covers the ground.

*Feeding habits:* Scratching with both feet, Fox Sparrows toss aside leaf litter and dig holes in the snow while searching for food.

*Description:* Noticeably larger than a White-throated Sparrow, the reddish-brown and heavily streaked Fox Sparrow has a central breast spot. In spite of its conical bill, the Fox Sparrow is decidedly thrush-like in general appearance.

*Fox Sparrow*
James F. Parnell

## Lincoln's Sparrow
*Melospiza lincolnii*
5¼–6 in. (13.5–15 cm)

*Range:* During its time in the Carolinas, the Lincoln's Sparrow is a silent, solitary, and rarely seen bird that skulks around brush piles and frequents damp brushy thickets bordering woods and fields. It is so hard to find, and once found so hard to identify, that we can assume the species is far more common as a transient and winter visitor than the few published records indicate. Occurring from mid-September to mid-May, the Lincoln's Sparrow is seen most often during fall migration, which apparently peaks in the month of October. The peak of spring migration appears to be in late April and early May. Winter records are from piedmont North Carolina (Raleigh, Chapel Hill, and Winston-Salem), coastal North Carolina (Dare, Pamlico, and Brunswick Counties), and coastal South Carolina (Bull's Island and Charleston). It is not clear, however, whether winter birds are transients or individuals spending the entire season in our region.

*Feeding habits:* See comments on family.

*Description:* Immature Swamp and White-throated Sparrows are easily confused with Lincoln's Sparrows. Reference to a field guide is recommended.

## Swamp Sparrow
*Melospiza georgiana*
5–6 in. (12.5–15 cm)

*Range:* In wet meadows, marshes, bogs, and wet woodlands bordering streams and ponds, but not necessarily in heavily wooded swamps, the Swamp Sparrow is a common winter resident throughout the Carolinas from late September to mid-May.

*Feeding habits:* This species feeds on or near the ground, taking insects and seeds in almost equal proportions.

*Description:* The Swamp Sparrow is larger than a Chipping Sparrow but smaller than a White-throated. Look for its rusty wings, rusty cap, dark streak through the eye, completely black bill, and white throat patch.

## Song Sparrow
*Melospiza melodia*
6–6¾ in. (15–17 cm)

*Range:* The Song Sparrow is a very common winter resident through-

*Swamp Sparrow*
Chris Marsh

*Song Sparrows*
William G. Cobey

out the Carolinas, frequenting weedy and brushy places such as hedgerows, ditches, railroad embankments, edges of woodlands and fields, and the margins of ponds and streams. Song Sparrows visit bird feeders, and they sing in all but the coldest winter weather.

The cutting of woodlands opens new habitat for the adaptable Song Sparrow, which continues to extend its breeding range in the Carolinas. The Mississippi Song Sparrow (*M. m. euphonia*) is a common permanent resident of the southern Appalachians, wintering only in the lower elevations but breeding at any altitude where suitable habitat is available. Song Sparrows also breed eastward across the piedmont to Roanoke Rapids, Raleigh, and Charlotte, N.C., and to Greenville and Clemson, S.C. On the North Carolina coast southward at least to Ocracoke, the Atlantic Song Sparrow (*M. m. atlantica*) inhabits sand dunes, marshes, and shrubby thickets.

*Nesting habits:* Typically, the female Song Sparrow builds the nest alone, using leaves, strips of bark, and weed and grass stems for the bulky outer part of the structure and lining it with fine grasses, rootlets, and hair. Locations of nests range from ground level to a height of 12 feet (4 m) or more in bushes and trees. Ground nests are the most common and are usually concealed under a bush, brush pile, or tuft of grass. Natural cavities and unoccupied buildings are also used. Song Sparrows prefer nesting sites near water, but they will build in dry places. Laying begins in late April or early May except in the higher mountains. The four or five bluish-white eggs are heavily speckled with reddish brown. Incubation is by the female and requires about 12 to 14 days. Although males sometimes sit upon the nest, they do not develop brood patches. Both parents feed the young, which may leave the nest anywhere from 7 to 14 days after hatching. At first newly fledged birds remain under plant cover, but they are ready to fly when only 17 days old. At this stage the female immediately deposits the eggs for her next brood, leaving the care of the previous one entirely to the male. By the time the second brood hatches, the older offspring can look after themselves, and the male again helps the female with the nestlings. In this manner as many as three broods can be raised in a season even in the mountains.

*Feeding habits:* The Song Sparrow eats insects as well as grass and weed seeds.

*Description:* Although quite variable in color, all Song Sparrows (except very young birds) have heavy breast streaks that converge to form a central spot. In flight the Song Sparrow pumps its long and slightly rounded tail.

# Lapland Longspur
*Calcarius lapponicus*
5½–7 in. (14–17.5 cm)

*Range:* The Lapland Longspur is a rare but apparently regular winter resident in the northern portions of North Carolina. Usually it is found amid large flocks of Horned Larks on sand dunes and in fields practically devoid of vegetation. Extreme dates of sightings are October 5 and April 20, but most known occurrences fall between mid-November and mid-March. On the Carolina coast the species has been found from the grassy runways of the Wright Brothers Memorial to an island at the mouth of the Savannah River. Lapland Longspurs have been recorded inland from Buncombe, Iredell, Wake, Northampton, and Moore Counties, N.C., and from Chester and Anderson Counties, S.C. In the past century more than 40 years sometimes elapsed between sightings of these northern wanderers. Recent records of single birds and flocks of 15 to 20 individuals from the Outer Banks, the Occoneechee Neck area of Northampton County, and the Lake Surf impoundment in Moore County suggest that the species is a more widespread and numerous winter resident in eastern North Carolina than previously suspected.

*Feeding habits:* In winter Lapland Longspurs eat grain, grass and

*Lapland Longspur*
Richard A. Rowlett

weed seeds, and a relatively small amount of insect matter.

*Description:* The Lapland Longspur is easily overlooked by bird students who are unfamiliar with its behavior. Longspurs habitually feed in the bottom of a furrow, and their coloration makes them very hard to see even when they perch on a hummock. When flushing a flock of Horned Larks, watch for the Lapland Longspur's more undulating flight and relatively short, notched tail. Listen for its low, staccato, rattling *ticky-ticky-tic* flight call, which is easily separable from the high, sibilant squeaks of the lark. Consult a field guide for help in separating the Lapland Longspur from the other longspurs and the Snow Bunting.

## Smith's Longspur
*Calcarius pictus*
5½–6½ in. (14–16.5 cm)

*Range:* Specimens of this very rare accidental from the Central Plains were taken in Chester County, S.C., on December 1, 1880, and February 9, 1889. On December 28, 1946, a Smith's Longspur was seen at the airport at Lumberton, N.C.

*Feeding habits:* See Lapland Longspur.

*Description:* Consult a field guide.

## Snow Bunting
*Plectrophenax nivalis*
6–7½ in. (15–19 cm)

*Range:* The Snow Bunting occurs erratically throughout the Caro-

*Snow Bunting, winter*
Jay Shuler

linas from late October well into spring. It is most likely to be found from early November to late February on the Outer Banks of North Carolina where flocks of 100 or more sometimes are seen, and on the grassy balds of certain mountains lying on the North Carolina–Tennessee border. Small flocks of Snow Buntings apparently winter regularly on Big Bald Mountain in Madison County and Round Bald Mountain in Mitchell County. No flock of 30 or more birds has yet been reported from the North Carolina mountains, any inland locality, or the Carolina coast south of Carteret County, N.C. Inland sightings, other than those on mountain balds, tend to occur along the major river systems and in most cases are associated with the spring and fall migrations.

*Feeding habits:* Snow Buntings glean grass and weed seeds in barren habitats, often depending on the wind to expose food by blowing away snow or sand.

*Description:* Large white wing patches provide a good field mark, but albinistic sparrows are easily mistaken for Snow Buntings. Reference to a field guide is recommended.

# Glossary

Note: Terms used to describe the residence status and relative abundance of birds are defined in the introduction to the species accounts (pages 33–36).

ADULT. Birds of breeding age, usually with adult plumage patterns.

AIR SACS. Outpocketings of the lungs extending into the spaces between organs and in some cases lying just beneath the skin.

ALBINISM. An absence of pigment (color) from skin, eyes, and plumage. May be partial or complete.

ALTRICIAL YOUNG. Birds that are born helpless, with eyes usually closed, and with little or no down.

ANTARCTIC. The south polar region.

ARBOREAL. Inhabiting trees.

ARCTIC. The north polar region.

AVES. The class of animals to which birds belong.

AVIFAUNA. All bird species of a designated region.

AXILLARS. The elongated feathers lying beneath the wing and close to the body, comparable to the human armpit.

BAR. A contrasting mark across a given part of the plumage.

BEND OF THE WING. The outermost moveable joint of a wing, comparable to the human wrist.

BROOD. The number of birds resulting from a single nesting effort. Birds may be single-brooded (one brood per year) or multibrooded (two or more broods per year).

CAMBIUM. The layer of tissue immediately beneath the bark of some shrubs and trees. The region of lateral growth in plants.

CANOPY. The upper portions of the tree layer of a forest.

CARNIVOROUS. Flesh eating.

CERE. A soft, swollen, and often brightly colored area at the base of the upper portion of the bill. Occurs in hawks and pigeons.

CLUTCH. The number of eggs laid by a single bird in a nesting.

COMMUNITY. Characteristic groupings of interacting plants and animals. Each community is usually named for one or more of the dominant plants, as in the pine-forest community.

CONIFEROUS. Bearing cones, as in pines, firs, spruces, and hemlocks.

COURTSHIP FEEDING. Ritualized feeding of a female by a male during courtship.

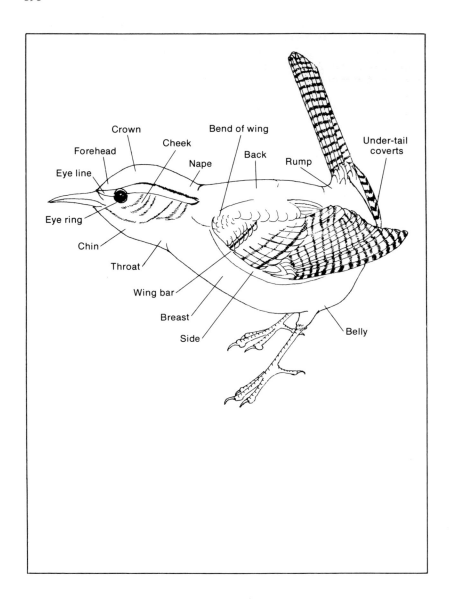

Crown

Bend of wing

Cheek

Forehead

Back

Under-tail coverts

Nape

Rump

Eye line

Eye ring

Chin

Throat

Wing bar

Breast

Side

Belly

*Topography of a bird*

COVERTS. Feathers covering the bases of the flight feathers of the wing and tail.

CREPUSCULAR. Active at dawn and dusk.

CREST. A tuft of feathers on the crown of a bird, as in the Cardinal.

CRUSTACEANS. Members of a large group of invertebrates including shrimp, crayfish, and crabs.

DECIDUOUS. Shedding or losing leaves (of plants) at the end of the growing season.

DECURVED. Curved downward, as in the bill of a Long-billed Curlew.

DISTRIBUTION. The geographic range of a species.

DIURNAL. Active during the day.

EAR TUFTS. Paired tufts of elongated feathers on each side of the head, as in the Great Horned Owl. Ear tufts are not actually associated with the ears.

ECOLOGY. The study of the relationships between organisms and their environments.

ENVIRONMENT. The sum total of the biological and physical factors that surround an organism.

EXOTIC. Not native, from another part of the world; an introduced species.

FACIAL DISK. A feathered area around the eyes of owls that gives them the appearance of having a face. The feathers of the facial disk assist in capturing sound waves and directing them into the ears.

FALL BELT. The zone of intergradation between the coastal plain and piedmont. Also called fall line.

FAMILY. A group of closely related genera. Members of a family usually share several important characteristics.

FEATHERS. Highly modified epidermal (skin) scales, peculiar to birds, which serve as their principal covering. Feathers may be of several types including primary, secondary, contour, down, bristle, and powder-down.

FECAL SAC. A clean mucous membrane containing the partly digested food that has passed rapidly through the digestive system of a newly hatched bird.

FLEDGLING. A young bird that is capable of flight but is still dependent on its parents.

FRONTAL SHIELD. An elevated portion of the base of the upper mandible.

GAPE. The open mouth of a bird.

GENUS (PL. GENERA). Unit of classification between the family and the species. The name of the genus becomes the first word of the scientific name for all species in a given genus.

GREGARIOUS. Occurring in groups.

GULAR REGION. A portion of the throat of birds. It forms the gular pouch of pelicans.

HABITAT. The type of environment in which a plant or animal lives; the place where a bird lives.

HYBRID. Generally considered to be an offspring derived from parents of different species.

IMMATURE. Not sexually mature.

INCUBATION PERIOD. The time between the beginning of incubation and the hatching of the eggs.

INSECTIVOROUS. Feeding primarily on insects.

INVERTEBRATES. Animals without backbones or spinal columns, including insects, worms, and shellfish.

IRIDESCENT. Having bright color produced by the selective reflection of light from feathers rather than from the production of pigments. Iridescent colors change with changes in light.

JAW STRIPE, CHIN STRIPE. A dark stripe extending downward from the jaw onto the side of the neck. Also called whisker, malar stripe.

LAMELLAE. Thin plates or scales, as along the margins of the bills of many waterfowl.

LARVAE. Immature stages of many kinds of organisms. Caterpillars are larvae of moths, butterflies, and various insects; tadpoles are larvae of frogs.

LENGTH. The total measured distance in a bird from the tip of the bill to the tip of the longest tail feather.

LOBED. Having lobes or flaps, as with the lobed toes of grebes.

LORES. The area between the eye and the bill of a bird. May be feathered or unfeathered.

MAMMALS. Warm-blooded vertebrates that have hair and produce milk to feed their young.

MANDIBLE. Either the upper or the lower part of the beak in birds.

MANTLE. The upper surface of the back and wings of birds.

MELANISM. The development of unusually large amounts of black pigment in the color of birds.

MIGRATION. The regular movement of a species between one part of its range and another. In our region, migration is usually associated with a movement southward in fall and a return northward in spring.

MOLLUSKS. Members of a large group of invertebrates that generally are encased in shells, for example, oysters, clams, and snails.

MOLT. The periodic shedding of some or all of the feathers. Birds molt at least once each year, and many have a second complete or partial molt.

MONOGAMOUS. Having a mating system in which a single male and a single female mate. The duration of the pair bond may be for a single nesting, for a single season, or for life.

MORPH. A color phase, as in red and gray Screech Owls.

NOCTURNAL. Active at night.

OMNIVOROUS. Eating both animal and plant materials.

ORDER. A major unit of classification higher than the family. All the birds living today are members of 27 orders and 155 families.

ORNITHOLOGY. The study of birds.

OVATE. Having the shape of the normal egg of a chicken.

PASSERINE. A term used for members of the avian order Passeriformes (the perching birds).

PELAGIC. Pertaining to the open ocean.

PELLET. A mass of undigested food materials regurgitated by some birds.

PLUMAGE. The total of all feathers on a bird.

POLYGAMOUS. Having a mating system whereby a bird may have more than one mate at a time.

POWDER-DOWN. Specialized feathers that grow in patches on the skin of some birds, notably herons. The tips of the feathers fray, forming a powdery substance that may be used to dress the feathers.

PRECOCIAL YOUNG. Downy chicks capable of locomotion shortly after hatching, as in ducklings.

PRIMARIES. The major flight feathers of birds. Primaries are elongated feathers attached along the rear edge of the wing from the bend of the wing to the tip.

RECURVED. Bent upward as in the bill of the American Avocet.

REGURGITATION. The casting out of food from the stomach or mouth.

RICTAL BRISTLES. Stiff hairlike feathers surrounding the gape of some birds, as in the Whip-poor-will.

SECONDARIES. A row of elongated feathers attached along the rear of the wing between the bend of the wing and the body.

SERRATED. Toothed, as in the bill of a merganser.

SIBILANT. Characterized by a hissing sound.

SPECIES. Commonly equated with a kind of organism. The term more properly refers to a group of interbreeding organisms that are generally reproductively isolated from other species.

SPECULUM. A brightly colored area, often iridescent, on the secondaries of some ducks.

SUBSPECIES. Geographic races of a species.

SUBTROPICAL. Characteristic of regions bordering the tropics.

TEMPERATE ZONE. A region in the middle lattitudes lying between the subtropics and the polar regions. The Carolinas are in the North Temperate Zone.

TERRITORY. A defended area. Territory typically refers to an area defended by a male against entry by other males of the same species during the breeding season.

TROPICAL. Characteristic of those regions, adjacent to the equator, that have uniform day lengths and constant warm temperatures.

TUNDRA. A major Arctic community that is characterized by low vegetation and poor drainage.

UNDERSTORY. The space beneath the canopy of a forest, often occupied by characteristic tree species such as, in the Carolinas, hollies and dogwoods.

VERTEBRATES. Animals with backbones or spinal columns, including birds, mammals, fish, reptiles, and amphibians.

WING BAR. A light-colored stripe extending across the folded wing of a bird. Usually visible only when the bird is perched.

WING LININGS. The coverts on the underside of the wing.

WINGSPAN. The total distance between the tips of a bird's outstretched wings.

WING STRIPE. A contrasting stripe running lengthwise the wing of a bird and often providing a useful field mark for the identification of birds in flight.

# Suggested Reading

FIELD GUIDES AND BIRD-WATCHING

Bull, J., and J. Farrand Jr. 1977. *The Audubon Society Field Guide to North American Birds, Eastern Region.* Knopf, New York.

Harrison, C. 1978. *A Field Guide to the Nests, Eggs and Nestlings of North American Birds.* Collins, Cleveland.

Harrison, H. H. 1975. *A Field Guide to Birds' Nests.* Houghton Mifflin, Boston.

Peterson, R. T. 1947. *A Field Guide to the Birds.* Houghton Mifflin, Boston.

Peterson, R. T. 1957. *The Bird Watcher's Anthology.* Harcourt Brace, New York.

Robbins, C. S., B. Bruun, H. S. Zim, and A. Singer. 1966. *Birds of North America.* Golden Press, New York.

Terres, J. K. 1968. *Songbirds in Your Garden.* Thomas Y. Crowell, New York.


REGIONAL: THE CAROLINAS

Green, C. H. 1933. *Birds of the South.* Republished 1975, Dover Publications, New York.

Norris, R. A. 1963. *Birds of the A.E.C. Savannah River Plant Area.* Contributions from the Charleston Museum XVI, Charleston, S.C.

Pearson, T. G., C. S. Brimley, and H. H. Brimley. 1942. *Birds of North Carolina.* Revised 1959 by D. L. Wray and H. T. Davis. N.C. Department of Agriculture, Raleigh.

Shuler, J. 1966. *South Carolina Birds of the Foothills.* Visulearn, Greenville, S.C.

Skinner, M. P. 1928. *A Guide to the Winter Birds of the North Carolina Sandhills.* Science Press Printing Co., Lancaster, Pa.

Sprunt, A., Jr., and E. B. Chamberlain. 1949. *South Carolina Bird Life.* Revised 1970 by E. M. Burton. University of South Carolina Press, Columbia.

Stupka, A. 1963. *Notes on the Birds of the Great Smoky Mountains National Park.* University of Tennessee Press, Knoxville.

WORLD

Austin, O. L., Jr. 1961. *Birds of the World.* Golden Press, New York.
Gilliard, E. T. 1958. *Living Birds of the World.* Doubleday, New York.


BIRD BIOLOGY, HABITS, AND BEHAVIOR

Bent, A. C. 1919–1958. *Life Histories of North American Birds.* 20 volumes. Bull. U.S. Natl. Mus. Republished by Dover Publications, New York.
Darling, L., and L. Darling. 1962. *Bird.* Houghton Mifflin, Boston.
Palmer, R. S. 1962–1975. *Handbook of North American Birds.* Volumes 1–3; loons through waterfowl. Yale University Press, New Haven, Conn.
Pasquier, R. F. 1977. *Watching Birds: An Introduction to Ornithology.* Houghton Mifflin, Boston.
Pettingill, O. S., Jr. 1970. *Ornithology in Laboratory and Field.* 4th ed. Burgess Publishing Co., Minneapolis, Minn.
Tinbergen, N. 1953. *The Herring Gull's World.* William Collins and Co., London.
Tinbergen, N. 1954. *Birdlife.* Oxford University Press, New York.
Welty, J. C. 1975. *The Life of Birds.* W. B. Saunders, Philadelphia.


JOURNALS

*American Birds.* Published by National Audubon Society.
*Auk.* Published by American Ornithologists' Union.
*Chat.* Published by Carolina Bird Club, Inc.
*Condor.* Published by Cooper Ornithological Union.
*Journal of Field Ornithology* (Formerly *Bird-Banding*). Published by Northeastern Bird-Banding Association.
*Wilson Bulletin.* Published by Wilson Ornithological Society.

# Index

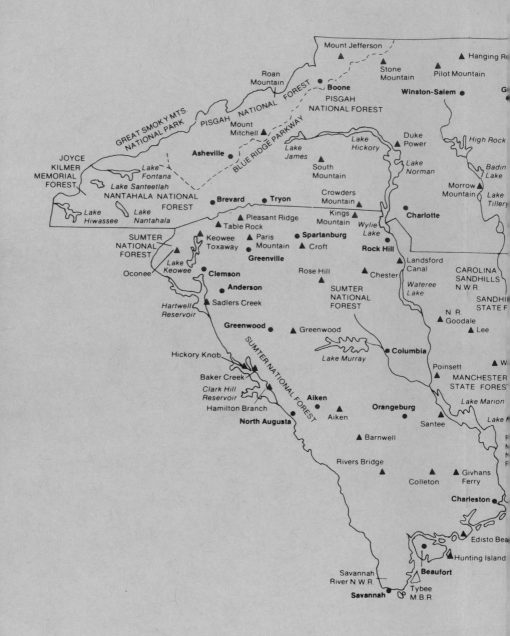